DEEPER THAN DARWIN

DEEPER
THAN
DARWIN

The Prospect for Religion
in the Age of Evolution

John F. Haught
Georgetown University

Westview
PRESS

A Member of the Perseus Books Group

Copyright © 2003 by Westview Press, A Member of the Perseus Books Group

Westview Press books are available at special discounts for bulk purchases in the United States by corporations, institutions, and other organizations. For more information, please contact the Special Markets Department at the Perseus Books Group, 11 Cambridge Center, Cambridge MA 02142, or call (617) 252–5298.

Published in 2003 in the United States of America by Westview Press, 5500 Central Avenue, Boulder, Colorado 80301–2877, and in the United Kingdom by Westview Press, 12 Hid's Copse Road, Cumnor Hill, Oxford OX2 9JJ

Find us on the World Wide Web at www.westviewpress.com

Library of Congress Cataloging-in-Publication Data

Haught, John F.
  Deeper Than Darwin: the prospect for religion in the age of evolution / John F. Haught.
    p.   cm.
  Includes bibliographical references and index.
  ISBN 0–8133–6590-2 (alk. paper)
    1. Evolution—Religious aspects—Christianity.   I. Title.
BT712.H377   2003
231.7'652—dc21

2002153464

The paper used in this publication meets the requirements of the American National Standard for Permanence of Paper for Printed Library Materials Z39.48–1984.

10   9   8   7   6   5   4   3   2   1

To
The Thomas Healey Family
for its generous support

Contents

Preface

Just how deep can evolutionary biology take us in the ageless human endeavor to understand life and its various manifestations? This is a question of great general significance today, but it is one of special interest to those who wonder if there is still room in an age of science for an illuminating religious or theological understanding of life. The present work addresses this issue.

This book's reflections on Darwin and religion are a sequel to those first presented in *God After Darwin: A Theology of Evolution* (Westview Press, 2000). The earlier book assumed the general accuracy, as well as the theological fertility, of Darwinian accounts of life, but it did not focus as extensively on the question of Darwinism's explanatory adequacy as does the present one.

Several chapters and subsections of the book are adaptations of recent articles that I have published elsewhere. Chapter 3 is based on "Science, Religion, and the Sacred Depths of Nature," *Quarterly Review*, Vol. 21, No. 4 (Winter 2001). Several paragraphs in Chapters 1 and 2, and a good portion of Chapter 9, will sound familiar to readers of *Commonweal Magazine:* "The Darwinian Struggle," Vol. CXXVI, No. 16 (September 24, 1999); "Evolution and God's Humility," Vol. CXXVII, No. 2 (January 28, 2000); and "The Darwinian Universe," Vol. CXXIX, No. 2 (January 25, 2002). Chapter 8 appeared in slightly different form as "Why Do Gods Persist? A Polanyian Reflection" in *Tradition and Discovery: The Polanyi Society Periodical,* Vol. XXVIII, No. 1 (2001–2002). Chapter 12 is a modified version of "In Search of a God for Evolution: Paul Tillich and Teilhard de Chardin," first presented at a meeting of the North American Paul Tillich Society in 2001 and later published in *Zygon,* Vol. XXXVII, No. 3 (September 2002). Finally, Chapter 13 is adapted from "Theology After Contact: Religion and

Extraterrestrial Intelligent Life," *Annals of the New York Academy of Sciences,*
Vol. 950 (December 2001).

I would like to express my gratitude to Westview Press senior editor Sarah
Warner and senior project editor Rebecca S. Marks for shepherding this project to completion. And my deepest appreciation goes to my wife, Evelyn,
not only for her unending support of my work but also for reading and criticizing the manuscript.

Introduction

In his strange new story of life, Charles Darwin exposed a depth in the natural world that we had never before fathomed. After Darwin, evolutionary science has continued to uncover extended pathways of life's struggle paved with pain, waste and death. It has also revealed a vast domain of creativity, but for many people today this is not enough to redeem so heartless a process. Evolution still often sounds like bad news, not only to religious believers but even to some biologists, paleontologists and philosophers troubled by the wickedness of natural selection. No matter how one interprets it, though, evolutionary discovery has taken us deep into nature, perhaps deeper than science had ever ventured before. Have we perhaps, through Darwinian eyes, stared into the very bottom of nature's well? Or may we look down even deeper?

The point of this book is to dig deeper than Darwin. I will assume here the fundamental correctness of evolutionary biology, but I want to question the nonscientific belief that evolutionary biology—or for that matter the cumulative body of natural sciences—amounts to an adequate explanation of living phenomena. Even though Darwinism is illuminating, it by no means tells us everything we need to know about life, even in principle. It certainly does not alone provide the space within which people, including the most devout Darwinians, can live their lives. Although evolutionary biology gives an enlightening account of some aspects of life, like all sciences it leaves out a lot. And although Darwinian concepts can even shed light on human existence, their explanatory power is easily exaggerated. To find the *deepest,* though certainly not the clearest, understandings of life and the universe, we may still profitably consult the religions of the world.

Religions, of course, are not uniformly pretty. Their lofty ideals, as Alfred North Whitehead observed, mingle with the crudest forms of barbarism.

Sometimes their scriptures are stylistically primitive and their moral teachings obtuse. And yet, as Whitehead goes on to say, religion is "our one ground for optimism."[1] Although certain traits of religion may embarrass us at times, it is hard—even in an age of science—to ignore completely its persistent intuition that the universe, beneath it all, makes sense. It is not easy for most people simply to shove aside the religious sense that, in spite of all evil, there is reason to hope for final deliverance. Unless there is some substance to the various creeds, mutually incompatible though they may often seem to be, our own lot is a sad one, and the end of all life, struggle and achievement is nothingness.

The question today, however, is whether we can embrace religious hope in an intellectually honest way. Numerous educated people are now convinced that science, especially evolutionary biology, has made religion implausible and obsolete. Some even see science as completely irreconcilable with religion. Others view religion as emotionally and morally tolerable, but intellectually superfluous after the rise of science. Many sincere people now believe that only science can understand fully what is going on in the universe. For them, reality consists fundamentally of material elements and physical processes. Even though contemporary physics has demonstrated that "matter" is much more subtle and slippery than previous generations had supposed, a lot of scientists and philosophers still embrace the conviction that, at bottom, "matter" or "matter-plus-energy" is really all there is.

In no sector of contemporary scientific culture is this materialist—now sometimes called "physicalist"—view so strikingly prominent as among evolutionists. We shall be surveying ample evidence of this fact in the following pages, but I would like to note even here what a remarkable reversal in the history of ideas it is that biology has now become such a stronghold of materialism. Michael Ruse, one of the most authoritative voices in the philosophy of evolution, declared recently that Darwinism is the "apotheosis of a materialistic theory."[2] Yet, at the beginning of the modern age, it was not biology but physics that reduced the universe to purely material stuff. So exceptional did life seem in comparison with inanimate nature that it required an extraphysical explanation. Even many hard-core scientists used to think that a supernatural agency was essential to lift dead matter up to the level of life. However, this so-called vitalist perspective has nearly vanished, at least as far as scientists are concerned, and the temper of evolutionary thought today is predominantly materialist.

Some readers may bristle at my usage of terms like "materialist" and "materialism" to characterize the still prevalent philosophy of nature assumed by evolutionary thought today. Nevertheless, I shall generally employ these terms rather than "physicalist" and "physicalism," especially since so many prominent evolutionists have no difficulty referring to their own thought as materialist.[3] Ever since Einstein, of course, the term "matter" has really meant "matter-energy," a subtler notion, and so some philosophers now prefer the term "physicalism" to earmark the belief that matter-energy, rather than just matter, is the ultimately real stuff in the universe. As we shall see, however, the term "materialism" will still do quite nicely. Numerous biologists, and evolutionists in particular, are quite comfortable with this designation.

In any case, it is the persistently materialist rendering of life and evolution that we need to keep examining. There are two important reasons for doing so. In the first place, materialist interpretations of life still offer the most intellectually serious challenge to religious faith. Religious beliefs continue to be of great importance to the majority of people in the world. And so it is enduringly important for them to ask whether there is really any substance to the materialist challenges to religion. And, in the second place, the kind of inquiry I shall undertake in this book is significant for the sake of science's own survival. I am convinced that materialist philosophical interpretations of the universe and evolution, whatever *prima facie* plausibility they have, are an obstacle to the advancement of science and our understanding of nature.

Of course, in its investigation of living phenomena, pure science legitimately employs a reductively physicalist or materialist method. There can be no justifiable objection to a "methodological" materialism in biology, for example, as long as its practitioners remain aware that their abstract mechanical or atomistic models are leaving out most of what common sense and cumulative human wisdom understand as "life." But when this modeling is taken too literally, it becomes in effect a belief system of its own, one that not only arbitrarily opposes religion, but also ironically imprisons and diminishes science itself. Once materialist approaches attain the status of a general view of reality, that is, of metaphysics, they become an impediment to the kind of open inquiry that we rightly associate with science. The intellectual clarity that materialist interpretations of life and evolution seem to offer is purchased at a great price: The very depth of life and the universe becomes lost to consciousness.

Reading the Universe

My proposal is that we can restore a sense of depth if we interpret our confusion about science and religion in general, and about religion and evolution in particular, as a "reading problem." Let us suppose that the universe is in some sense comparable to a written text and that its intelligibility cannot emerge until we have learned how to read it. Both religion and science may then be seen as distinct ways of "reading the universe." The idea that the cosmos is something like a book is recurrent in the world's post-literate religions. But, in modern times, science also has pictured nature as a book to be read. Galileo, for example, in the earliest days of the scientific movement compared the universe to a book, insisting that it "cannot be understood unless one first learns to comprehend the language and read the letters in which it is composed. It is written in the language of mathematics, and its characters are triangles, circles and other geometric figures, without which it is humanly impossible to understand a single word of it; without these one wanders about in a dark labyrinth."[4]

However, it may be that science itself cannot read in depth the full content of nature's book. Aside from leaving out the qualitative meanings that religions had previously read in the cosmos, or in what has been called the "Book of Nature," the quantitative readings of nature by modern science are liable to overlook, or render merely incidental, the fact that the cosmos has also gradually shown itself to have a narrative complexion. Over the last century and a half, science itself has shown that the universe has a *history*, but the new historical understanding of the cosmos has yet to make a truly significant impact on intellectual culture. Celebrated academicians, for example, often think of the cosmos as a pointless swirl of mindless stuff on which a patina of life and mind glimmers feebly for a cosmic moment.[5] The narrative texture of nature still lies largely unacknowledged. However, once we develop the habit of thinking of the cosmos as a story—as geology, biology and astrophysics now demand that we do—the universe again becomes something to be read, possibly at many levels of depth. We not only now find in nature features analogous to codes, alphabets, grammars and information. We can also make out the outline of a dramatic adventure. But shall we be able to find a "meaning" written there also?

Not if we persist in our literalism. Like all texts and stories, nature is susceptible to shallow readings that fail to get to its inner substance. Today, it seems to me, evolutionary materialism is a kind of "cosmic literalism" stuck on the surface of nature, satisfied with groundless claims that there is simply nothing beneath the "fundamental" laws of physics and natural selection. Just as biblical literalism remains content with a plain reading of scripture, the modern decision to understand the universe and the evolution of life as "merely material" is essentially a literalist flight from the depths of nature.

Today, we are all painfully aware of religious literalism and its sometimes hideous consequences. Literalism, of course, is one of the side effects of literacy. Once writing emerged in history, the human sense of the sacred began to register itself formally in the various scriptures that we still study and revere. But as religious classics grow old, people often lose touch with the depth that inspired them, and so the texts become frozen. A rigidity in reading follows, and it shows up most poignantly when devotees of the various religious traditions discover, often to their enormous sorrow, that they cannot reconcile their sacred literature with the new universe of science. Having lost the ability to read beneath the surface of sacred scriptures, they mistakenly interpret science as a threat to the very substance of their faiths. This has been especially the case after Darwin and the discovery of evolution. As we shall see, the question of science and religion has to do, at least in great measure, with how to interpret the texts of scripture in the light of Darwinian narratives of nature.

The arrival of literacy, as I have just noted, brings with it the possibility of literalism. And it is often scriptural literalism that leads religion into apparent conflict with science. However, in a parallel way, a literalist interpretation of nature—one that goes no deeper than Galileo's quantitative symbols or Darwin's idea of natural selection—can also lead scientists to dismiss religion for the shallowest of reasons. Scientific deciphering of nature has been the occasion for great gains in knowledge, but it has also permitted the emergence of a most soul-deadening "cosmic literalism." Our recently acquired scientific expertise in reading the text of nature has led us into such a trance-like fixation on surface codes and signifiers, and on life's evolutionary grammar, that we fail to look into the depth that lies beneath them. I hope in the following pages to burrow beneath both religious and cosmic literalism. Only in the depth beneath the texts of nature and holy writ shall we find a way to reconcile science and religion, evolution and the idea of God.

Beneath Evolution

I have written this book especially in response to numerous claims by contemporary Darwinians that we cannot expect to surpass the profundity of evolutionary explanations of life. Today more than ever, biologically informed thinkers claim that Darwinian concepts, updated by genetics, provide the deepest and perhaps the ultimate explanation of life. Even when life manifests itself in human religion, they believe we can trust Darwinian concepts to provide the final accounting. If this supposition is true, of course, then Darwinism rules out altogether the ultimate explanation of religion given by religious people themselves, namely, that religion is a consequence of the presence to consciousness of an Absolute Reality. If the "sense of God" comes not from God but *only* from biological factors, then religion is groundless.

In *God After Darwin* (Westview Press, 2000) I made the case that not only is evolutionary biology compatible with religious belief but that it is even a great gift to theology. I argued that evolution is not atheism, as some opponents and proponents of Darwinism have claimed. After Darwin, our thoughts about God may not be exactly the same as before, but evolution does not inevitably diminish trust in a creative and providential deity. In fact, for many thoughtful theists today, evolution arouses a deeper understanding of the divine than a pre-Darwinian worldview could ever have authorized.

The present book, going beyond the earlier one, looks more deliberately at the question of how, after Darwin, religions may plausibly claim to be bearers of *truth* and not just of meaning and adaptive consolation. The question is especially interesting now that so-called evolutionary psychologists claim to have found a deep Darwinian explanation for why we tend to be religious in the first place. After "explaining" religion as an evolutionary adaptation, or as the by-product of the peculiar kind of brains our ancestors acquired during their Pleistocene evolution, it seems easier than ever to conclude that Darwin has therefore exposed religion as "airy nothing" (see Chapter 8). We need to examine carefully the inference that Darwinism (or neo-Darwinism), by explaining religion, also explains it away.

While I am appreciative of any light Darwinism can shed on religion, the question still remains as to whether evolutionary biology can in principle give an unsurpassably deep explanation of religion or, for that matter, of life as such. Darwin, I agree, has brought considerable depth to our understanding of life. It is time now to look deeper.

I

Religion and
Darwin's Truth

What religions have said about the universe does not always appear to correspond with what science reports. Religion and science even seem incompatible at crucial points. And so we are now divided. Some of us look to science to tell us what is real or true. Others, ignorant of science, or distrustful of its methods, continue to fill our minds and hearts with religious images and ideas. A few can keep their scientific knowledge separate from their religious sensibilities and in this way apparently avoid conflict. But, as everyone knows, science now questions the factual basis of much of the Bible, the Quran and other religious texts. How then can those of us who cherish our faiths and live joyfully within their visions of the universe also claim that they place us in touch with *what is?* Aren't religions essentially fiction, merely imaginative constructs? Can we any longer take them seriously as pathways to truth?

The Darwinian picture of life, more dramatically than any other development in modern science, tempts us now to place the whole of religion in the realm of illusion. Perhaps nothing challenges the religious notion of a purposeful universe more directly than does evolutionary biology. Moreover, recent versions of Darwinism even claim that our ethical and religious inclinations are nothing more than adaptations, survival mechanisms "put in place to help our genes get into the next generation."[1] Our moral and religious aspirations are guileful evolutionary contrivances deluding us into the groundless *belief* that we are cared for by a providential reality. Prominent evolutionary psychologists now believe they have exposed all of religion as a grand illusion.[2] Religious beliefs, they say, make us feel at home in an otherwise unbearable universe and in this way contribute to our race's reproductive fitness. But in fact, they claim, religions are empty of referential substance.

In Darwinian perspective the *ultimate* reason why ideas about the gods persist and religions continue to survive is because they are biologically adaptive. As vehicles of evolutionary cunning, religions motivate us to work hard, raise families and communicate a spirit of trust to our offspring. But now, with Darwin's help, we have found out what is *really* going on underneath our religious posturing. It is simply this: Our genes are seeking to get themselves into the next generation. All the rich layers of religious symbolism are, in the final analysis, nothing more than the consequence of our genetic endowment seeking out a circuitous path to immortality. Genes may not be the direct or immediate cause of our specific religious ideas, but they are the ultimate explanation.[3]

By explaining religion, therefore, evolutionary ideas also seem to explain it away. In Darwinism, if we are to believe some of its adherents, the world is now finally handing itself over completely to human understanding. Francis Bacon's sensational dream that the human mind can force nature to spill forth all of its innermost secrets appears close to realization. Today an increasing number of scientists think Darwin's ideas, updated by genetics in the form of "neo-Darwinism," are about as deep as we can go in our efforts to understand life. It is not surprising then that religious skeptics and critics of theology are also turning to Charles Darwin. If they want science to back their suspicions about the reality of the sacred, they look not so much to Vienna and continental Europe as to Down House in the English countryside. Freud and Marx have lost much of their former luster, and the anti-theistic disciples of Nietzsche, Sartre and Derrida are not interested in getting the seal of science anyway. But for those who still think that science is both authoritative and essentially ruinous to religion, Darwin has become more compelling than ever.

Not only does Darwin's picture of nature's indifference seem to give the most convincing reasons yet for scientific atheism, but his powerful idea of natural selection, in combination with our recent knowledge of the gene, also apparently provides the cleanest explanation of why our species became religious in the first place. An increasing number of Darwinians, after countless centuries of human ignorance, claim now to have reached rock bottom in explaining both our own existence and the motivating power of our religions. Science has not only found out what is really going on in nature. It has also found out what is really going on in our religious longing for the sacred.[4]

Heartwarming Fiction

Obviously it is hard for religious people not to be distressed at the starkness of what Darwin's net has dredged up from the depths of life. Intriguing as it may be intellectually, the Darwinian account of life hardly provides a space within which spiritual and ethical aspirations can flourish. This is not a logically sound argument for writing it off, of course, but it is reason enough, even for those of us who accept evolution as factual, to ask just how deep Darwin does in fact take us into the heart of the real. Impressed and grateful though we may be for his clarifications, we still have cause to wonder whether his limpid accounts lead us, after all, to the foundational levels of life and religion. To satisfy our longing for meaning in an age of science, some of us may turn to piety or poetry. But enlightened evolutionists caution us that religion and art are merely heartwarming fiction.[5] Our genes, they claim, have created adaptive but essentially deceptive brains and emotions that spin seductive spiritual visions in order to make us think we are loved and cared for. But in fact it is all illusion. Darwin has allowed us at last to naturalize religion completely.[6]

A "naturalized" explanation accounts for religion without having to appeal either to cultural factors or the notion of the "supernatural."[7] The naturalizing of religion and other facets of human culture has gained enormous appeal recently among some Darwinians. What would happen, though, if everyone on Earth suddenly took seriously the claim that religion has a purely natural explanation? Suppose that tomorrow all humans became convinced that their most cherished beliefs are *ultimately* the products of their genes alone. Wouldn't all the poetry and piety that had reassured our ancestors lose their power to comfort us today? Having seen religion for what it really is—brilliant illusions fabricated, at least remotely, by mindless genes—won't even the noblest spiritual visions inevitably fall flat before all lovers of truth? And if religions lose their power to attract us because they are now cognitively suspect, what then will happen to our genes? By learning the "truth" about religion—that our spiritual dispositions are purely natural vehicles in the service of genetic interest—won't we contribute to species suicide? If the naturalizers of religion really cared about the human future, why don't they keep their Darwinian revelations to themselves?

Ironically, by alerting us to the genetic flow beneath our religious and ethical "constructs," the Darwinian psychologists risk making the river run dry. If they follow the dictates of logic, the newly awakened will conclude that all the ideas of ultimacy cherished by naive religious souls throughout generations past are empty of any real content. And religion will no longer have a transformative effect on us once we become assured that it does not lead toward Absolute Reality. If it was adaptive at one time because we thought it was true, religion can no longer be so once we have acknowledged its referential emptiness.

At our best, after all, we humans are truth-seeking beings, and eventually we realize that only candid contact with *what is* can bring us lasting satisfaction. Certainly the Darwinian debunkers of religion cannot deny this point without self-contradiction. Otherwise, why are they such devout seekers of the ultimate truth about religion? If we were all to assume with them that science alone can retrieve the deepest or most "fundamental" truths about the universe, then our sense of "the sacred" would soon appear to us as emotionally charged fiction at best. We would see through the filminess of religion, recognizing it to be nothing more than a cozy cover-up protecting us from the ultimate meaninglessness lurking beneath the benign surface of nature. If we come to suspect that our religions are not in some very deep sense true, then honesty should compel us to abandon them, once and for all. To tolerate religious ideas as charming inventions or as pre-scientific holdovers of frail human conjecture would be unworthy of truth-seeking beings.

Can Religions Give Us Truth?

Yet, what does it mean to be truthful? To scientific skeptics, there can be no surer road to truth than science. To some so-called postmodern thinkers, neither religion nor science can be "objectively true" because nothing in the arena of thought can claim to be truthful (except, of course, that judgment itself!). But it is still the authority of science, much more than any academically sequestered expressions of postmodernism, that makes religion seem dubious to most sincere skeptics. To many people, both in and beyond the academy, religious ideas do not connect easily with the world that science has opened to our view. And even though skeptics sometimes concede that religion continues to have ethical, aesthetic or emotional import, they find it hard to believe that it contributes anything to our knowledge of *what is*.

Religions, however, no matter how "counterintuitive" or "counterfactual" they may seem to the scientifically literate, are to their followers profoundly *truthful* ways of reading the universe. Religious people themselves are convinced that their myths and metaphors are *about* something, indeed about Absolute Reality.[8] If their religious ideas were not taken to be representative of something eminently real, then these same ideas would have no ethical or aesthetic power either. When beauty and goodness are divorced from truth they grow too hollow to stir us.

Even Sigmund Freud, who thought of religion as made up totally by the human imagination, realized that at least to its devotees it is about something real. He himself was convinced, of course, that religion is only a matter of our projecting childish wishes and fears onto an inhospitable cosmos. But he acknowledged that to religious believers themselves faith has a truly cognitive rather than purely projective status. Freud knew that it is only to outsiders such as himself that religion seems to be a mere construct. As far as the devout themselves are concerned, God, salvation, heaven, nirvana, enlightenment and so on are much more than simply aesthetic or ethical adornment of an inherently pointless life. On the contrary, religion is about the deepest of all realities. And although today most theologians grant that, viewed psychologically, there is an imaginative aspect to all religious expression, this does not mean—at least to most of us—that religion is *nothing but* human projection. Religion, to anyone who takes it seriously, is about what is Most Real.[9]

Freud predicted that religious people, as they become imbued with the spirit of science, will eventually abandon the conviction that faith conforms to *what is*. They will come to see the real world as the province of scientific inquiry alone. In his view, if we could only agree that there are no dimensions of reality deeper or more comprehensive than those accessible to empirical investigation, religion would be fully exposed as the enemy of true knowledge. Religious people would then relinquish any notion that there is in fact a transcendent reality or an ineffable depth of meaning that underlies the universe.[10]

If we add to Freud's the now even more influential ideas of Darwin, a religious reading of the universe may seem more implausible than ever. The known facts of biology appear to contradict the ideas of religion. It is hard to reconcile evolution's blind rigor and aimless meandering with the nearly universal religious sense that we live in a purposefully ordered world. Consequently, today, many prominent evolutionists dismiss abruptly any speculations that locate the story of life within a spiritually endowed universe. Rather than fitting nature to religion, it is more appropriate, they argue, to fit religion to a Darwinian account of nature. In this fascinating new perspective, our ancestors became religious only because sacred symbols and stories adapted their scientifically uninformed minds and hearts—and ultimately their genes—to a harsh universe. In a roundabout sort of way, religion promoted their reproductive fitness. In neo-Darwinian perspective, religious symbolism amounts to just one more aspect of adaptive evolution. As for its actual content, religion is pure fantasy bearing no relationship to reality itself.[11]

Gould's Overtures

Some evolutionists actually enjoy telling us that Darwinian accounts of religion have made our species' sacred dreams completely unbelievable, and that we must therefore choose between science and religion. Sometimes, however, they break the news more gently. Recently, for example, America's most prolific—and justifiably honored—evolutionist, Stephen Jay Gould (who died after a long illness while this book was in press) tried mightily to soften the devastating theological implications of his own understanding of Darwin. Science and religion, he said, can peacefully coexist. He proposed that any alleged conflict between the two may be overcome if we would just learn to view them as "non-overlapping magisteria" (NOMA). Science and religion, he claimed, are talking about two entirely disparate sets of topics. They should be "equal, mutually respecting partners, each the master of its own domain, and with each domain vital to human life in a different way."[12]

The realm of science, according to Gould, is that of "factual knowledge," and that of religion is "values and meaning."[13] Situated in these separate domains, "how can a war exist between two vital subjects with such different appropriate turfs—science as an enterprise dedicated to discovering and explaining the factual basis of the empirical world, and religion as an examination of ethics and values?"[14] Gould was trying to put a distance between himself and the more publicly anti-theistic neo-Darwinians. While candidly professing his own agnosticism, he had awakened apparently to the prospect that in a theistic culture the cause of science education is hardly served by tying Darwin's ideas as tightly to atheism as do his neo-Darwinian rivals, especially the Tufts philosopher Daniel Dennett and the Oxford evolutionist Richard Dawkins.[15] The latter two clearly enjoy brandishing the godlessness they claim to be implicit in Darwin's revolution. Gould, on the other hand, considered such antics heartless as well as pointless.

However, a closer look at Gould's writings about science and religion will show that he could reconcile them only by understanding religion in a way that most religious people themselves cannot countenance. Contrary to the nearly universal religious sense that religion puts us in touch with the true depths of the real, Gould denied by implication that religion can ever give us anything like reliable knowledge of *what is*. That is the job of science alone. As far as Gould was concerned, our religious ideas have nothing to do with objective reality. Scientific skeptics may appreciate religious literature, including the Bible, for its literary and poetic excellence. But they must remember that only science is equipped to give us factual knowledge. Doubters may enjoy passages of Scripture that move them aesthetically, or they may salvage from religious literature the moral insights of visionaries and prophets. After all, the exhortation to live a life of justice and love is always humanly respectable. Still, Gould could not espouse the idea that religion in any sense gives us truth. No less than Dennett and Dawkins, when all is said and done, he too held that only science can be trusted to put us in touch with *what is*. At best, religion paints a coat of "value" over the otherwise valueless "facts" disclosed by science. Religion can enshroud reality with "meaning," but for Gould this meaning is not intrinsic to the universe "out there." It is our own creation.

In the wake of modern scientific understanding, and especially evolutionary biology, the persistent question, then, is whether religion can claim coherently that the universe is *in fact* purposefully influenced by an ultimate, transcendent reality, one that exists independently of our own projections. It is clear from his own writings on Darwin that Gould himself was dubious about such a possibility. He unremittingly maintained that what makes Darwinism so difficult for people to swallow is not the science of evolution as such, but the "philosophical message" that comes along with it. According to Gould this message is that life has no direction, that there is no purpose to the universe, and that matter is "all there is."[16] As far as he was concerned, this "philosophical message" cannot appropriately be disengaged from Darwin's science. It is Darwinism, not religion, that has read nature down to its final depths.

Thus, beneath his benevolent overtures to religion, Gould held on tightly to the assumption that only a materialist philosophy can appropriately contextualize evolutionary science. We should note that Gould himself, like many other modern and postmodern thinkers, was not at all disappointed by this state of affairs. An inherently meaningless world, he submitted, allows us humans to give our own meanings and values to it, and in this way realize our creative human vocation.[17]

Condescension

The consequence is that if Gould was correct in tying Darwin's theory inalienably to the idea of a purely material cosmos, a universe intrinsically devoid of overall significance, then no conceivable theistic belief system, by anyone's definition, could ever live comfortably with science. Gould insisted that "no scientific theory, including evolution, can pose any threat to religion."[18] But his persistent approval of the materialist ideology in which allegedly "scientific" presentations of Darwin's great ideas so often come packaged subverted his own claim.

Gould's neat separation of religion and science as non-overlapping magisteria may appeal to scientifically educated humanists who acknowledge the cultural importance of the Bible and religion, and who view all religions as essentially illusory. However, such an approach will inevitably seem condescending to believers. For those who take their beliefs seriously, authoritative scriptures and teachings refer to an Absolute Reality to which only a transformation of their whole being and consciousness can give them access. The biblical writings, for example, invite believers to look with trust and hope toward a promising and saving God. But only if people believe that this God *actually exists* will they be enflamed by hope, empowered to embrace the moral ideals of the prophets or truly caught up in the movements of biblical narrative. Without a genuine trust in the *actual* coming of God in a new creation, the Bible's moral and aesthetic dimensions would be ultimately vacuous to earnest devotees of Yahweh.

Gould's approach, while trying to rescue some of the Bible's literary and ethical residue, in effect dismisses religious hope as excess baggage incompatible with scientific modernity. But this is hardly to encounter the ancient texts on their own terms. We may legitimately dispute the biblical authors' pre-scientific cosmology, but we cannot ask them to surrender their fundamental trust that the universe *in its depths* is shaped by a divine promise. If we do insist that they give up their idea of a promising God, we should be candid enough to confess that such a deletion would take the soul out of their poetry and the passion out of their moral commitments as well.

Whatever poetic beauty or ethical inspiration the biblical texts embody was originally inspired by their authors' sense of the dawning of a saving future that would be brought to completion by a truly living God. If the psalmists and prophets had embraced the modern assumption that their hope is merely imaginative projection or Darwinian adaptation, they would never have felt empowered to write and speak as they did. A necessary condition of their poetic creativity and ethical passion was a sincere belief that religious claims have to do with reality in the deepest sense of the term. The lyrical beauty of the psalms and the moral challenges issued by the prophetic books are responses to what their authors took to be the *reality* of a creative and redeeming God. The biblical authors and their communities of faith, therefore, would be deeply puzzled if they saw us enjoying the products of their religious inspiration while at the same time viewing their trust in God as childish illusion.

For scientific skeptics, however, what pre-scientific people took to be "revelation" is merely the product of human longings imaginatively run wild. Our ancestors allegedly projected onto an indifferent universe creative fictions so palpable that the imaginings seemed to be inspiration from "beyond." So graphic was their picturing of God that the illusion of deity even aroused in some people the most exquisite poetry and the most intense commitment to the unfortunate poor. But scientific modernity, postmodern historicism and Darwinian anthropology now profess to have exposed this commitment as a grand, though perhaps poignant and even noble, deception.[19]

Representatives of evolutionary anthropology, for their part, do not always despise religion, but their estimation of it goes something like this: "It is fortunate for us that people in the past were oblivious to the biological facts that drove them to produce their inspired works, for if they had been fully aware (as we Darwinian biologists and psychologists are) that religion was ultimately the work of selfish genes, they could never have felt the illusory compulsion from 'beyond' that drove them to their extraordinary aesthetic and moral accomplishments. Lucky for us and our genes, they did not yet know the Darwinian facts, for their freedom from evolutionary understanding allowed them to unleash powerful fantasies that laid out the foundations of the cultural and ethical constructs that have shaped culture and civilization to this day!"[20]

The Road Ahead

Something, it seems to me, is terribly wrong with this picture. Here we are, scientifically enlightened moderns (and historically conscious postmoderns), in effect telling all the psalmists, seers and prophets of ages past that there never was any basis in reality to their hopes and ecstatic utterances, but that it is nice of them to have graced us with their inspirations nonetheless. In effect we are saying to them: "If you really knew what we know now about the purely natural causes of religion, you would have rid yourselves of any pretense that there actually exists a transcendent ground of value and meaning. But thank you anyway for passing on to us the beautiful words and ideals that your touching illusions of ultimacy have provoked, so that we can delight in them and even live by them."

We will avoid such condescension, I believe, only if we sincerely ask once again whether religions can lead us to a level of depth and truth that we cannot discover through science alone. But is there anything in the real world "left over," any dimension of depth to be plumbed, after science has finished its own reading of nature? Is there room for theological explanation of nature alongside of, or in addition to, that of science, and especially evolutionary biology? What indeed is the cognitional status of religion or theology in an age dominated by the Darwinian paradigm? After Darwin can we still read the universe as something grounded ultimately in God, as overflowing with promise? Can we do so while at the same time paying serious attention to what the Darwinians are saying about nature and life? While all the interesting things that evolutionists talk about are indeed going on, is it possible also that something even more fundamental is occurring—something that runs too deeply in the nature of things to fit fully on the rich platter of evolutionary understanding?

While expressing an appreciation of evolutionary *science,* and without in any way contradicting it, the ensuing chapters will argue, one step at a time, that we may go much deeper than Darwin in our attempts to understand both life and religion. In doing so, we can learn a lot from the ancients, who at least had the suppleness of mind to allow for layered explanations when looking at complex phenomena. For example, in Plato's *Phaedo,* the imprisoned Socrates, commenting on the question of why he was sitting there in his cell, weighed an "explanation" not entirely unlike the series of physical causes evolutionary materialists might point to today in explaining religion. This kind of explanation would contend, Socrates fumes, "that the reason why I am lying here now is that my body is composed of bones and sinews, and the bones are rigid and separated at the joints, but the sinews are capable of contraction and relaxation and form an envelope for the bones with the help of the flesh and the skin, the latter holding them all together; and since the bones move freely in their joints the sinews by relaxing and contracting enable me somehow to bend my limbs; and that is the cause of my sitting here in a bent position."[21]

Socrates admits, of course, that he would not be sitting there without such physical factors. But these essential conditions are not the ultimate explanation. To suggest otherwise is analogous to saying that voice and air are the causes of our conversation. A deeper, but still not the deepest, explanation for Socrates' sitting there in prison is that the Athenians had condemned him and he had thought it right and honorable to accept their penalty. But such deeper explanation, Socrates admits, is much harder to locate, much dimmer and more difficult to bring into focus than are purely physical accounts. Perhaps the same is true of the deepest explanations of life and religion. Socrates knew, but could not specify with physical precision, that the *ultimate* reason for his being there in prison was the attractive power of "the good." It was the transcendent realm of value, of "what is best," that had grasped hold of him and moved him to accept his fate. Perhaps something analogous to "the good," something deep and barely perceptible, is the ultimate explanation of life, evolution and religion as well.

2

A Reading Problem

In the academic world today, it is not at all uncommon to encounter the claim that religious ideas carry no cognitive weight. Intellectuals often view religion as essentially a matter of feeling and inspiration, but seldom do they publicly endorse it as a way to truth. Religion is "mere metaphor" or at best useful fiction. Today's skeptics, with a few notable exceptions, do not generally rage against religion but are instead content to ignore it. Some evolutionists, as we have just seen, even appreciate the adaptive role that religion has played in ethical and cultural evolution, but they doubt that religion can tell us anything about the way things really are. Even where there is abundant goodwill and open-mindedness, scientifically enlightened thinkers often find it difficult to understand how religion could possibly lead us toward reality or truth. They allow at times that religion can give us consolation, moral motivation and even meaning. But they find it hard to imagine how it could put us in touch with *what is*.

What we have here is a reading problem. How are we to read sacred writings in an age of science? And how are we to read the universe that has just become visible to us as an evolving story? Is the cosmic narrative filled with meaning or is it essentially pointless? Ever since the invention of writing, the universe has often been compared to a book. And because books may be read at many levels, the assumption of religions has been that the universe itself is a great teaching, one whose wisdom could be mined if only the reader is properly trained.[1] I believe it is useful for us to experiment once again with the idea that the cosmos is something like a *book*. This venerable analogy may open up fresh ways of thinking about evolutionary science and its relationship to religion while giving us access to a depth in nature that has become almost inaccessible because of shallow reading habits. The book analogy may allow us to understand Darwinism and religion as different "reading levels" rather than as incompatibles. It will also lead to distinct understandings of truth, so that we need not dispense with the idea that religion can give us access to a kind of truth that science cannot reach. And picturing the universe as a book may help us spin off other ideas associated with "reading." These satellite notions may help us address the question of whether we can trust our religions to lead us beneath surface impressions, into the depths.

Reading Levels

Let me introduce my theme by way of a simple parable.[2] Suppose Herman Melville's novel *Moby Dick* is lying open on the floor of my house. My dog comes along and pokes its nose into it, excited by the book's peculiar odors. At the level of dog perception Melville's great work has a special significance that it does not have for me. The dog lives in a world of smells. Its senses are sharper than mine, and they help it grasp dimensions of the book that will forever elude my own awareness. Nevertheless, dog-awareness has clearly left something out as far as the book's content is concerned.

Let us now imagine that a monkey opens up the same book, curiously and randomly turning its pages. The monkey will "read" the novel as a set of white pages dappled with small black marks. Again, the monkey is not wrong to apprehend the novel at this elementary level, but the book just may have more to it than this. Next, a five-year-old child, having recently learned her ABCs, looks into *Moby Dick* and observes that the book is a treasury of letters of the alphabet, a content missed by both the dog and monkey. Again, the child's reading is quite accurate, but deeper levels of meaning still remain buried in the book. I wrote a book report on *Moby Dick* when I was about fourteen years old. At that time the book seemed to me to be a very long—and tedious—adventure story. I grasped the narrative outline at the time but missed all of the artistry, pathos and wisdom beneath the narrative's surface. I was not *wrong* to read the novel at the level of sheer storytelling, but having spent some time with Melville's book later in life, I realized how much of its substance my earlier readings had left out. Today, I can assume that a great deal of the book's substance still escapes me, calling for even deeper readings in the future.

Perhaps the universe is at least in some sense comparable to such a book. If so, the natural sciences, while able to read it at a certain level, are still leaving something out. For that matter, religions likewise leave out a great deal in their own readings of the universe, while perhaps also being able to retrieve levels of depth that science cannot. If so, it would follow that learning to read the universe in multiple ways would enrich all of us. But literalism, both scriptural and cosmic, stands in the way. Scientific literacy has made it possible to decode nature, life and even aspects of the human brain. We now know about elementary particles, DNA chains, amino acids, neurons and natural selection. We have cracked nature's code at several levels. But knowing a code does not mean knowing how to read. Our situation today is not unlike that of the child who has just learned the alphabet without having yet probed Melville's novel for a more profound content.

Academic science is skilled at decoding nature. But it is not equipped—and rightly so—to probe for deeper meanings beneath the deconstructed surface of nature. Science has gained control over the chemical alphabet of life and is now deciphering its genetic lexicon and evolutionary grammar. It has brought us to the point where we believe we can manipulate living processes to serve our own goals. But our enchantment with the close-up, fine-grained view of life that science provides may divert us from reading the depths below. Having reached a high level of scientific literacy, we now have the problem of how to avoid getting stuck at the level of a "cosmic literalism," made possible, ironically, by our new literacy. Fixation on the scientific understandings of nature, including the Darwinian, threatens to make cosmic literalists of us all.

Scientific Literacy and Cosmic Literalism

A recent article in *Scientific American* claimed that over ninety percent of the 1,800 members of the National Academy of Sciences profess to being atheists or agnostics.[3] To many of them, the idea of God, and any corresponding sense that we live in a meaningful cosmos, are not only superfluous but contrary to scientific understanding. Even among the less elite classes of scientists in the United States, only about forty percent or so would say they believe in a personal God, although this is a figure that has remained almost constant since early in the twentieth century. What "God" means in these surveys is not always clear; but, whatever spin we put on the polls, there is clearly a wide gap between scientists and the public at large on the question of the credibility of belief in God. To scientists, the universe is apparently not bursting with revelations of the divine. The ancient psalmists may have read the heavens as declaring the glory of God, but the majority of today's scientists find no message there whatsoever.

Why is this so? There are many complex historical reasons, and it is useful to know these. But let me suggest again that we are dealing here with what is essentially a reading problem. It is the problem not only of how to read religious texts in the context of contemporary scientific cosmology, but also of how to "read the universe" against the backdrop of the sacred texts and teachings of religion. In parallel with the religious world's persistent textual literalism, a cosmic literalism has settled into the scientific domain of contemporary culture. And if textual literalism is a way to avoid the deeper dynamics of sacred texts, cosmic literalism for its part now keeps out of view the vast domain of nature's own depth. If the biblical literalist defensively repudiates all challenges to the plain meaning of Genesis, the advocate of evolutionary materialism just as fiercely protests the claims of poets and mystics who, in Wordsworth's terms, see nature as "deeply interfused" with a meaning that science cannot discern.

Literalism in the religious community is especially conspicuous in the phenomenon of biblical "creationism," notorious among scientists for its repudiation of evolutionary biology. An interesting subset of the creationist camp is "scientific creationism." Longing to bolster religion's cognitive status in a literalist scientific culture, the scientific creationists place the Bible in direct competition with Darwinism. They insist that the biblical book of Genesis provides a scientifically accurate explanation of life and that Darwin's ideas are scientifically weak by comparison. Rather than seeking to understand life at an altogether deeper level than that of science, scientific creationists have decided—most ironically—to embrace scientism's own cosmic literalism. They have implicitly conceded that only a scientific reading of nature will command respect today. And after making this concession they declare that an ancient religious text gives a more accurate scientific reading of life than Darwin does.

Where creationists read things with a biblical literalism, however, evolutionary materialists approach the world with no less shallow reading habits of their own. Both readings, as far apart as they may be in other respects, characteristically share an aversion to understanding things on many levels simultaneously. If creationism collapses explanation of life onto one level, this is no less true of countless contemporary interpretations of Darwinism. By proclaiming that natural selection of adaptive genetic ensembles is *fully* explanatory of life's diversity and complexity, some well-known evolutionists exhibit a literalism that matches, in its flight from depth, anything in the world of contemporary religious fundamentalism.

Neo-Darwinian science, of course, can give lucid explanations of life. For example, it rightly "reads" the specific design of organisms as the product of natural selection, and it does this in a way that appropriately leaves out any sense that life is of God. This methodologically godless way of reading nature is uncontroversial and justifiable as far as science itself is concerned. But what deserves comment is the quite nonscientific conclusion that Darwinism therefore *excludes God* as an explanation of life's design.[4] If "excludes God" means that there is no room *at any level* for theological explanation, then at this point Darwinians have become literalists, too. Such a claim says in effect that there is no need to pierce any deeper into the text of life than Darwinism does in order to grasp what is *really* going on there. If we follow the *Moby Dick* analogy, however, it may turn out that—once we take into account the full scale of being—evolutionary science will be exposed as having taken us, comparatively speaking, only a little way past the reading levels of the dog, the monkey, the child or the fourteen-year-old. The Darwinian reading, like theirs, is not wrong, but conceivably it leaves a lot out, as all sciences inevitably do. It is one of the tasks of the present book to propose that alongside the Darwinian, and *not* in competition with it, there are other truthful ways of reading the life-story. Without in any way spurning the insights and advances of evolutionary science, these alternative ways of reading may take us deeper into the life-story than Darwinism can by itself.

From a purely scientific point of view, of course, all phenomena need to be understood *etsi Deus non daretur* (as though God were not a factor). Natural science, for the sake of its own integrity, has to leave out all appeals to divine explanation. From the point of view of science, a theological reading of nature is always out of place. The question remains, however, whether the scientific reading takes us deeper than all other readings. Are there perhaps in the universe even more fundamental levels of meaning, levels that the sciences, including evolutionary biology, may have missed? Is it possible that the clarity given by science does not inevitably bring along with it the depth that the human quest for truth is really after?

If there are any deeper dimensions, we should not be surprised that, in order to discover them, we would have to undergo a disciplining of consciousness—at times involving struggle and some pain—that would "train" us to perceive them.[5] Such a requirement should not disquiet us, since even within the sphere of the sciences, accurate understanding is possible only after we have undergone a rigorous transformation of our mental faculties. We must undergo a *training* in the respective methods of inquiry appropriate to each field of science before we can see what is going on in its own unique vista on the natural world. We cannot understand what the physicist discovers in nature, for example, without first learning calculus or without acquiring the discipline of suppressing questions that do not pertain to this particular science. Some tutoring of the mind—even a kind of asceticism—is a prerequisite for reading the universe through any scientific discipline.

It should not be surprising, then, that religions also demand a change of mind, as well as heart—a *metanoia* as the Gospels call it—as an indispensable condition for reading in a deep way what is going on in the universe. One function of religious exercises is to train us to see beneath the surface of the world so as to encounter what otherwise would remain buried beneath our notice. Religions, as we shall see in the next chapter, prepare us not so much to grasp as to be grasped by a dimension of inexhaustible depth in the cosmos. They instruct us, no less than the natural sciences, in what is *really* going on in the universe. They set before us images and stories that represent, often in a crude and unlettered way, the graciousness that seems to lie beneath the world's ambiguous surface. And the main reason they appear to conflict with science is that we are so stubbornly literalist in our approach to both scriptures and the cosmos.

Religious scholars today are willing to admit that in some sense our religions (like the sciences) are constructive enterprises. There is always an element of imaginative creativity going on in religion, just as there is in science. But religions no less than science understand themselves primarily to be *responses* to something real, to a presence that beckons. They are reactions to a dimension of reality that lies far deeper than what we can imaginatively concoct. This dimension takes hold of us long before we attempt to take hold of it, so we have to be extremely careful and tentative in the ways we represent it. Because of the distortive tendencies of human imagining, the great religious teachers even exhort us to submit at certain points to the discipline of *silence*. A posture of waiting quietly and patiently without images—for we know not exactly what—is essential to religion's authenticity. Religion carries with it a tacit sense that, beneath the surface of our sacral images and ideas, there resides infinitely "more" than we can ever express. Literalism, however, is not interested in this "more."

I am proposing, then, that our human penchant for literalism accounts for most of the apparent skirmishes between science and religious belief. But we can move beyond seeming conflicts only if we learn to distinguish carefully among possible reading levels. Whenever either scientists or religious believers sense an apparent clash, it is because, for one reason or another, they have decided to read a religious text or the universe *only* on one level, usually the one in which they are most competently trained. Thus, in the controversy about Darwin and God, the so-called scientific creationists and their evolutionist opponents both implicitly agree that everything should be read at a plain or literal level of understanding. "Scientific creationists" ironically read the accounts of creation in Genesis less religiously than through *scientifically* trained eyes (though these eyes are typically more Newtonian than contemporary), thus compacting a richly layered sacred text into a prosaic source of scientific information. And their decision to read the Bible at the level of science inevitably makes Darwin's ideas appear contradictory to religious beliefs.

Meanwhile, scientifically enlightened thinkers, and especially evolutionary materialists, are at times as literalist in their reading of the Bible as are their creationist opponents. For example, the philosopher Daniel Dennett, reading the Bible at the same information-hungry level as his creationist foes, claims with them that Darwin's great idea is indeed incompatible with religious belief. Because to him the quality of scientific information in the Bible is inferior, he feels obliged to announce that "science has won and religion has lost," and that "Darwin's idea has banished the Book of Genesis to the limbo of quaint mythology."[6] In his discussions of Darwin's "dangerous idea," he patently shares with creationists the assumption that biblical literature is in the business of dishing out science. It is not his scientific learning so much as his biblical literalism that leads him to claim that evolution has rendered Genesis obsolete.

Similarly, the noted Harvard biologist E. O. Wilson expresses wonder that anyone would try to reconcile the Bible with biology. In league with his creationist opponents, he puts Darwin's science into direct competition with Genesis, a work that frustrates him by failing to provide reliable information about evolution. Surely, he complains in his celebrated book *Consilience,* if the Scriptures were inspired by God, they would not have given us so deficient a picture of nature![7] Although Dennett and Wilson differ from creationists by declaring Darwin right and the Bible wrong, they share with their religious opponents an anachronistic literalism that demands from ancient texts nothing less than a body of reliable contemporary scientific information.

Hybrid Readings

Of course, while the creationists are trying to subject Genesis to a scientific reading, they cannot avoid simultaneously reading it religiously, also. Undeniably the biblical text brings them spiritual consolation along with (allegedly reliable) scientific information. What is remarkable is that they remain untroubled by their imposing modern scientific expectations on a pre-scientific composition. They defend as *scientifically* accurate certain symbolic and mythic expressions that were never intended to be fonts of scientific information. When they are reading the symbolic, narrative and metaphorical content of Genesis, they are moved religiously at one level, but simultaneously they are locating the material representationally at another, in fact at the same reading level as that at which science conducts its own work. They may be grasped by the narrative depth and symbolic power of the texts, but at the same time they force this content into scientifically shaped cognitive containers. This "hybrid reading," conflating metaphysical with scientific inquiry, is one of the most characteristic features of contemporary literalism. It is symptomatic of the reluctance by many in the religious and scientific communities to distinguish reading levels.

The only cure for literalism, and hence for hybrid reading, whether in religion or in the realm of science, is to gain an appreciation of the hierarchy of distinct reading levels through which we may approach both sacred texts and the universe. This awareness, however, demands a textured appreciation of the *dimension of depth* that underlies both classic religious texts and the universe itself. I shall say much more about this dimension of depth in the following chapter, but for now it is enough to note that as our reading skills develop, we may achieve competency at one level in our pursuit of understanding without necessarily becoming qualified to read things at another level. Whenever we forget this point, we end up reading things appropriate to one reading level with eyes schooled only by familiarity with another. As the *Moby Dick* comparison implies, one may not be wrong to read religious texts or the world of nature at levels parallel to the dog, monkey, child or adolescent, but these elemental readings inevitably leave out substance that can only be encountered by deeper readings.

Once again, however, it is not biblical fundamentalists alone who practice hybrid reading. Eminent scientists also often find it hard to restrict their reading to the levels demanded by the methodological requirements of their separate disciplines. They may start off innocently enough reading the universe with great clarity at the level of atoms, genes or evolutionary mechanisms. But then, without warning, they sometimes begin to read their material with eyes that are more appropriate to philosophical or theological metaphysics than to science. Without being explicitly aware that they have jumped from a scientific reading level to that of metaphysics, they begin to hold forth on the *ultimate* nature of things. There are countless examples of this hybrid reading in the writings of well-known scientists today, but let us look at two in particular.

We may turn first to the physicist Steven Weinberg. Weinberg asks whether physics, which he dignifies with the competency to take us down through layer after layer of nature to the "fundamental" levels of reality, will eventually find God.[8] The question of God, as Weinberg would have to agree, is not one that physics itself appropriately asks, since science deliberately leaves out any religious considerations. Nevertheless, reflecting on the implications of his own branch of science, Weinberg cannot resist asking whether physics will find God.[9] He claims—quite rightly, of course—that it will not. But from this truism he suddenly catapults, without any warning to the reader, to a metaphysical or theological conclusion that *therefore* the idea of God is dubious. Because reading the universe at the level of physics—for Weinberg the most "fundamental" of sciences—will not find God, it is unlikely that God exists. Forgetting, at least momentarily, that physics is neither fundamental (it is actually quite abstract) nor equipped to read the universe for answers to what we usually call the "big questions," Weinberg in effect decides that physics is competent after all to decide the question of God. This is an unusually clear illustration of what I am calling hybrid reading.

A second example is that of evolutionist Richard Dawkins, who claims in almost all of his books that we can learn the deepest truth about life only if we read it at the level of genes.[10] Taking note of all the clever things DNA does to get itself passed on from one generation of organisms to the next, Dawkins's genes-eye reading of life is illuminating at a certain level. It is not wrong to read the life-process at the level of genes, any more than it is wrong for the five-year-old child to read *Moby Dick* at the level of alphabetical ciphers. However, for Dawkins the genes-eye approach becomes the *fundamental* way to read the life-story. In his rendering, we cannot expect to go any deeper than the level of genetic activity in our understanding of life on Earth. No other reading levels lie deeper than the genes-eye approach. Having made this assumption, Dawkins is already on the way to concluding that *therefore* evolution must entail atheism.

If we look at evolution only from a genetic perspective, of course, what we shall see is a purposeless, impersonal flow of genes—and that is all. Dawkins is right so far. The interesting point, however, is not that we don't see God through a genes-eye reading of life. Clearly we don't—just as the five-year-old, at her reading level, cannot see Melville's meaning in *Moby Dick*. What is interesting is Dawkins's heedless mixing of levels, a hybrid reading that oscillates upward and downward, construing life now at the level of science, now at the level of metaphysics. In his books, helpful observations about genetic activity become alloyed time and again with spurious personal convictions about the ultimate nature of reality. This is why he cannot envisage religion or theology in any other way than as conflicting with science. As Ullica Segerstråle observes in a very helpful discussion of the sociobiology debate, Dawkins is convinced that "the ambition of religion is to explain the *same* things as science! For Dawkins, religion occupies exactly the same slot in people's mind—a world-view slot—which is why they are in direct competition."[11] Once he decides that there can be only *one* reading level available to our understanding of life, the only way for a metaphysics or worldview to have its say is to hybridize with science, as it persistently does in Dawkins's books.

Reading Nature in Depth

If there is anything deeper to life or the universe than what physics or evolutionary biology can provide us with, then the readings by Weinberg and Dawkins will turn out to be shallow. But does nature in fact have the dimension of depth that would expose this shallowness and allow for alternative, and perhaps more fundamental, readings? Today it seems to experts like Weinberg and Dawkins that science is bringing everything in nature up to the surface with such clarity that nothing remains to be illuminated by other avenues of exploration. Religious intuitions that the world is *inexhaustibly* deep seem harder to sustain than ever before. And it is very difficult for many scientific thinkers to believe that there will be any real mystery left over after scientific probing into the cosmos has finished its work.

Nature, says physical chemist Peter Atkins, is just "simplicity masquerading as complexity." In other words, beneath its overt display of complexity, nature's "depth" turns out to be nothing more than an unadorned elementality that has now been uncovered by physics. And beneath that austere simplicity there lies—absolutely nothing.[12] Science has already penetrated to the very bottom layer of nature's illusory profundity. In agreement, the late physicist Heinz Pagels wrote that in the future "the universe will hold no more mystery for those who choose to understand it than the existence of the sun. As our knowledge of the universe matures, that ancient awestruck feeling of wonder at size and duration seems inappropriate, a sensibility left over from an earlier age."[13] Today, numerous scientists and philosophers believe that only a scientific reading can put us in touch with rock-bottom reality. Life, accordingly, turns out to be *nothing but* lifeless matter, and mind is *nothing more than* neurons.[14] Evolution is *merely* the result of blind chance and impersonal law working algorithmically on mindless stuff. There is "literally" nothing else going on.

If there is an inexhaustible depth to nature, the materialist perspective will turn out to be a shallow one, and I shall argue in the following chapters that this indeed is the case. However, if scientific materialism only skims along the surface of nature, so also do theological readings that fail to take into account the raggedness of Darwin's portrait of life. An aversion to nature's depth is noticeable in the kind of religious thought that dares not look beneath the veneer of "design" in nature into the tortuous evolutionary story of life's long struggle. The anti-Darwinian tenor of so much contemporary religious piety is no less a flight from nature's depth than is evolutionist reductionism. How then are we to get beneath both scientific and religious literalism into the depth of nature?

To start with, we would have to acknowledge that nature, like a book, can be read on several different levels without any contradiction. It is not hard to show that we can do this with written texts. For example, we can approach the Bible religiously or simply to mine whatever information it provides about ancient Near Eastern culture, or to satisfy other kinds of intellectual curiosity. In the academic world today, it is often in very nonreligious ways that scholars look into what others have taken to be sacred texts full of mystery and meaning. We can learn a great deal in our purely secular reading of such texts, for this kind of reading is not wrong. But perhaps we may also still read sacred literature in such a way as to find inspiration for our lives. We may immerse ourselves in traditionally revered writings in a manner that allows them to have a transformative effect on our hearts and minds. For example, by attending to the constant encouragement to trust in the promises of God that leap out from nearly every book of the Bible, countless people are still moved from despair to hope. And in finding a reason to hope, they discover a reason for living lives of goodness as well.

However, can we read the universe in a parallel way? Without contradicting any particular scientific reading, can we perhaps also ascertain that the actual shape of the universe and its evolution conforms more compliantly to the contours of hope than of despair? Cosmic pessimists claim that science gives us no reason to hope, but religions—or at least some of them—have encouraged us to read the cosmos on a deeper level as a source of meaning that can have a reconstructive effect on our lives. But in order to carry out such a project, do we have to place the transformative readings of nature into a competitive relationship with the scientifically informative? Or can we view the distinct readings as occurring on different "levels"? If it is possible to read a sacred text on both informative and transformative levels without contradiction or hybrid conflation, may we not also do likewise with the universe, especially now that it is showing us its fundamentally narrative character?

Of course, there can be no immediate transition from a scientifically informative reading of the cosmos to a religiously transformative one. Just as holiness of life will not make us experts in the sciences, so also scientific insight into nature does not lead us inevitably to lives of authenticity. No matter how impressive our command of scientific knowledge is, we may miss something significant about the universe if we fail to let our encounters with it transform our hearts as well as our minds. On the other hand, we cannot expect the universe to disclose its inner meaning to our hearts if we stubbornly refuse to let the various sciences change our minds. To agree that the transformative and informative readings are logically incommensurable does not mean that we can keep them perpetually apart at the core of our consciousness. Even though the two readings record their content on separate scrolls, our need to unify knowledge cannot settle indefinitely for a standoff. The overwhelming wealth of information now coming to light in the fields of physics, astrophysics, scientific cosmology and evolutionary biology must be incorporated into any deeper reading of the universe that expects once again to recover its religious import. The fact that nature can now also be read as a narrative may facilitate this union.

For the universe to transform our hearts as well as our minds it must allow itself to be read—in one way or another—as having a purpose. To say that the universe has a purpose means quite simply that it is in the process of realizing something that is undeniably good, and that this good is also in some sense imperishable. A process that brings about something self-evidently and *permanently* valuable is worthy of the label "purposive." But can a reading of the universe today honestly discern any such overarching purpose in it? Isn't our sense of cosmic purpose an illusory creation of the forlorn human heart seeking a hospitable home in an indifferent universe? Isn't our habitual human belief in purpose—a proposal characteristic of most religions—simply an evolutionary adaptation?

A growing assumption in the contemporary scientific world, especially among the biologically literate, is that the human heart is conditioned, perhaps even genetically hardwired, to read a purpose into nature that may not really be there. Scientific method alone, we are told, can be trusted to read things *out of* nature as nature actually exists. It is a common opinion of intellectual culture that the human heart, especially in its religious yearning, is purely projective, whereas science alone is awarded the status of being cognitively objective. Endorsing this duality, Joseph Wood Krutch remarked in an early essay that the difference between religion and science is that the former can only tell us what we *wish* the world to be like, while science alone can tell us what the world is *really* like.[15] Many other modern writers concur: if we truly desire to *know* the cosmos, we must read it with the impersonal and heartless methods of science, no matter how pessimistic the conclusions we would then have to draw from it.[16]

Is it possible then to read the universe as a meaningful story without contradicting scientific readings? In the chapters ahead, I intend to address the modern (and postmodern) denial of our capacity to find a transformative meaning in the depth of the natural world. This means, above all, learning how to read the narrative we call evolution. Commenting on neo-Darwinism, Daniel Dennett has stated that the only message in evolution is that "the universe has no message."[17] Philosopher David Hull has written that the evolutionary process is "rife with happenstance, contingency, incredible waste, death, pain and horror."[18] In the eyes of many scientific thinkers, the randomness and blindness of evolution have now shown that nature is forever incompliant to the heart's longing for a personal universe. For some prominent evolutionists Darwin has decisively destroyed the credibility of any claims that life is the product of divine "design."

My thesis, however, is that cosmic purpose lies deeper than either Darwin or design. Cosmic purpose is more appropriately thought of in terms of nature's *promise* than of the "design" that appears on the surface of this great text. The idea of "design," in any case, is too brittle to represent the richness, subtlety and depth of the life-process and its raw openness to the future. Life is more than "order." Life requires also the continual admittance of disruptive "novelty," and so the idea of "promise" serves more suitably than "design" to indicate life's and the universe's inherent meaning. In conversation not only with contemporary biologists, but also with philosophers and theologians who have probed beneath the surface of classic religious texts, I shall set forth a way of "reading" evolution that I believe to be consistent with science but also with religious hope. I shall propose that the processive character of the universe—both biologically and cosmologically speaking—is quite consistent with its being read once again as the embodiment of promise.

If we placed ourselves imaginatively in the remote cosmic past—say seven hundred thousand years after the Big Bang—how many of us, after looking out at the massive sea of radiation and emergent atoms all around, could have predicted such eventual outcomes of cosmic process as life, mind, culture, art and science? But these precipitates have indeed occurred, and so the *promise* of their appearance was latent in the inauspicious monotony of the primordial cosmic stuff. At the present point of cosmic unfolding, a cursory survey of the extravagant—but still ambiguous—story of evolutionary achievements that have occurred so far should do nothing to dampen our anticipation of yet more creative outcomes in the cosmic future. Our sensitivity to nature's ageless straining to erupt in an array of aesthetic diversity allows us to read the universe once again as having a transformative meaning. What the story of the universe seems to be "teaching" us—and this in a way that we could not have appreciated in a pre-evolutionary age—is that there may be reasons, after all, for hope.

3

The Depth of Nature

S cience and religion both take for granted that the universe is much deeper than it seems. The whole thrust of science, for example, is to dig beneath what appears on the surface of nature. Scientists make a tacit assumption that the world is always more than what first impressions yield. But religion also assumes that there is more to the world than what appears on the surface, indeed infinitely more. In theologian Paul Tillich's terms, religion is a state of being grasped by the inexhaustible depth that lurks beneath the surface of our lives and of nature too.[1] In religious experience we do not so much grasp this depth as allow the depth to grasp us. Depth takes hold of us in such a powerful way that we can neither deny it nor master it, though of course we may try to flee from it.

Although they are distinct ways of approaching the dimension of depth—and should never be confused with each other—science and religion share a concern to take us beneath the surface of things. Without a sense of reality's depth, there would be neither science nor religion. Religion exists only because beneath the surface of mundane experience, many people have felt—some more palpably than others—that something inexhaustibly important and mysterious is going on. At times the dimension of depth powerfully carries them away, and in doing so provides an unexpectedly solid grounding to their lives. To those who have experienced this depth, it strikes them—even in all of its vagueness—as more "real" than any of the focal objects they encounter on the surface of their world. They long to enter more deeply into it. But they also hesitate, lest they become lost in its immensity.

Even though science and religion are expressions of our longing for depth, they are repositories of our attempts to avoid it as well. Each is tempted to rest in a literalism that hides what lies deeper beneath the surface. I believe, for example, that this is especially the case with both creationist and materialist readings of evolution. Yet there are special moments in both science and religion when the dimension of depth breaks through with such compelling and self-authenticating force that it assumes an almost revelatory character. To those who have been grasped by it, everything else then pales in significance, including all previous renditions of reality. This "revelatory" experience is most obvious in religion, but there are occasions in the history of science also when the depth of nature surprisingly breaks through and shatters all conventional assumptions. This happened in the case of the Copernican revolution, but perhaps even more dramatically in the more recent discovery of evolution. Because Darwin's new science exposed us to the terror as well as the fascination of new regions of depth, religion cannot justifiably remain indifferent to it. Moreover, religious thought must ask if the depth that Darwin exposed perhaps provides an entry to even deeper regions beneath.

Science and Religion in Search of Depth

Let us look more meticulously into the metaphor of "depth," for here too it is all too easy for us to skim along the surface. Everybody already knows at least something of what it means to be grasped by depth. If you have ever felt that you are being called to make a sacrifice for the sake of something you value, you have already allowed yourself to be grasped by depth. If you are a scientist and have felt the call to honesty and truthfulness, even in the face of great inconvenience, it is because you have somehow been drawn down into the depths. Any scientist who wants to move beyond mere impressions about the natural world is in the grasp of depth. In fact, it is only because scientists have already dimly glimpsed new levels of depth that the great geniuses among them are able to break through the shallowness of conventional ideas. Not unlike religious prophets, such scientific adventurers also suffer at times from the loneliness and social isolation that accompanies a call from the depths.[2]

If at this moment you are wondering whether what I am saying is true, it is because you want to go deeper than the surface of my words. You too are in the grasp of depth. Ultimately, since "depth" and "truth" are one, to be taken captive by your longing for truth means that you have already gone beneath the surface into the depth. In order to value truth you must at some level already have surrendered, perhaps not without pain, to truth's claims upon you. Even to raise a critical question—to suspect, for example, that my remarks here are oversimplifying things—you have already allowed the depth to envelop your life.

But what is this depth? Are there any other names for it? Listen to these shocking words of theologian Paul Tillich. Another word for depth, he says, is "God." And so, if you want to know what "God" really means, think first of the dimension of depth that you have already experienced. "That depth is what the word God means." And if the word "God" still means nothing to you, then don't use it. Think instead about the depth that has taken hold of you—or from which you may have fled—in your life or in your work. "For if you know that God means depth, you know much about Him. You cannot then call yourself an atheist or unbeliever. For you cannot think or say: Life has no depth! Life itself is shallow. Being itself is surface only. If you could say this in complete seriousness, you would be an atheist; but otherwise you are not. He who knows about depth knows about God."[3]

Of course, it is quite possible that you know something about depth but prefer not to use the word "God" as a name for it. Perhaps the word "God" seems too small to represent the endless reaches of reality that your scientific and other experiences have uncovered. This is not entirely unlikely. But when I use the term "God" in this book I intend, nonetheless, to follow Paul Tillich's claim that God really means depth. "God" also refers to much else besides, but let us at least start with the suggestion that "God" means the inexhaustible depth that perpetually draws us toward itself, the depth without which no enduring joy or satisfaction or peace is possible. And if God means depth, then "religion"—underneath all its elaborate apparel—is simply the grateful and obedient posture of surrendering to the depth without which your life and work have no substance, no future and quite possibly no point either. To the extent that you allow yourself to be taken into the depth there is an essentially religious character to your life, even if you have never thought of yourself as religious.

But why attach the label "religious" to the surrender to depth, especially since this term is now odious to many sincere seekers? The reason quite simply is that, in their own deepest moments, the social entities that we commonly identify as "religions" have been more explicitly concerned than anything else in human history with awakening us to the dimension of depth that underlies the shallow world of appearances. Indian religion, for example, instructs us that the Most Real lies beyond *maya,* the veil of illusion in which our lives are ordinarily enmeshed. Taoism looks for the Way or the Truth that hides itself humbly in the depths of the mundane world and everyday life. Buddhism seeks an awakening to a liberating "reality" concealed beneath the everyday misrepresentations spun by our greedy longings. Platonic contemplation directs us to a realm of permanence that transcends the becoming and perishing of the world of appearances. Hebrew faith orients us toward a saving future, beyond our idolatrous enslavement to things too small for us. Jesus speaks about the presence of God's Kingdom hidden "in our midst," a reality that only hearts trained to be like the poor, or like little children, can receive. No word other than "religion" is more indicative of humanity's passionate quest for the depth beneath the shallowness of the ordinary—even if religions themselves often decay into a literalism that confuses surface with depth.

The Depth of the Universe

We may appreciate the notion of depth—in a deeper way—if we recall the process whereby we once developed our own reading skills. To understand the written word, at first we had to memorize an alphabet, corresponding sounds, vocabulary, grammatical structures, etc. Then we began to probe into simple texts and later into more challenging ones. And in the process of our education, good instructors helped us penetrate "deeper" into the great classics. They invited us to journey beneath the plain sense of a novel or essay into a "depth" of which our first reading gave us only an inkling. And even though we may have struggled and even suffered as we learned to read a play or a poem in a less literal way, we eventually arrived at a more profound level. Then we began to experience a surprising satisfaction, a sense of being on more solid ground than before. We had been grasped by depth.

The experience of learning to "read in depth" is applicable to the natural world also. Nature itself has a dimension of depth that invites both scientific and religious readings. Science and religion may each "read" the universe in search of what is going on beneath the surface. The quest for depth motivates both enterprises. But if we ignore the question of exactly how to read, then science and religion are likely to become entangled with each other beneath the surface. Viewing them as ways of reading can give unity to science and religion; but viewing them as *distinct* ways of reading can help us avoid the "hybrid reading" that I discussed in the preceding chapter. Because both science and religion originate in the human desire for deeper understanding, their mutual outcomes may at times seem to compete. But wherever conflict occurs, it is because we have not yet gone deep enough, either in our scientific or our religious reading.

Whenever scientists and theologians have persisted on what Tillich calls the long and lonely road to depth, recognizing the inexhaustibility of reality on the one hand, and the poverty of their own insights on the other, what seemed to be a good reason for conflict at one time turned out to be the occasion for breaking away from the surface even more decisively later on. The emergence of modern science and its own way of reading the universe may have disturbed a shallow religious literalism, but in the long run scientific discovery has helped religious thought abandon the textual superficiality that had shielded it from its own depth. The encounter with Galileo, Darwin and Einstein has been good for religion and theology.

Theology, then, has nothing to lose and everything to gain from its "dangerous" encounters with new scientific discovery. Today this is especially true of its engagement with evolutionary biology. Darwin's surprising portrait of life, though initially terrifying to a certain kind of religious mentality, is really a fresh invitation into the depth of nature, a depth that can also help us understand both ourselves and the divine more profoundly than before. But the quest for nature's depth cannot stop with Darwin. For the sake of truth, it must keep digging deeper.

In keeping with the "reading" analogy, I am employing the term "literalism" as equivalent to a shallow perusal, one that skims along the surface, whether of religious texts or of nature. And I believe that we live at a time when many members of both the scientific and religious communities have settled into a literalism that in both cases blunts the sense of reality's depth. Literalism, in fact, is the outcome of a refusal to look into the depth, whether of religious texts or of the universe. And it seems that literalism becomes all the more desperate whenever an abyss begins to open up beneath the surface. One example of the flight into literalism is creationism. But another is the current obsession with "design" that causes some Christian thinkers to turn away from the disturbing depths of natural history churned up during the last two centuries by the harrows of geology and evolutionary biology. Intelligent Design Theory, as it is called, seems to me to be a sophisticated way of avoiding the depths of nature. In its fixation on instances of present design in living organisms, it ignores the dark and tragic depths of nature's evolutionary creativity. By associating divine wisdom almost exclusively with shallow samples of natural order, and by overlooking the disturbing novelty and struggle that evolution entails, it leads only to an impoverished sense of both nature and God.

The avoidance of nature's depths, however, is not restricted exclusively to creationists and Intelligent Design advocates. The scientific community also sports its own brand of literalism. Scientism, the belief that science alone can put us in touch with the ultimate depths of the world, is a blatantly literalist evasion of depth as well. No less than biblical literalism, scientism (and its attendant "scientific materialism" or "physicalism") settles for an absolute clarity devoid of the ambiguity that always accompanies a genuine openness to depth. Scientism arises from an intolerance of uncertainty no less repressive of nature's depth than biblical literalism is of the religious depth of sacred texts. In fact, some of today's most fervent scientific literalists (whom I would prefer not to mention here by name) were at one time in their lives biblical or religious literalists of one kind or another. What remains constant, even after conversion, is an obsession with clarity at the price of profundity.

In keeping with current scientific literalism is the sentiment that we are close to reaching rock bottom in our exploration of the universe. A few scientists are even quite certain that physics will soon have arrived at the most "fundamental" layers of the world. Having dug down to the irreducible units of physical reality, they conjecture, we will have reached "the end of science."[4] Once we have attained the "Final Theory," there will be no digging any further, since everything significant in the natural world will already have been brought up to the surface. Nature will then show itself to have no remaining depth to be fathomed.

On the other hand, most scientists are not really literalists at all. They have little patience with the suffocating idea that the arena for further scientific exploration is growing progressively smaller. They would insist that no matter how illuminating our current scientific reading of the cosmos may be, there is yet more depth beneath the surface, and even more beneath that. Indeed they generally suspect that we shall never gain complete intellectual control over the downward, upward and outward reaches of nature. Science would lose its vitality if its practitioners truly felt close to exhausting the universe's profundity.

Religion and the Loss of Depth

Both science and religion are stirred to life especially when the sense of an endless abyss opens up beneath them. However, even though science and religion both presuppose the reality of depth, they do not read it in the same way. Science does not formally attend to the dimension of depth at all. In fact, it employs methods that push aside, for the moment at least, our tacit awareness of the inexhaustibility of the world. Each science abstracts in its own way from the rich dimensionality of the real, biting off only what it decides to chew. Every explanation is an abstraction begging to be complemented by yet other kinds of explanation.

No given scientific field, therefore, can legitimately claim to have swallowed reality whole. For while it savors its own little bite, the full platter of being remains out of view. But sometimes scientists become so satisfied with the tastiness of the morsel they have chomped off that they forget how much remains on the table unconsumed. This is what happens, for example, when a physicist claims, by dint of mathematical expertise, to have found the "mind of God," or when a biologist asserts that the secret of life lies in chemistry or that evolution is nothing more than the consequence of selfish genes seeking immortality. Allegedly "scientific" readings of nature, having mastered the alphabet and grammar of a particular level, may claim that they have read the text of nature all the way down to its "fundamental" levels when in fact they have shaved off only an abstract veneer. It is cosmic literalism that brings scientists into conflict with religion, just as biblical literalism inevitably leads religious people to reject aspects of science.

Whenever it takes its founding metaphors and symbols too literally religion also loses its own depth. For example, Judaism, Christianity and Islam represent the depth of nature in personal or anthropomorphic terms. They do so in order to render vivid their intuition that the universe is grounded in an all-encompassing love and promise. Since impersonal reality is incapable of caring about anything, let alone making promises, a meaningful cosmos must apparently be rooted in a reality endowed with the capacity to care. Thus, the Abrahamic religions, along with many others, have always insisted that in its ultimate depths the universe must be *at least* personal. However, the sense of nature's infinite depth can sometimes be pushed aside by religious fixation on certain images of a personal God. The danger here is that the deity may then come to seem smaller than the universe itself. The "size" of God becomes too middling to command the response of genuine worship. And if our sacred traditions become too literalist in their understanding of a personal God, the universe of science may seem to open up a deeper and more enticing context for spiritual adventure than do the religions.

For this reason many scientifically educated people today have little or no interest in formal religion. This indifference testifies to the failure of our theology and religious instruction to integrate the revelatory experience of a personal, promising God into an expansive cosmological setting. A profoundly religious need for endless horizons and inexhaustible depth has led many scientifically excited seekers away from the shallowness of what they rightly take to be religious literalism. After Darwin, Hubble, Einstein and Hawking, cosmic boundaries have inflated unimaginably, and the newly discovered immensity of time and space appears now to swallow up our narrowly human images of God. Likewise, the world of the infinitesimal seems to open up endlessly more fascinating frontiers. Religions concerned primarily with healing the foibles and hurts of human history have begun to seem rather paltry when silhouetted against the newly discovered cosmic ranges. Contemplation of the universe has become more intriguing and spiritually satisfying than participation in official religion.

Meanwhile religious spiritualities often direct us to look only inward. Tillich himself had modeled his "depth" metaphor for God in part on the new inward-looking psychologies of "depth" associated especially with Sigmund Freud and C. G. Jung. Following psychology's disclosure of the inscrutable abyss within each psyche, the religious quest for depth has often taken the form of a one-sidedly "inward journey." But the religious and theological importance of natural science is that it now allows us to discover "depth" also in the endless outward horizons of cosmic reality that are opening up to our ongoing exploration. The biologist and professed non-theist Ursula Goodenough implies as much in her 1998 book *The Sacred Depths of Nature.*[5]

Goodenough finds in the vastness and "mystery" of the universe a refuge from the anxiety of our own human finitude and perishability. By contemplating an endlessly expansive cosmos, she claims to have "found a way to defeat the nihilism that lurks in the infinite and the infinitesimal." She says, "I have come to understand that I can deflect the apparent pointlessness of it all by realizing that I don't have to seek a point. In any of it. Instead, I can see it as the locus of Mystery." The universe, she continues, is "inherently pointless," but acknowledging the "sacred depths" of the universe can be emancipating: "I lie on my back under the stars and the unseen galaxies and I let their enormity wash over me. I assimilate the vastness of the distances, the impermanence, the fact of it all. I go all the way out and then I go all the way down, to the fact of photons without mass and gauge bosons that become massless at high temperatures. I take in the abstractions about forces and symmetries and they caress me like Gregorian chants, the meaning of the words not mattering because the words are so haunting." Forming a "covenant" with cosmic mystery is all Goodenough needs as a scientist to satisfy the spiritual side of her nature.[6]

The favorable reception that her elegantly written book has received confirms my suspicion that theology has for too long ignored the spiritual fertility of taking the cosmic route into the domain of depth. Contemporary spirituality has instead typically undertaken the search for depth in terms of the personal "inward journey," and the result, I believe, has been to prolong the modern sense of our isolation from the universe. If each fragmented psyche is borne afloat a limitless ocean of unconscious depth, it has seemed that the way to overcome our isolation is to embark on the long and painful pilgrimage into our own untapped inwardness. There and there alone, spiritual directors have told us, will we find the connection to meaning, or to God, that ordinary life in the outer world cannot provide. But meanwhile we have lost touch with the Earth, the heavens and the abyss of evolutionary time.

The inward passage to depth often seems to be our only spiritual option, however, since so much modern science claims to have demystified the outer world, unveiling the apparent "pointlessness" of an essentially lifeless and mindless universe. Science seems to have found only a spiritual void in those vast astral realms where countless people in the past, and even a considerable remnant of scientifically uneducated people today, have looked for a grounding significance. The sense of an utterly desacralized cosmos now apparently leaves only our own interior depths as the place to look for religious meaning. The inward journey, however, has merely taken us into a subjective world that modern thought had already severed from any enlivening connection to the physical universe. The spiritless cosmos of modern mechanistic science is one in which we feel our own souls—if these too have not been demythologized away—to be complete strangers. As we seek psychological or spiritual fulfillment, therefore, we understandably turn our backs on a universe that has already been drained of meaning. And since science has apparently expelled any meaning from the immense universe outside of us, the "inward journey" leads only to an even deeper sense of human alienation from the cosmos.

Goodenough's proposal, as we shall see, is not without problems of its own. But it at least has the merit of suggesting that we are now at a point in our scientific and spiritual history when we may once again take the universe, rather than the isolated self, as our primary point of entry into depth. Or if we still wish to enter through the door of our subjective lives, then at the bottom floor of our own psyches let us allow that there is an opening that sluices downward into the temporal and spatial immensities of an unfathomably deep universe. We may now entertain the thought that the circumscribed world of the self—and of human history too—blossoms forth from the subsoil of an immeasurable cosmic evolution. The spiritual dramas involving the self and human history do not occur simply on the outer face of a natural world whose meaning is exhausted in being the theater for such adventures. Rather, the self and human history are now to be thought of as eruptions from the depth of nature itself. And by allowing ourselves to be embraced by this depth, even with all of its ambiguity, Goodenough and other religious naturalists believe it is now possible to discover a kind of redemption and even cause for ecstasy. The proposal is at least worth examining.

Deep Enough?

What response might thoughtful religious believers make to this new religious naturalism? One approach is to keep on ignoring the universe of science as essentially irrelevant to religious faith. In this case, the assumption is that what really matters religiously is only the human sphere, whether public or private, and its relationship to God. Concern with our personal destiny, or with the affairs of people and the outcome of human history, still seems to be more than enough to hold the interest of most devout believers. Most of us remain relatively uninformed about cosmology or biological evolution. We may have a vague apprehension that the universe began fifteen billion years ago, that life has evolved slowly and that genes constrain our behavior. But this knowledge remains notional rather than real. Most of the time, theologians, religious educators and pastors avoid thinking in depth about the universe and our place within it.

It is not surprising then that the new picture of an immensely deep, still evolving universe arouses a kind of cosmic religiosity that some scientists find healing. For more than a few science-minded spiritual pilgrims the "epic of evolution" is now supplanting the historically limited narratives about Israel, Jesus and the church as the place to look for religious satisfaction.[7] The new cosmic story appeals to their need for breathing space and a sense of adventure. On the other hand, the cult of a deity concerned primarily with human history is for them too provincial to evoke the sentiment of worship. The great mystery of the universe with its indefinitely expanding boundaries, on the other hand, provides an outlet for human longing to celebrate and surrender to the infinite. The "universe story" or the "epic of evolution" then becomes the new "creation myth," one that surpasses in scope the culturally confining narratives recited by our religious traditions. In the new science-based cosmic story the ancient religious narratives, including those about the promising God of Abraham, get pushed into the background, and at times abandoned altogether, as too diminutive to satisfy the religious craving for limitless depth.

Still, I wonder if this cosmic piety is as deep as we can go, even after encountering the expansive depths of cosmic and biological evolution. I would propose that another—and much deeper—approach is available to us. It is one that sacrifices neither the rich symbolic images of a "personal" God nor the imposing magnitude and profundity of the evolving cosmos. It argues that there is no compelling reason to separate the idea of an unfathomable principle of care, or of an infinitely generous source of promise, from the expansiveness and depth of the new universe story. After all, the logic even of the most classical forms of theism has always disallowed any delimiting of God, the ultimate source of "all things visible and invisible," by the universe, regardless of how extravagantly large the latter is construed. If we understand God not only as inexhaustible depth but also as the infinite source of boundless promise, by anyone's mathematics such a reality can never be surpassed by a *finite* universe, no matter how expansive the latter may be.

For this reason, religious thought must not be afraid to engage the enormous universe of contemporary cosmology. No immensities and abysses that we shall ever discover in the cosmos could conceivably outreach the bottomlessly resourceful promise that religious experience senses in the inexhaustible depths of being. More than that, the mysterious universe of religious naturalism remains itself too shallow to accommodate our religious longings for an infinity of depth. Undoubtedly there is considerable religious appeal in the exhilarating new awareness of an ever-expanding and indeterminately self-organizing cosmos. But I find myself still asking such questions as the following: Can the fathomless night sky, the unfolding complexity of the cosmic story, the world of the atom and the epic of evolution all by themselves speak adequately to the human need for *infinite* depths, especially after Einstein and the discovery that the universe itself is a *finite* set of interrelated entities? And even if we attributed some sort of mathematical infinity to it, could an ultimately *impersonal* cosmos ever speak adequately to the personal human heart and its longing for infinite love and perfect fidelity?

Can an unfathomable cosmos, at least so long as it is pictured as essentially pointless itself, arouse from slumber the human inclination to hope? Naturalistic ecstasy or tragic resignation perhaps—but hope? Can a large but still fundamentally meaningless universe be the final context for the basic confidence without which our moral aspirations may flag and fade? Can an impersonal universe, all by itself, really inspire us across many human generations to heroic lives committed to the virtues of justice, peace, love and promise keeping? Can the scientific story of biological and cosmic evolution, deep and fascinating though it certainly is, be the *ultimate* repository of our trust? In short, can nature all by itself respond proportionately to the *cor inquietum,* the restless heart, with its native capacity for the infinite?

No doubt, the religious naturalists will claim that it can. My own apprehension, however, is that devotion to the "new cosmic story" or the "epic of evolution" can all too easily lend itself to a literalist reading, one that keeps us from pushing even more penetratingly into the sacred depths of nature. I cannot fathom how the universe as now construed by natural science alone could ever adequately respond to our religious longing for infinite depths, at least so long as we take it simultaneously to be ultimately *impersonal,* as do religious naturalists such as Goodenough. Without being grounded in the reality of an "interested God"—if I may use an expression of the famous physicist and self-styled atheist Steven Weinberg's—any derivation of religious meaning from the universe alone will prove in the end, I think, to be spiritually illusory, morally impotent and logically incoherent. In saying this so bluntly, I wish, at least on this matter, to express my agreement with Weinberg. He rightly insists that a universe uncoupled from the idea of a personal God would be not only inherently "pointless" but also ultimately devoid of religious depth as well. Here the hard-core atheist seems to me to be much more logically consistent than the devotees of cosmic piety.[8]

No matter how much its expanding breadth and timeless creativity rescue me from spiritual claustrophobia, I wonder if my religious aspirations—and perhaps even the foundations of a coherent moral existence—would not be shipwrecked ultimately on the rocks of an essentially senseless universe. Bathed in "mystery" though it may be, an immense but impersonal universe, as both Bertrand Russell and Albert Camus correctly noted, is somehow *less* than I am.[9] Even though its apparent depths may invite me to prostrate myself before it and lose myself in it, I have to ask whether I can surrender myself completely to any reality that in its deepest strata lacks the qualities of intelligence, concern or the capacity for self-sacrificing love and promise keeping that I associate with the very highest ideals of my own species. Even though it may be immeasurably larger than me, a universe that is not rooted in something "personal" would be less intense in its mode of being than I am. I fear that I cannot bow religiously to a finally unpromising, impersonal universe, no matter how far its boundaries in time and space extend, without becoming less than a person myself.

A person, as Tillich correctly insisted in his famous reply to Einstein—after the great physicist proposed that religion must now grow up and eliminate the idea of a personal God—can be healed only by that which is itself personal.[10] What I choose to worship, therefore, must be *at least* personal in order to attract me at the center of my own specific kind of existence. Anything less than personal, no matter how large it is, cannot reach into the depths of my heart or heal my soul, even if it does appeal to my need for breathing room. Of course our ideas of God must include nonpersonal (or superpersonal, or transpersonal) aspects. "God," as I said earlier, means *at least* inexhaustible depth. But this depth also must be *at least* personal, or else persons could never surrender themselves religiously to it. We cannot, without diminishing our own being, worship an *It,* no matter how big It is, or how roundly It seems to dwarf us by its enormity.

However, we do not have to choose religiously between a seemingly dwarfish personal God on the one hand and an expanding impersonal universe on the other. There is no reason why we cannot take the recently revealed cosmic immensities and the evolution of life as the extravagantly sacramental self-expression of a transcendent personal divine power of renewal. Deeper than any contemporary cosmological ideas and Darwinian depictions of life can reach, perhaps there lies a wellspring of promise that opens up the universe to an ever new future of evolution and new creation. The character of our expanding and evolving cosmos is consistent with its being the embodiment of such a divine promise.

Our still unfinished universe does not exhibit unambiguous evidence of "intelligent design," and for this reason I resist making the issue of design the focus of dialogue between science and theology. The universe strikes me not so much as an exhibition of God's designs as a still quite unfinished creation, permeated with present ambiguity but also pregnant with promise. Nature is neither completely chaotic nor clearly ordered. It is *in via,* but even in its presently unfinished status it may be the carrier of an infinitely extravagant promise. It is not without a dark side, but even nature's ambiguity is consonant with its being "promise" as well. If everything at the moment were perfectly clear, completely ordered or mathematically certain, there would be no promise of a future. Neither would there be the boundless openness of the cosmos to surprising new evolutionary outcomes. Nor would life be possible. The notion of promise is suggestive because we currently find ourselves in a life-process where evil is mixed with good, ugliness with beauty and disorder with order. Trusting in a promise does not magically dissolve present ambiguity, but it does propose that confusion and chaos may not be final. And trusting in the "promise of nature" gives us confidence to explore its sacred depths as well.

I suspect that the reconciliation of science with religion today can best be accomplished in company with the idea that nature, in its sacred depths, is a great promise—and this means deeply personal. Nature, as Darwin reminds us, is not paradise, or at least not yet. Nature is filled with beauty, but also with violence and death. We cannot deny the evolutionary travail that compels many noble souls to spurn the idea that there could be any "point" or purpose to the universe. But even without dispelling ambiguity, it is still possible to appreciate the world as the carrier of a momentous promise in its depths. Sensitive to this promise, religious hope can read the universe at a level deeper than Darwin alone can take us. Darwin's science fractures the benign surface of life, exposing a troubling abyss. But in every abyss, there may also reside a hidden ground, and it may only be through religious surrender that we allow this ground to emerge as the foundation of our lives and hopes.

It is not by exhibiting flawless "design" but by carrying a promise that the cosmos also finds its fundamental "purpose." Putting things this way allows us to affirm cosmic purpose without having to deny the realities of evolutionary struggle, innocent suffering and moral evil. Those who see the universe as pointless often do so because of the pain and evil that life on Earth (and possibly elsewhere) has to endure. And, of course, if suffering were the final word, the absurdist would be correct. But there is no certain evidence that the absurdist will have the final word. The claim that the universe is pointless, a position that cosmic pessimists usually consider to be scientifically certain, may turn out after all—as we dig deeper beneath the surface— to be quite unrealistic, perhaps itself too literalist in its representation of the way things really are in their final depths. The cosmos is imperfect, as are our lives within it, but even in this imperfection, there is room for promise. And in promise there may well be purpose enough.

4

Deeper Than Despair

Suppose someone asked you to explain the world's current ecological predicament. How many different ways could you do so? I believe you could account for it simultaneously, and without mutual contradictions, on a number of distinct levels. For example, you could appeal to the insights of chemistry, biology, ecology, economics, politics, ethics or intellectual history. Each of these disciplines can "read" our planet's environmental troubles in ways that the others cannot. Indeed, at its own level, each discipline can strive for *complete* explanation of the problems. Yet horizontal completeness, that is, explanatory adequacy at any particular level, does not forbid your leaping vertically to other levels of understanding. And so you may legitimately cite the "causes" of ecological distress at each new level without rejecting what you have learned at others.

At the level of physics, to start with, ecological damage can be quite tidily explained in terms of entropy, whereby complex life-systems are irreversibly breaking down into disorder, obeying invariant laws of nature. From the point of view of the Second Law of Thermodynamics, this is *all* that is going on in environmental degradation. It would hardly be appropriate for physics to give a biological, ethical or political explanation. Most of us can live with such a self-limiting understanding, as long as we realize that other ways of reading are also available.

From the point of view of other sciences, the "real" explanation of the ecological crisis will be quite different from that of physics. For example, to the

41

chemist, the cause of ecological degradation will be located at the level of the laws of nature that permit the transformation of organic into inorganic material. From a certain point of view, we can read Earth's ecological degradation as a change in the chemistry of the planet. The biologist, however, looks for an explanation of ecological breakdown at the level of the interaction of organisms and the complex conditions essential for sustaining their viability. The environmental scientist, in turn, may "explain" the breakdown of Earth's life-systems as the consequence of hurtful (usually human) intrusions into the delicate web of relationships and mutual dependencies among diverse populations of organisms.

Moving beyond the physical and life sciences, an economist may legitimately "explain" the ecological crisis as the result of human patterns of consumption, unsustainable market growth or the inequitable distribution of the world's wealth. The political scientist may locate the "real" cause of the crisis in centers of governmental power that push the pace of economic development far beyond sustainability. Then the ethicist may come along and tell us that the "fundamental" cause of the present quagmire can be found in the human arrogance, greed, injustice or obsession with power that shapes political and economic policy. And finally, the intellectual historian may locate the deepest roots of the crisis in dubious anthropocentric philosophical or religious assumptions that lead some cultures to neglect or exploit the nonhuman natural world.

A Hierarchy of Explanations

It is easy to see from this example that multiple levels of explanation can all easily coexist, each giving its own answer to the simple question of why there is an ecological crisis. Moreover, each discipline offers its own reading of the ecological situation without any conflict with other levels. A *hierarchy* of explanations allows for a much richer understanding of the ecological situation than any particular reading can provide by itself.

A multiplicity of reading levels, or an "explanatory pluralism," may, for all we know, pertain to all phenomena, including the universe and the evolution of life. The necessity of distinguishing different reading levels *within* the world of the sciences is uncontroversial. Each scientific discipline, as we have just seen, inevitably leaves out a great deal—precisely in order to give the distinct kind of explanation characteristic of its approach. Each scientific explanation is an abstraction. It leaves something out that other sciences may be able to compensate. But is it perhaps conceivable that the totality of sciences, considered as a unit, still leaves out a great deal of the world's inherent substance, intelligibility and depth? Can we plausibly move beyond the natural and social sciences to other illuminating ways of reading the whole universe, perhaps at levels of depth completely unknown to science itself? Can we have an "extended hierarchy of explanations," one that gives a legitimate place to metaphysical and even theological understandings of the universe and evolution?

The "cosmic literalist" would forbid such a transgression. Modern intellectual life has brought along with it the powerful temptation to limit our reading of nature to what scientific disciplines alone can uncover. Accordingly, some scientists and philosophers have claimed that all natural phenomena are to be understood—at their deepest and "most fundamental" level—simply as manifestations of invariant chemical and physical laws. Since these laws are inviolable, it should be possible in principle to predict their future manifestations in all physical occurrences. And so, if we are to understand what is "really" going on in the universe, we need to read no deeper than the level of elementary physical principles and properties operative in all natural phenomena.

To those impressed by the explanatory power of evolutionary biology, it is also tempting to think that Charles Darwin has taken us about as deep as we can possibly go in the understanding of life. And when evolutionists are simultaneously inclined toward philosophical materialism—not an uncommon propensity—they are likely to suppose that an even "deeper" explanation of life lies at the level of chemistry or physics. For example, Daniel Dennett, in *Darwin's Dangerous Idea,* claims that in order to understand what is *really* going on in the evolution of life, our reading of nature needs to dig down no deeper than the level of invariant physical processes that obey simple mathematical rules known as algorithms. We can read all the complexity of life, along with human history, as "really" nothing more than the outcome of automatic atomic, molecular and genetic operations.[1] Life's evolution, in this reading, lies on the surface, and the depth beneath it consists ultimately and exclusively of "fundamental" algorithmic physical processes. In Dennett's search for nature's depth, the narrative "drama" of life in the universe becomes only incidental, since *at bottom* evolution is a purely material process.

The question, though, is whether Dennett's mechanistic explanation of life is in fact very "deep" or "fundamental." I have suggested earlier—and will press the point more fully later on—that purely physical accounts are more abstract and more shallow, not deeper, than evolutionary and other kinds of explanations. Some evolutionists, including the Harvard biologist Ernst Mayr, for example, argue that evolutionary biology, not physics and chemistry, furnishes the "ultimate" explanation of life.[2] To Mayr, Darwinian explanation is *more fundamental* than chemistry and physics. Biological evolution could never be adequately understood in terms of the knowledge proper to mathematics or the physical sciences. Mayr realizes that there is a dramatic or historical aspect to evolutionary understanding, and this narrative dimension of living processes will never show up in a chemical, physical or algorithmic reading of nature. He would object strongly to Dennett's literalism here.[3]

Our task in this book, however, is to ask just how deep the Darwinian reading takes us. Mayr contends that Darwinism gives us the "ultimate" explanation of life. It is not clear whether he means "ultimate" only in terms of the hierarchy of natural sciences, or if he means it in both a scientific and a metaphysical sense—I suspect the latter.[4] In any case, his criticism of purely physicalist accounts of life is appropriate, and he takes us a step deeper in the understanding of life than do Dennett's mechanistic abstractions. But is it also conceivable that there is something going on in life and the cosmos that lies much deeper than either physics or evolutionary biology can make out? Without contradicting what either of these sciences can discern, it is not cognitionally irresponsible for us to suppose that, given the abstract nature of all scientific explanation, they both leave out a great deal.

As a matter of fact, in order to read nature at the level of any single scientific discipline, we have to learn the difficult skill of *leaving out*—or abstracting from—the kind of reading done by other disciplines. To become qualified students of high energy physics, for instance, we cannot allow ourselves to be distracted by the concerns of biology, psychology or human history. Physics is the most *universal* of sciences. It is applicable to the understanding of everything in nature, but it arrives at this generality only by leaving out much specificity.[5] One of the things physics leaves out is all of the drama that—at least to another kind of reading—gives genuine depth, along with tragedy and promise, to nature. Although physicists often claim to be dealing with the *fundamental* constituents of nature, this does not mean that they have looked very far into the *depth* of nature.

We need to distinguish carefully between what is really deep on the one hand and what physicists call "fundamental" on the other. Physicists deserve our admiration, it goes without saying. But precisely because their science prescinds from the narrativity or historical drama that carries us toward what another reading may consider the real depth of the universe, they cannot plausibly claim that their science penetrates to the bottom layer of it all. Physics must be part of any informed understanding of nature; but in order to appreciate nature's depth one does not have to understand the intricacies of quantum or relativity physics any more than the evolutionary biologist has to be an expert in biochemistry in order to understand Darwinian selection.

Theology, Scientism and the Flight from Depth

Contrary to the modern suspicion that religion or theology can only read meaning *into* nature, my proposal is that our sacred symbols and myths may, at a certain level of understanding, come closer than science to registering what is *really* going on in the narrative depths of the universe. A religiously informed consciousness—especially one that is both acquainted with suffering and skilled in the habit of hope—may be able to detect signals arising from the depths of nature that the methods of science, proficient in abstractive, mathematical and nonnarrative conceptualization, will inevitably (and quite appropriately) overlook. A wholesome theology is ready to face the fact that it is not easy to look into nature's depth, any more than into the depths of a great literary classic or one's own soul. The reason is that true depth inevitably confronts us initially as a cavernous abyss, one that threatens totally to consume us. And so we instinctively recoil from it. Only when we have allowed the depth to grab hold of us, often in the face of fierce resistance, do we begin to love it and be grateful for it.

Within the massive bombardment of our perceptivity by the universe, religious awareness claims to discern, at least vaguely, a dimension of reality that science must deliberately ignore in order to establish its own distinctive identity as science. That the theological reading will always be "dim" or "vague" is not a defect; rather, it is the consequence of religion's referring to a reality that lies *too deep* for human thought and language. Since the effort to arrive at scientific clarity impels us to ignore so much of reality's complexity, only a cloudier but richer kind of medium—that of myth, symbol or metaphor—can put us in touch with the ultimate depths of things. By permitting ourselves to be grasped by religious symbols, we are pulled down into a domain that often unsettles us at first, but one that eventually leaves us more satisfied than before. This dimension, at least to those who have allowed themselves to be grasped by it, will impress them as being much closer to *what is* than any of the abstractions of science can claim to be.

Science rightly seeks clarity, though an obsession with clarity leads only back to literalism. But readings of the universe that move us most deeply, or that mean the most to us personally, *must* inevitably be unclear.[6] If they were perfectly clear they would not move us. Modern thought, however, has been obsessed with clarity. Starting with nominalism in the late Middle Ages and fortified by René Descartes's concern for "clear and distinct ideas," the

modern intellectual world has idealized the quest for crisp lucidity in repre-
senting the universe. But as Dennett's work demonstrates, modernity often
ends up confusing clarity with depth.

A preoccupation with clarity appears to be benign, of course, and in ordinary life it is essential. In writing this book, for example, I am striving for at
least some degree of clarity on the complex topic of evolution and religion,
employing an all too simple analogy of "reading levels" as a first step toward
understanding what is in fact a much more convoluted matter than such elementary modeling can represent. Clarity is important. But it should not be
confused with depth. In fact, clarity in understanding is almost inevitably
going to be purchased at the price of depth. So the closer we come to the
universe's true depths, to *what is*, the more our clear and distinct ideas will
have to give way to symbol and metaphor.

Once again, I do not intend here to dismiss the mind's search for clarity as
unnecessary. Teachers justifiably require clarity from their students' written
and oral presentations. Without attempts at clarity, communication could
not occur. In the absence of clarity, science and good philosophy are impossible. And yet, at a certain level in our encounter with the deeper dimensions
of *what is*, a striving for absolute lucidity becomes inappropriate. Perhaps if
the universe were in fact a one-dimensional Flatland, we could expect its full
substance to be brought out into the daylight of full transparency. The need
for clarity indeed is the driving force behind purely physicalist readings of
life. But a universe (or a text) that has real depth cannot become completely
subject to intellectual clarification. Consequently, we must search for a kind
of expression that can represent the depth of reality without succumbing to
literalism. This is where we need to take seriously the role of narrative discourse, poetic metaphor and religious symbolism.

As Whitehead has observed, "those elements of our experience which
stand out clearly and distinctly in our consciousness are not its basic facts."[7]
They are abstractions. And to abstract means "to leave out." Our clear and
distinct scientific abstractions leave out most of the depth of nature. Abstractions, necessary though they may be to focus our thought, are not adequately
representative of what is really going on in the universe. To represent reality
in depth, we need a kind of expression that leaves less out than does scientific
discourse. And it is the enormous virtuosity of myth, metaphor and symbol
to keep before us at least a dim awareness of the depths of the real. The most
powerful, moving and meaningful human discourse—even in an age of science—inevitably takes on a metaphoric, symbolic or mythic form.

For that matter, even evolutionary explanation employs a metaphoric and
narrative mode of expression not found so generously in physics or biochem-

istry. To those evolutionary biologists affected by "physics envy," the inevitable fuzziness of their narrative-historical accounts of life can be a source of embarrassment. At times they apologize for telling evolutionary stories, promising us that as their science progresses it will be able to dispense with narrative and embed the information in mathematics. They will find Dennett's approach appealing because it tries so hard to replace narrative with algorithm as the language most suited to the factual representations of life.

However, instead of apologizing for their narrative and metaphoric depictions, evolutionists should instead embrace these as more richly explanatory of what is going on in life than any equations could ever hope to capture. Life, after all, *is* a story. And only a narrative mode of expression could ever hope to represent it accurately. Of course, by leaving less out than physics or chemistry does, a narrative kind of explanation inevitably sacrifices the narrower road of clarity. But in doing so Darwinian stories take us deeper than nonnarrative accounts are able to do. The question, once again, is whether they take us deep enough.

If we are accustomed to literalist readings, we will find the vagueness not only of religious but also evolutionary metaphor especially frustrating, and perhaps even cognitively vacuous. We may then try to replace metaphor with mathematics, in the way that Dennett idealizes. But Whitehead's advice is that, as we progress in understanding the world, we must learn to mistrust our abstractions, not because they are wrong but because they fail to take us very far beneath the surface. On the other hand, as religions would insist, myth, metaphor and symbol have the power to lead us toward the depths.

Readings that are clear and distinct may be intellectually satisfying, but they are existentially trivial. Complete conceptual clarity, therefore, is certainly out of place in religious awareness. This is necessarily so because the depth into which religions initiate us comprehends us much more than we can comprehend it. We cannot intellectually encompass that which already enfolds our own being. We can have an awareness of being grasped by depth, an awareness that we may call "faith."[8] But if we attempt to subject the depth of the universe to our scientific control, this depth will slip even further beneath the surface. And in response to its elusiveness, we may be inclined to deny that it has any reality at all. Nature will then seem to be nothing more than "simplicity masquerading as complexity."[9]

In order to appreciate beauty and truth we have to allow ourselves to be carried away by them. Likewise, to experience depth we must allow ourselves to be drawn down into it. We will resist, of course, for it seems at first that we are being hurled into a bottomless pit. But it is only by surrendering to the depth beneath the surface that we will find real satisfaction, and possibly even joy.[10] Only in the depths shall we find truth—or better, allow truth to find us. Even beneath the surface of scientific work, which methodologically leaves out our human concerns about the deeper meanings that the religious quest seeks, there is nonetheless a kind of surrender to depth that coincides with "faith." To be effective as scientists, we must allow ourselves to be grasped by values such as honesty and integrity. Above all else, we have to allow our minds to surrender to truth. Only by allowing ourselves to be *drawn into* reality's depth can we look beneath surface appearances.

It is not science, therefore, but *scientism* (the belief that we can arrive at truth only through science) that sponsors cosmic literalism's flight from depth. From its very beginning, modern science decided, as it were, that it would not ask questions about the purpose, meaning or the value of things. Its methodological bracketing of such "existential" concerns is still rightly considered essential to the very enterprise of science. Theology has no objection to this deliberate self-limiting, a restriction that allows science to have its distinct ways of (abstractly) reading the cosmos. But what theology cannot accept is the very nonscientific belief that the sciences, taken either individually or together, will ever give us an exhaustively deep and adequate reading of the universe. In fact, the belief that science can encompass the full scope of *what is* must be recognized to be utterly nonscientific itself. Nothing in science justifies the assumption that its method of reading puts us in touch with *all* dimensions of the real. Scientism is not the logical outcome of scientific inquiry, but a supposition that has no basis in science at all.

Scientism, nonetheless, continues to be a prevalent, academically sponsored way of avoiding the depth of nature. It is a "literalist" reading more akin to biblical creationism than to the open-minded, depth-seeking quest for truth. Thus, any alleged conflicts between science and religion do not arise from either science or religion as such, but from arbitrary decisions by either scientists or religious believers about the explanatory adequacy of different reading levels.

Reading an Unfinished Universe

How then can we overcome religious and scientific literalism and learn once again to read life and nature in depth? Before modern times, the universe seemed deep beyond measure. It was the expression of an eternal wisdom. People thought of the cosmos as a "great teaching," one to which we must closely attend if we are to learn wisdom ourselves.[11] In literate cultures, the natural world even appeared to be a sacred text. By approaching it with reverence, people could read it and make sense of it. Reading the universe, of course, was not an exercise lightly to be undertaken, for beneath the surface lurked layer upon layer of challenging mystery and meaning along with realms of terror. And in penetrating toward the world's innermost substance, the interpreter would have to undergo a purifying self-transformation. One could not really *know* the universe without being changed in the process.

The universe no longer appears this way to most of us. With the help of science, we can now read it quite clearly—or so it seems—but we seldom discover any deep meaning in it, and we are not significantly changed by learning about it. Often it appears that the farther our scientific facility in decoding nature has advanced, the more vacant the cosmos is of any transformative significance. While scientific proficiency progresses at an accelerating rate, our lives do not necessarily become deeper, better or happier. Information about the universe piles up, but our sense of its significance does not keep pace. For many of us, the cosmos is no longer anything like a sacred book, but a blank and mindless tablet onto which we may, if we wish, inscribe our own purely human meanings.[12]

How then can we begin once again to envisage the cosmos as a rich repository of deep meaning? I believe a good place to start is with our new evolutionary awareness that we live in an unfinished universe. By our best reckoning, the universe is a story in the process of being told. Evolutionary narrative clearly implies that the cosmos is still coming into being. The sciences of geology, astronomy, Big Bang physics, astrophysics and evolutionary biology have all contributed to a new consensus that the universe remains an ongoing project. But if this is so, whatever "meaning" the universe may have can be glimpsed only fragmentarily at the present. At best our perspective can be only akin to the vague intimation we may have of a great novel's message and meaning when we are still at the point of just beginning to read it. In an evolving and unperfected universe, any cosmic "purpose," if we may use the term, must likewise still be coming to expression. It cannot yet have manifested itself in a transparently definitive fashion; and so any attempt on our part to say what the universe is all about will always fall short of precision. Nevertheless, even an unfinished universe may be the coming to expression of an unfathomably deep *promise*. And in attuning ourselves to the sense of nature's promise, we may be not only informed but transformed as well.

But a promise conceals as well as reveals. Consequently we cannot expect the universe to be here and now an absolutely clear and final revelation of its ultimate meaning. Exactly what the outcome of cosmic process will be we cannot say. We can only trust. Even from a theological point of view, it is inappropriate to view what religions call "revelation" as giving us any supratemporal vantage point that would lift us suddenly to the end of the story and vanquish all obscurity. Revelation is an eruption from out of the depths, but an inexhaustible depth can never manifest itself in a temporally final way. Consequently, any religious meaning we might discern in the recesses of a cosmos still-in-the-making could at best take the form of a hint or intimation of final enlightenment. If there is a broad purpose to cosmic reality, it would reveal itself indistinctly—and only to a consciousness that is transfigured more by hope than by an obsession with absolute clarity.

Deeper Than Dennett

However, isn't hope an unrealistic attitude, especially after Darwin? Certainly cosmic literalists would say so. But just as I could not appreciate music if I were tone deaf, I could not detect any promise in nature's depths unless my awareness were shaped beforehand by the "virtue" of hope. A posture of entrenched despair would render me opaque to any harbingers of final meaning that an unfinished cosmos might hold. A mind and heart formed by hope, on the other hand, would more likely be sensitive to such signals, if indeed there are any. One implication of our living in an unfinished universe is that we can become attuned to the deep promise of nature only by *wagering* to indulge our native propensity to hope. Unfortunately, however, modern intellectual culture has discouraged such a leap, habituating our minds and hearts to cosmic pessimism, often laying out allegedly scientific reasons for a tragic "realism" about things. As Dennett's work illustrates, the dominant schools of philosophy today almost universally assume that the cosmos is inherently devoid of meaning. And in this intellectual atmosphere the findings of evolutionary biology seem to be final proof of the ultimate senselessness of the universe.

Nevertheless, given the unfinished state of nature, such a reading may very well turn out in the end to be a misrepresentation. In any case, it is certainly premature. After all, if the universe is in the process of coming into being, its story is still being told. And like all interesting stories, it may be riddled with ambiguity as it ambles along. But ambiguity is quite consistent with hope, and hope cannot be dismissed as naively out of touch with truth until we have seen things through to the end. Perhaps if we were to assume that the cosmic story is virtually completed, we might have more reason for despair. But, as things stand, there is no crystal-clear reason, scientific or otherwise, for us to approach the cosmos in a spirit of despair rather than trust. Even the prospect of an eventual physical "death" of the entire universe need not undermine this trust, at least so long as there remains a way in which the perishing of everything in time can somehow be redeemed. How to think of such a prospect after Darwin will be the topic of Chapter 11.

In any case, religion—or at least some important versions of it—can shape our hearts in such a hopeful way that our minds may be enabled to attend to promising features of nature that a more stoical perspective, or a more literalist reading, would cause us to overlook altogether. Objectivity, at least in matters of great importance, requires an appropriately fashioned subjectivity; and such a subjectivity may require especially the courage to hope. Daniel Dennett, whose sensibilities are clearly shaped by a metaphysics of materialism and cosmic pessimism, not surprisingly reads the universe as "really" nothing more than an entropic algorithmic movement of dead matter momentarily tolerant of the improbable aberration known as life. But another kind of scientific thinker—biologist Louise Young, for example, in her book *The Unfinished Universe*—without in any way denying the Second Law of Thermodynamics, can plausibly argue that what is "really" going on in the universe is an orientation toward ever richer modes of ordered complexity and beauty.[13] Even after science has laid out the naked facts, the universe remains open to more than one way of reading it.

Contemporary scientists and philosophers, however, will often persist with the claim that science demonstrates indubitably that the universe is purposeless. Any overarching meaning eludes detached empirical inquiry, so we may justifiably conclude that the cosmos is pointless.[14] Biologists know, of course, that there are numerous instances of "teleonomic" behavior in living organisms. For instance, the eye has the purpose of seeing, or the heart for pumping blood. But such local organic functioning provides no warrants for attributing purpose to the universe as a whole. It still seems likely to many, if not most, scientists and philosophers that any sense of cosmic purpose arises from illusory yearnings of the human heart rather than from dispassionate inquiry.

Scientists, however, decided from the time of science's early modern origins not to deal with questions of purpose at all. Consequently, we cannot be surprised that science has not found any point or purpose to the universe. It is not the business of good science to deliberate about something so empirically evasive as the overall meaning or significance of things. It is interesting, though, that scientific impressions of the universe today are lending themselves to an undeniably narrative presentation. The cosmos now seems to be much more like an unfolding story than a timeless and frozen state of affairs. So our asking whether there is any "point" to an unfinished universe is not the same as asking about the meaning of an eternal swirl of essentially mindless matter. If we can view the universe as a story instead of a merely algorithmic explication of an inflexible set of laws, it is not at all inconceivable that, at least in some "loose" sense, the story is filled with promise, and hence with a purpose that makes human hope the most realistic of outlooks.

Today, the universe undeniably shows itself to be a flowing story rather than an established state. Carl Friedrich von Weizsäcker observed some years ago that the most significant discovery of the twentieth century is that nature itself is inherently historical.[15] And science now depicts the whole cosmos as a kind of journey. We find ourselves somewhere—we really don't know exactly where—in the midst of a work-in-progress. Immersed in the flux, we can have no omniscient perspective on it; and so we cannot pretend to speak with clarity about the meaning or meaninglessness of what is apparently still so incomplete. Still, what *is* undeniable is both the irreversible temporal sweep of the process, and the net increase in organized complexity leading to life, mind and other manifestations of beauty over the course of time. These are at least hints or suggestions worth looking at in more depth than contemporary intellectual culture seems to be interested in doing.

How then are we to greet the new narrative of the universe? Increasingly since the late sixteenth century, modern intellectual life, based largely on the impression that the universe is governed by impersonal physical laws, has chosen a fatalistic approach. Meanwhile much of the religious world has responded to modern cosmology by reverting to the time-worn path of mystical renunciation. That is, it has sought in effect to nullify the passage of cosmic time, reading the temporal universe only as a place of exile, as something we must eventually put behind us altogether in the soul's spiritual expedition to the beyond. The search for a timeless eternity outside of nature has made the physical universe seem to be only a staging area for the human religious passage.

However, the emerging new scientific sense of an unfinished universe allows us to dig deeper than either scientistic fatalism or mystical renunciation has taken us. As long as the cosmos seemed to have no future, and human history was the only interesting arena of dramatic activity, fatalism and mystical renunciation were our only options. As a result, discussions of the relationship of science to religion often came down to a confrontation between cosmic pessimists who claimed that the universe is fundamentally indifferent to life, and religious pilgrims who agreed with the fatalist cosmology but who looked "above" to a realm of timeless perfection beyond the futile flux of becoming. But developments in science itself have now made the apparently forced option between cosmic fatalism and world-fleeing piety less constraining than before. Although both alternatives still have numerous adherents, the universe that stood motionless as the background of their former disputes has now been seen to move dramatically.

The stage on which the human drama unfolded, in other words, now shows itself—through scientific discovery itself—to be nothing less than an adventure. Science formerly seemed to shore up the fatalist position, but it now lets us envisage a universe that has a future full of surprises. The specter of an immeasurable cosmic future now overshadows the diminutive human story while still allowing us to site our ephemeral span within an enormous and momentous project, one to which our own species may also contribute something unique and valuable. The universe that we now know to be *in via* leaves both the logical and cosmological space for us to speculate about much more interesting outcomes than cosmic pessimism or religious mysticism had entertained. A cosmos manifestly still in the making allows us, at least in principle, to retrieve once again a religious posture of hope for the future of the universe.

What kind of promise or purpose can we possibly discern in the depths of a universe upon which we cannot yet train our sights in any settled way? The transience and expected death of the cosmos defy our attempts to state clearly what the "point" of it all might be. And the long tortuous epic of life's evolutionary struggle and suffering only adds to our disquietude. We need to remain fully aware of all the travail and messiness, and not just the astonishing complexity and creativity, in life's coming into being. As we look for purpose, we cannot close our eyes to the disorder and pain in the life-story by focusing only on instances of obvious "design."

For this reason, I propose that we cease looking for design as evidence of purpose and instead look deeper—into what I have been calling the promise of nature. The notion of promise is more flexible and more realistic than that of design. Unlike design, promise is logically consistent with the ambiguity that evolutionary science finds in the natural world and that we encounter in human history. The notion of cosmic purpose need not be forced to coincide simplistically with the stiff and lifeless idea of divine "intelligent design." There is wonderfully intricate patterning in nature, of course, but there is much disorder and suffering as well. By anyone's reckoning, this universe is not a perfectly ordered one, and all instances of order eventually dissolve into the torrent of entropy. Thus, if today we are to speak once again of cosmic purpose with our eyes wide open, it must be in such a way as to take nature's present disorder and eventual demise fully into account. It is for this reason that I am contemplating here the possibility that the universe may be thought of in depth—and without in any way contradicting science—as a story filled with *promise.*

Promise of what? Again, we cannot really say. The cosmos is a book still being written, and so we *cannot* yet read it with full comprehension, either through the eyes of science or through those of theology. Both disciplines are humbled by the vast distances the universe apparently has ahead of it.

Today, as never before, we are aware that nature is an always meandering river of creation. This means that we cannot expect any contemporary reading of it to be completely unambiguous. At any given time there will be some uncertainty about what is really going on now. And there will be some anxiety about what is going to happen in the future. What we *can* say, though, is that the universe, at the very minimum, has already given rise to instances of beauty, experience, enjoyment, personality and love. We can read these, of course, as accidental outcomes of a purposeless process, with no significance and no inherent connection to the whole scheme of things. On the other hand, recognizing the possibility that the universe is still barely emerging from the cosmic dawn, we may take them as promissory symbols of the ultimate depth into which all things are being drawn. In the following chapters, we shall attempt to dig deeper into the narrative depths of nature.

5

Beneath Evolution

It often takes the shock of new information, either about the world or about ourselves, to make us reflect critically upon the assumptions that lie beneath our explicit ideas. Not uncommonly, however, when we meet something previously unimaginable, we take refuge in a literalist haven of certitudes, whether religious or naturalistic, that shield us from raw encounter with new realities. Many who have lived joyfully within a religious milieu, for example, have found that the emergence of evolutionary science has shaken to the roots their presuppositions about life and the universe. Contact with evolutionary biology has been so disquieting that countless devout believers have either ignored it or rejected it altogether. Some, of course, have assimilated the riches of evolutionary science and, as a consequence, have come to read the universe with renewed appreciation. Still, I believe that the vast majority of people today are at least somewhat dubious about whether there are grounds for a robustly religious endorsement of evolution.

Can we honestly connect religious hope with the world as it appears to us after Darwin? A mere glance at the elements of evolutionary theory would seem to discourage such a project. Charles Darwin theorized that the entirety of terrestrial life flows from a common ancestor and that the wide diversity of living species on our planet can be accounted for by "natural selection" (along with the equally impersonal and seemingly unfair process he called sexual selection). He observed that living organisms produce more

offspring than are capable of surviving and reproducing and that the vast
majority of organisms die without leaving descendants. Those that survive
and reproduce do so only because *by chance* they have been favorably endowed with qualities that give them a competitive advantage in the struggle
for existence. During the course of millions (and today we would say billions) of years, blind selection and replication of minute adaptive advantages
bring about all the various kinds of life, including eventually the human
species. In a synthesis known as "neo-Darwinism," most biologists today still
embrace Darwin's original ideas, simply adding to them our more recent
knowledge of genetics. And although there are sharp differences among neo-
Darwinians on some of the details of evolution, most scientists today consider Darwin's notions of descent and selection essentially accurate.

Our question then is whether Darwinian explanations still leave any room
for a religious reading of life. Beneath the surface of evolution is there perhaps a dimension of depth that only religious symbolism can permit us to
plumb? Emboldened by the success of evolutionary science, a good number
of Darwin's followers now insist that there can be no more fundamental understanding of living phenomena, including human life, than that provided
by Darwin. Ernst Mayr, as we noted in the previous chapter, allows that
other sciences like biochemistry may help fill in some of the less consequen-
tial gaps in our understanding, but he thinks that Darwin gives us the deepest explanation of life we can hope to find.[1] Venturing beyond Mayr, Richard
Dawkins and others have declared that, prior to Darwin, our own existence
may have been an unexplained mystery, but now Darwin and the new understanding of the role of genes in evolution have provided a fully adequate
account of how life works and why humans are here. For others, Darwinism
offers the deepest explanation not only for why we are here but also for why
we are the way we are. Darwin can even explain why we are ethical and why
so many of us are religious.[2]

In view of such forceful claims, theological readings of life may now seem
more suspect than ever. Any proposal that we may tunnel beneath evolutionary biology to an even more profound understanding of life, therefore,
would imply that Darwin, though possibly correct as far as he goes, does not
give us a completely adequate understanding of what is going on in the story
of life. Many Darwinians, though, are not willing to concede this much. So
if religion or theology is to have an illuminating and explanatory role alongside of, or in addition to, Darwin's account, it first has to demonstrate that
there are levels of depth beneath life and evolution that somehow remain
unilluminated and unexplainable by Darwinian biology.

However, today more than ever, it is tempting to believe that Darwin's rich account of life in terms of natural selection provides not only a trenchant but also a conclusive understanding of life. What intelligibility could a theological reading possibly add to the allegedly "ultimate" explanation of life that a Darwinian account already gives us? What need is there for talk about anything like divine creativity, promise, providence or purpose if, over the course of time, a purely blind process can gradually give rise to life's complexity and beauty all by itself?

Traditional theological responses to this question—and henceforth I am speaking primarily of the Western religious context—have generally appealed to the notions of primary and secondary causation. God is said to be the primary cause of nature, while nature and its laws are secondary causes, contingently created by God, but endowed with enough autonomy and resourcefulness to bring about the scientifically observable effects in nature on their own. The idea that secondary causes, rather than direct divine intervention, can account for the evolution of life may even be said to enhance rather than diminish the doctrine of divine creativity. Isn't it a tribute to God that the world is not just passive putty in the Creator's hands, but instead an inherently active and self-creating process, one that can evolve and produce new life on its own? If God can make things that can make themselves, isn't that better than a magician-deity who pulls all the strings, as theological "occasionalists" have supposed?

Even St. Augustine (354–430 C.E.) argued that the Creator in the beginning endowed the universe with "seed-like principles" that would later give rise to the marvelous diversity of nature.[3] A universe that could "evolve" from within itself, rather than requiring constant divine tinkering from outside, is surely a more marvelous handiwork than one that requires constant infringements and patchwork repair. In the spirit of Augustine's theology, God could be said to be the final explanation of evolution, residing at a deeper level of the world's being than even Darwinism can reach. God, as Paul Tillich might add, would not be one cause among others, but the Ground of all causes. Thus, theology may arrive at the ultimate explanation of life without in any way competing with Darwinian biology's specification of the more proximate mechanisms of evolution.

The distinction between primary and secondary causes is still attractive to many theologians and scientists, especially since it concedes that nature has no need for *ad hoc* supernatural interventions. And, at the same time, it can reserve a place for God as the deepest explanation of life—inasmuch as God is the Ground of all being. However, restricting the creative role of God to that of primary cause can also easily give the impression that God is removed, in deistic fashion, from what concretely goes on everyday in nature and life. Such a distancing of the divine may have a kind of intellectual appeal, one that even Darwin entertained on occasion. But, religiously speaking, it seems inconsistent with the idea of a caring, responsive and intimately involved God. A primary cause is not quite the same as the infinitely loving, promising and "interested" God about which biblical religion, for example, tells us. Thus, without abandoning the notion that God is indeed the Ground of the world's being—and in that sense the deepest explanation of evolution—it seems appropriate for theology to search for ways in which to relate divine reality more intimately and intricately to evolution.

A Theological Reading

Even after we have assented to the impressive theory of evolution by natural selection—and let us concede that it is indeed impressive—it still leaves many questions unanswered. And while we can respond to some of these by moving into other natural sciences such as physics, chemistry, astrophysics and cosmology, even a thicker scientific account will still leave abundant room for a theological reading of life as well.

How is this conceivable? To begin with, Darwinian science itself does not spring forth from a vacuum, but makes several grand assumptions that, if we are to make good sense of them, open up a fertile arena for theological speculation. Darwinism takes for granted the existence of at least three generic cosmological features that make the evolution of life possible, but which themselves call for a deeper kind of exposition than either Darwinism or the body of other sciences can give by itself. In the first place, biological evolution requires a universe that is open to accidental, undirected or "contingent" events. For example, nature has to allow room for the novel combinations of chemicals that permit the spontaneous origin of life. Then, after life appears, there must be room for random mutations in genes as well as for "accidents" in natural history such as asteroid impacts and sudden climatic changes that contribute to the unpredictable unfolding of life. A universe that permits life and evolution cannot at every level be so dominated by draconian determinism that it leaves no room for the emergence of the kind of novelty and diversity we witness in the sphere of living phenomena. It is through the portals of *contingency* that what is truly new enters into the universe, and life acquires a historical status. Events that we confusedly refer to as random, accidental, undirected or indeterminate are essential to evolution's recipe.

Second, nature must also possess a set of invariant and inviolable physical constraints, namely, the laws of physics and chemistry. These regularities give consistency and reliability to natural processes. Without the predictability and stability provided by nature's lawful routines, there would be no way for life to take hold and persist. Life relies on the unbreakable laws of chemistry and physics. In the realm of deterministic invariance, we may also locate what is loosely referred to as the "law" of natural selection. Like other consistent features of nature, natural selection performs its work with remorseless fidelity, making no exceptions. As life ratchets itself gradually toward a net gain in organized complexity, it is natural selection that engineers the project.

The unbending rigor of natural selection need not, however, lead to a philosophical fatalism, as it has done so often among Darwinians. Nature's predictable laws, abstracted in one way or another by every science, can instead be read as necessary grammatical rules that any incarnation of deeper meaning must adhere to if it is to receive embodiment. Just as the sentences on this page have to obey inviolable grammatical regulations, the novelty that emerges in evolution can become actualized only if there is an underlying constancy in the laws of nature. The rigidity or "necessity" that we associate with the laws of nature is not opposed to contingency but provides a bass note of continuity that prevents emergent novelty from bringing in only dissonance. By connecting the creativity of God closely to the monotonous invariance, as well as to the more colorful contingency, in natural process, we may abolish the deistic overtones associated with the idea of a purely primary cause. The divine fidelity to promise is always and everywhere intimately embedded in and creatively working through the laws of nature as well as the novelty that breaks in through the accidental. This divine presence need not be thought of as manipulative but instead as persuasive. And it is also a presence that suffers and struggles along with the world's creative advance.

Third, and finally, Darwinian process requires a vast amount of time to lock into replicative consistency the new possibilities that emerge contingently in the life-story. Without such generous temporal amplitude as the universe's long duration makes possible, the evolution of life would be either nonexistent or extremely trivial. Our awareness of the enormous age of the cosmos and the 3.8 billion years of life's terrestrial journey is relatively new. And the true dimensions of cosmic time are still beyond the power of our imaginations to contemplate. But the discovery of time's vastness has considerably deepened our sense of nature and biological evolution. From a theological perspective, deep time may be thought of as the consequence of God's opening up the world to a luxuriantly creative future.

Let us now focus more deliberately on the remarkable blend of the three generic cosmic conditions underlying evolution—contingency, invariance and deep time. Reflection on these three features, traits that conjointly make the life-story possible, may lead us much deeper into what is going on beneath the surface of life than a Darwinian account can take us all by itself. An in-depth reading of evolution leads us to sink our thoughts into what lies deeper than life, beneath the contingency, lawfulness and temporality of nature that provide the subsoil of organic evolution. What possible meaning, then, can we make out in this depth?

The Narrative Character of Nature

Contingency, as we have just seen, renders nature open to *novelty*, an essential element in evolution. The consistency embedded in physical laws and natural selection endows the evolutionary process with a *coherence* that gives organic unity and continuity to life across time. And nature's irreversible temporality, in conjunction with the elements of contingency and consistency, marks the universe with the stamp of *historicity*. After Darwin—and even more so after Einstein—nature has revealed itself, beneath previous impressions of it, as being an immense story. And the significance of the three features we have just isolated is that they make it possible for the universe to have a narrative disposition. Thus, even at a minimum, the "meaning" that we may find in the cosmos, at a level deeper than Darwinism itself, is that our three generic features confer on the cosmos the kind of constitution that allows it to become an unfolding story. And this story, in turn, may very well be open to many levels of reading.

To be perfectly clear here, Darwinism *presupposes*—since by itself it cannot account for—the narrative cosmic tablet on which the life story becomes inscribed. Or, to put it in other terms, our three background ingredients must be waiting on the cosmic table long before Darwinian process begins mixing and cooking them. It is only because nature is *already* composed of the stuff of narrative that the evolution of life can occur at all. And it is this narrative texture that allows us to entertain the prospect of an even deeper reading of nature and life than evolutionary science offers by itself. Neither Darwinian science nor any of the other sciences can satisfactorily tell us "why" nature is constituted in just such a way as to allow the universe to unfold narratively. The sciences may describe and measure, and to a limited extent predict, natural occurrences, but the question of why nature in its ultimate depths is made for story is one that invites theological comment.

Let me be even more explicit. A story obviously requires time, a sequence of moments in which the narrative can unfold. And if time is deep, then there is the possibility of a deep story as well. A story also needs a strain of consistency or predictability on which the moments of the narrative can be woven into a coherent set of events. Otherwise, the story degenerates into purely episodic droplets, devoid of any connecting thread. Finally, a story also needs to be open to contingent, unpredictable or surprising events that give it a dramatic and suspenseful bearing. All evolutionary portrayals of life presuppose this three-plied narrative underpinning. My point, then, is that at least one appropriate place for theological explanation is in response to the question: Why does nature have a narrative character at all? I believe we must look much deeper than Darwinian science for any satisfying answers to this question. Biological evolution, after all, jumps astride a cosmos already primed for stories like those that Darwin and his followers have been telling us. And it is theologically relevant to ask why nature is so primed.

At its very foundations, the universe appears to have been shaped by what I would like to call the "narrative cosmological principle." The longing to penetrate to the foundations of life leads us down into a narrative cosmic infrastructure beneath the Earth's life-story and any other life-stories that may be emerging elsewhere in the Big Bang universe.[4] Hence, we need to place our quest to understand terrestrial evolution within the framework of a whole cosmic story. Biologists today, however, are often uncomfortable with this widening of the evolutionary milieu, for it seems to wrest away from them the newly won autonomy of their discipline. However, biotic evolution on Earth has become possible over the last three and half billion years only because the universe was already getting ready for life's dramatic emergence as far back as the Big Bang, fifteen or so billion years ago.

Today science can no longer take for granted that the universe *had* to have been so wide open to story and hence to life's evolution. Other kinds of universes, nonnarrative varieties powerless to sponsor evolutionary adventures, are now conceivable from the point of view of physics. The Big Bang universe depends for its exquisitely narrative orientation upon initial cosmic conditions and physical constants for which science itself can find no inherent necessity. For all we know, the physics of the universe may easily have been such as to disallow the kind of narrative performance that evolution requires. An alternative physics might have given rise conceivably to a cosmos too tightly bound by the rigidity of lawful necessity, or one too peppered with contingency, or one whose temporal span was too abridged, to carry a story. What is certain is that in the absence of the exquisite blend of physical features that subtends our actual universe, evolution and the dramatic emergence of life and human history could never have occurred.

One may, in response, imaginatively multiply universes, as the British astronomer Martin Rees does, conjuring up countless versions incapable of

carrying life and Darwinian evolution.[5] Surrounded or preceded by number-
less cosmic failures to hit upon the right blend of contingency, necessity and
time, our own story-prone universe could then be thought of, in statistical
terms, as purely accidental. In that case, chance rather than providence
would be the ultimate explanation for the cosmological features that underlie
biological evolution. But it is interesting to note that even our notion of
"chance" comes from the fact of contingency that we experience in *this* universe. We cannot even invent the multiple-universe idea without injecting it
with the pulse of randomness we experience in our own cosmic setting. Furthermore, our quasi-mythic theorizing about multiple universes has a narrative quality itself that is rooted in the specific character of *this* universe. The
whole ensemble of universes, in the multiverse account, is imaginatively held
together by the very blend of contingency, lawfulness and temporality that
underlies what we know as story. Indeed the extravagant generation of many
universes would have to be a story itself, and it would therefore beg the same
theological question we are raising here: Why any story at all? The point is,
we cannot help embedding all of our speculation about other worlds within
a "narrative *a priori*" in accordance with which evolution has forged our own
brains. Our minds, religions and even all our scientific ideas are strapped in-
dissolubly to a narrative style of understanding that itself is inseparable from
the fundamental cosmological characteristics (contingency, law and deep
time) of *this* universe. Thus it is that we cannot even talk about other conceivable universes without assimilating them somehow into the story of our
own.

Rees's brand of speculation, drawing on ideas of physicists such as Andrei
Linde, may have already taken us deeper than Darwin. However, it is indicative of the contemporary appeal of Darwinian explanation that today even
some cosmologists are applying the principles of randomness, selection,
competition, successful adaptation and, at times, replication to their imagined multiplicity of universes.[6] Accordingly, our own universe could be said
to have survived only because it is somehow more adaptive to the rigors of
existing than are other random "attempts." Notice once again, though, that
this Darwinian cosmological account can be narrated at all only because its
storytelling cosmologists, like the rest of us, abide within the womb of narrative
features particular to *this* universe. The possibility of our telling stories at all
is rooted in the triadic blend of physical features that pertain to Big Bang
cosmology. The very structure of the modern cosmologist's consciousness, no
less than that of the ancient mythmaker, is irremediably narrative. And so
our question still festers, perhaps at a deeper level than before: Why is the
world, or the ensemble of worlds, made for *story?*

Here, it seems to me, we have arrived at a question that Darwinism by itself cannot answer. And here also there remains plenty of room for theology. What lies beyond dispute is that the cosmos is endowed with a narrative structure that allows genuinely new things, such as life and evolution, to happen in the course of time. This is not a trait that we can simply take for granted. What will always remain open for theological speculation, therefore, no matter how extensively the particular sciences fill in the gaps at their various levels of explanation, is the question of why nature is made for narrative. Theology, of course, turns the question around and asks why God would create such a world at all. Is it perhaps because God loves stories?[7] And not only small stories, but large ones also?

Promise or Prediction?

Whatever lawfulness nature now exhibits is itself contingent upon how the universe was "set up" at the moment of its origins. There is no need to imagine a facile connection between this initial "setup" and the simplistic designer deity of natural theology. Yet perhaps at least the *promise* of an eventual emergence of life and evolution was already present at the cosmic dawn. As far as science can now surmise, the universe might very easily not have been so bursting with such creative potential as it in fact is. Perhaps the "meaning" of the universe's narrative character is, at least in part, that it allows for the unfolding of an enormous promise.

Why, we may ask again, is the universe so unaccountably composed of the compound of contingency, predictability and temporality that are essential to story? Why, in other words, is nature narrative to the core? Why does it possess the openness to novelty that is resident in the accidents essential for evolution? Why does it have the regularity and reliability that we associate with the "laws" of physics, chemistry and natural selection? And why does it unfold in such an irreversibly temporal and prodigiously prolonged manner?

Although the natural sciences also have something to say in response to these questions, I strongly suspect—on the basis of our previous discussion of the need for explanatory pluralism and hierarchies of explanation—that there need be no *exclusively* scientific answer to them. One may, of course, assert gratuitously that it is all an accident, that the universe's felicitous blend of contingency, necessity and temporality itself has no explanation itself, just as the naked existence of the universe is said at times to be inexplicable. However, such a claim is no less metaphysical than a theological one would be. Moreover, the idea that the existence of our story-bound cosmos might be an absurd accident in a void of ultimate meaninglessness suffers from the disadvantage of not cohering well with the ongoing scientific search for intelligibility. Our view of what reality is like in its ultimate depths must be in consonance, rather than competition, with scientific understanding if the latter is to have a future. Were we to suppose that the universe at bottom is an abyss of absurdity, this would hardly encourage the ongoing quest for deeper and deeper insight. On the other hand, a theological conviction that the cosmos, in its ultimate depths, is endlessly intelligible goes very well with science. A trust that the world is intelligible "all the way down" allows science to breathe, and to have an indefinite future. Such trust can only encourage the ongoing scientific adventure of trying to figure things out. At the same time, a trust in the world's endless intelligibility will discourage all dreams of final theories. It will shatter the pretense that physics can capture the mind of God, or that Darwinism can give us the deepest available understanding of life.

But can't the Darwinian get by quite well without entertaining the possibility that the universe's narrative character makes it a place of promise? At the level of biological explanation, yes. From a strictly scientific point of view, what is *really* going on in biological evolution is simply adaptation and selection. And as the Darwinian reads the life-process, this is *all* that is going on. Everything can be explained, all biological knowledge unified, and perhaps other attempts at understanding life made to seem obsolete, by the notions of selection and reproductive success. However, beneath all of its Darwinian experimentation, nature still exists in such a way as to have the character of a story. And stories can be read on many different levels simultaneously. We may wish to focus on life's alphabetical code as does genetics, or on chemical pathways as does molecular biology. Or we can become entranced by the grammatical rules of selection that give consistency and coherence to evolutionary accounts of life. But nature also has a foundationally narrative structure, and this means that it may be the carrier of a "meaning" deeper than Darwinism or other sciences can decipher.

A theological reading may enter into the wider search for life's intelligibility without in any way competing with legitimately roped-off scientific regions of exploration. If nature is narrative, then theology can take its place in a rich hierarchy of interpretations that articulate—each at its own reading level—what is *really* going on in evolution. In order to avoid needless conflicts, a theological reading will enter at a level distinct from that of physics, chemistry or evolutionary biology. Conflicts between science and theology appear only when we attempt to read the universe on one level alone, a reading that I have been referring to as literalism. Without in any way interfering with neo-Darwinian grammarians, theology may legitimately join in the enterprise of apprehending what is *really going on* in the story of life and evolution. Theology, for example, may read the generically narrative features of the universe, including its biological evolution, as the place of *promise,* something to which science as such could not, and should not, be sensitized. Science has taught us that the universe is a process unfinished in time, contingently open to novelty, yet lawful enough to have coherence. But only by reading all of this at a level more fundamental than the abstractions of science could an awareness emerge that the universe, in its ultimate depths, is the carrier of an immense promise—one that gives ample place to religious hope. Such a perspective, moreover, is one that understands God to be more intimately involved in cosmic evolution than the idea of a remote first cause generally suggests.

Familiarity with biblical narrative, in which anticipation of a fulfilling future is the dominant motif, prepares the mind as well as the heart to read nature dramatically, as a story bearing an incalculable future of new creation. At the heart of biblical wisdom, and in the traditions that have interpreted its sacred scriptures, there lie three fundamental beliefs. First, there is the trust that an inexhaustible and incomprehensible Mystery eternally grounds, encompasses and cares for the cosmos. Second, there is the belief that in self-abandoning and vulnerable love this inexhaustible Mystery (or depth) gives itself away unreservedly to the universe. And third, there is a conviction that this divine Mystery continually invites the universe toward a future fulfillment that remains unpredictable and full of surprises.[8] The many "doctrines" associated with biblical faith are all historically conditioned ways of expressing these three core principles. Teachings about divine personality, creation, revelation and redemption all point back to these three central tenets. My point then is that there is a tight coherence between these teachings and the newly discovered narrative character of the universe. When we read the universe with eyes and hearts prepared by the motif of promise, there emerges a palpable consonance between the narrative character of a life-bearing evolutionary cosmos, on the one hand, and the general thrust of religious hope on the other.

Objections

I realize, of course, that some readers will choke on my suggestion that faith in a promising God can live comfortably with the scientific, and especially the Darwinian, way of looking at the world. After all, the predictable and law-abiding world depicted by modern science seems to be closed off to any truly *surprising* future such as that anticipated by the biblical vision. The world of classical science is one in which there is very little room for surprise. Whatever happens, science instructs us, there can be no violation of the inflexible laws of nature. We can only bow to the impersonal necessity of the universe. Even the evolution of life, as Daniel Dennett has already reminded us, is at bottom nothing more than an "algorithmic process." There is no room in nature for the truly unexpected. Everything that happens is the product of what has already taken place in the temporal past.

In the world of the Bible, on the other hand, the prospect of an indeterminate future is preeminent, and the present is always open to future surprise. Faith is most authentic when it looks forward to the unexpected. Those are called "blessed" who trust that God's promises will be fulfilled.[9] Running steadily across the diverse historical and religious layers of the biblical writings is the persistent theme that what is most important and most real lies up ahead, in the uncontrollable future. The past and present have meaning because they are filled with promise for the future. Even present circumstances that tempt us to despair may conceal a surprisingly salvific outcome. Abraham's advanced age is no obstacle to starting life over. Sarah's present sterility is no barrier to future fertility. David's weaknesses will not prevent the implementation of God's plan for Israel. Killing the prophets only liberates their message. In the disaster of Jesus' death lies the power of a new creation. The biblical vision invites us to anticipate a future whose character will be one of fulfillment beyond imagining. "Eye has not seen, ear has not heard . . . ." "The lion will lie down with the lamb." "There will be abundant rejoicing." "Every tear will be wiped away." "The kingdom of God is at hand." "Nothing is impossible with God." Naive as we modern scientific realists may consider such imaginings to be, any serious appropriation of the biblical vision(s) entails our immersion in the stream of hope that flows from the Abrahamic font. Only by being open to an unimaginable future can we sincerely claim that we are sons and daughters of the promise.

But the whole of modern science seems to outlaw such a wide vision of hope. Even the new science of "chaos," though emphasizing the practical impossibility of our predicting the future states of certain systems, still lends itself to deterministic interpretations. Daniel Dennett's work exemplifies the view of many scientists that the apparent contingencies of evolution do not wipe out the more dominant strain of inevitability in nature. Even where evolutionists such as Stephen Jay Gould have given much weight to accidental events in the history of life, the truly scientific evolutionist can allow no deviation from the fatalistic necessity of physical laws underlying it all. And so, if evolution is simply the working out of a deterministic set of laws, there is no reason for our expecting the unexpected. The future is already implied in the present state of things, and it will unfold only in a manner already dictated by the past.

Here there appears once again the ages-old clash between a world-picture dominated by fate and one open to eventualities that cannot, even in principle, be predicted on the basis of our knowledge of the past and present. Evolutionary theory springs from the world of science, where every contingent surprise must eventually be "reduced" to the predictable routine of known physical laws. The biblical sense of God, on the other hand, emanates from a consciousness imbued with a sense that the future can always be unexpectedly new. The biblical God is one who comes into the world from the realm of the future and who makes and keeps promises that always transcend our petty powers of prediction. So how can we fit the religious hope for new creation together with the dour news of scientific inevitability?

I believe that our newly emergent awareness of the fundamentally narrative character of nature—together with the proposals I have been making about the need to avoid literalism by distinguishing reading levels—now allows us to bring some resolution to these two apparently dissonant viewpoints. Scientists, once they experience the fact that the cosmos is a story, can learn to read physical laws not as final explanation but as the grammatical framework or *constraints* for emergent narrative novelty. Here the book or story analogy we have been using is especially helpful. In writing a book or a story we have to follow inviolable grammatical rules—along with other more subtle principles of storytelling that we need not recite here—without which the narrative would crumble into a pile of meaningless particulars. When I write a story, for example, I am compelled by grammatical necessity to use the right verb tenses, agreement of subject with predicate, proper sentence structure and so on. Nevertheless, this unbending grammatical grid does not prevent me from weaving onto it an unpredictable story, one full of surprises. The decrees of grammar are not so deterministic that they preclude a creative liberty that gives dramatic tension to any interesting narrative. Rather, the rules are enabling conditions for telling any story that has both an internal consistency and a surprising outcome.

The grammatical rules are essential, recurrent, predictable constraints. They are necessary conditions for bringing a story to expression. Analogously the strict Darwinian "rules" of adaptation and selection, along with the laws of physics and chemistry, are "grammatical" requirements of any conceivable life-story. No matter how extravagantly life unfolds in opulent diversity, it must never violate the laws of physics, chemistry and natural selection. In any story, the grammatical rules must be obeyed or else the narrative will fall apart. So also nature's strict and apparently inviolable adherence to the statutes of Darwinian selection is essential for the evolution of new kinds of life. Try to imagine what the history of life would have led to, for example, if in the past the Darwinian rules had occasionally been relaxed, and the weak and the sick, instead of the strong and healthy, had won out in terms of reproductive advantage.[10]

However, just as we do not have to consult the grammarian in order to understand the meaning of a story, we do not have to confer with the evolutionary biologist (or evolutionary psychologist, anthropologist, and so on) in order to understand, at its *deepest* level, what life in this universe is really all about. This implies, furthermore, that we may immerse ourselves in the considerable accumulated wisdom of the religious and literary past, without constantly devaluing it—as Darwinian literalists do—simply because its authors knew nothing about evolution. Contemporary Darwinians are progressively refining our understanding of the grammar of life, just as molecular biologists and biochemists are improving our understanding of life's alphabet. But none of these developments logically rule out our learning much about the universe from readings of life other than science. Even if we concede that evolutionary biology, especially its clarification of the rules of reproductive success, has refined our sense of life's grammatical constraints, this in no way precludes a potential retrieval of meaning from the life-story through a different kind of reading than that of biology. At the same time, however, an appreciation of evolutionary biology and cosmology can both constrain and enrich what theology has to say about what might be going on in the universe. The following chapters will amplify the points I have just made.

6

Deeper than Dawkins

In 1859 Charles Darwin published *On the Origin of Species,* one of the most important works of science ever written. Experts today still consider it to be generally accurate, and recent scientific expertise seems to confirm its explanatory power. Theologically speaking, however, as everyone knows, Darwin's work has aroused a storm of controversy, and we are still wrestling with the question of how to read it. Does Darwin's theory—or any of its neo-Darwinian offshoots—signal the end of a coherent notion of God? Or can we find beneath the evolutionary picture of life reasons for deepening our thoughts about deity? In the depths of a universe that gives rise to Darwin's luxuriant but troubling story of life, is it possible to make out anything like divine wisdom, or any evidence of divine providence? "Where can I flee from your presence?" the psalmist asks God. "If I go up to the heavens, you are there; if I make my bed in the depths, you are there" (Psalm 139:8). But after Darwin, the depths seem destitute, empty of any providential presence.

The psalmist's reading of things now seems strange, since for many scientists and philosophers Darwin has taken us about as deep into the fabric of life as we are ever likely to go. Indeed, according to many evolutionists, what Darwin has brought up from the depths is a universe empty of any meaning other than what we humans project onto it. In fact, the physicist Steven Weinberg asserts that biological evolution demonstrates the impersonality of the universe much more decisively even than do the remorseless laws of his own discipline.[1] The ways of evolution are so lumbering and inelegant that even if life on the surface points to divine intelligent design, right beneath this deceptive veneer lurks a mindless and haphazard netherworld in which an infinitely wise deity could not possibly have played any role. Nevertheless, I would like now to persist with the previous chapter's proposal. If we burrow a bit further beneath the disconcerting story that geology and biology have unearthed, perhaps we may find ourselves once again being drawn down into a depth that only a religious consciousness like that of our psalmist can properly plumb.

On the surface, of course, the ideas of God and evolution do not seem to match each other very well. The reasons are now very familiar. Darwin observed that all living species produce more offspring than ever reach maturity, but that the number of individuals in any given species remains relatively stable. Since more young are produced than ever reach maturity, this means that most living organisms die off before reproducing. The relatively few that do survive must, by sheer accident, be better "adapted" to their environments and so are able to survive and reproduce. Most organisms lose out in the struggle for existence, leaving no offspring. Still, during the extended journey of evolution an amazing diversity of life comes about, and occasionally entirely new species arise, including eventually *Homo sapiens*.

What, then, is so theologically challenging—at least on the surface—about this account of life? What is there about evolution that, even for many people today, almost a century and a half after the publication of Darwin's *Origins,* places the very existence of God in question? First, as we have already seen, the variations that lead to differentiation of species are said to be purely *random,* in the sense of being "undirected." The apparent absence of intelligent control over the contingencies of evolution suggests that the novelty in nature is at bottom "accidental" and that no providential influence governs the world after all. Today, the sources of life's variations have been identified as genetic mutations, and most biologists still follow Darwin in attributing the variations to "chance." In the second place, the fact that individuals have to struggle for survival, and that most of them suffer and lose out in the contest, points to the underlying *indifference* of natural selection, the mechanism that so mercilessly eliminates the weaker organisms. Finally, as a third ingredient in the recipe of evolution, life's experiments have required an almost unimaginably extensive amount of *time* for the diversity of species to come about. That the origin of life would take so many billions of years to bring about intelligent beings seems, at least to many scientifically educated people today, to be clear evidence that neither life nor mind is the consequence of an intelligent divine plan for the universe. We humans, had we been able to design a universe, could have done a much quicker and more competent job of it.

Evolution seems to be the outcome of mindlessly combining the three constituent elements: randomness, the blind natural law of selection and the immensity of cosmic time. These ingredients seem sufficient to account for all the phenomena we associate with life, including ourselves. The comprehensiveness of this rather elementary evolutionary recipe now leads many scientifically informed commentators to doubt that life and mind require any additional illumination. Especially irrelevant are theological ideas about the special creativity of a truly "interested" God. How could we ever reconcile the tattered evolutionary panorama with the idea of a benign, intelligent divine providence? Darwin himself, reflecting on the accidents, impersonality, pain and temporal protraction of evolutionary process, abandoned the idea that nature could have been ordered, at least in its particulars, by an intelligent designer. It is not clear that he ever completely renounced the idea of God, and at times his writings suggest that he settled for a very distant divine lawmaker. But he gradually became convinced that we can account for the design in living beings in a purely naturalistic way. After Darwin, many others, including prominent neo-Darwinian biologists today, have nearly equated Darwin's science with atheism. And countless religious believers have likewise concluded that they cannot harmonize Darwinian biology with theistic belief.

The sentiments of our psalmist, in other words, seem scarcely resonant with the depths that Darwinism has disclosed:

> *For you created my inmost being;*
> *you knit me together in my mother's womb.*
> *I praise you because I am fearfully and wonderfully made;*
> *your works are wonderful, I know that full well.*
> *My frame was not hidden from you*
> *when I was made in the secret place.*
> *When I was woven together in the depths of the earth,*
> *your eyes saw my unformed body.*
> *All the days ordained for me were written in your book*
> *before one of them came to be.*
> *How precious to me are your thoughts, O God!*
> *How vast is the sum of them!*

(Psalm 139:13–17)[2]

Can we prayerfully recite these words with the psalmist, and mean them sincerely, after we have peered into the Darwinian depths? There are at least three distinct sets of answers to this question. The first claims that if Darwin is right, then the idea of an "interested" God, that is, of divine providence, must be wrong. Embracing this position are evolutionary materialists, biblical creationists and advocates of Intelligent Design Theory, the last of whom I shall discuss in the next chapter. All parties in this Conflict circle are bound together by a common agreement that a Darwinian understanding of evolution is incompatible with any realistic trust in divine providence. The diverse participants in this group reject or ignore the possibility that there might be a hierarchy of explanations in which theological and Darwinian accounts can complement each other by occupying logically different levels. Instead, for all of them, there is only one "explanatory slot," and it must be filled by either science or religious/metaphysical categories, but not both.

A second set of answers to our question comes from religious believers, including many scientists, who accept in principle the evidence for evolution, but who remain unmoved by it all. To them, the discovery of evolution does not require that we deepen our understanding of nature or God in any significant way. The new biology is theologically inconsequential since theology has to do not so much with the cosmos as with humans and their unique relationship to God. The assumption here is that even if human beings evolved from nonhuman ancestors, our species and its cultural pursuits are now virtually discontinuous with the rest of life. So there is no longer any need to be concerned about evolution, or even the universe as such, except for the fact that the latter is the physical setting for human culture and, to those who embrace religion, a point of departure for the spiritual journey. Science in general is acceptable as a way of understanding the natural world, at least for those who are interested in doing so; but it can shed very little light on either the human domain or that of God.

We may call the partisans of this second approach Separatists, since they assume not only that humans are intrinsically split off from the rest of the universe but also that evolutionary science and religious traditions are concerned with two entirely different issues. Within this separatist camp, we may find a considerable sector of modern and postmodern religious thought, as well as the implicit theology of most churches, mosques and synagogues. Advocates of this approach allow for a hierarchy of explanations that has room for both science and theology, but they are not interested in coordinating the scientific levels with the theological.

A third response to Darwin, however, differs considerably from the Conflict and Separatist approaches. It consists of those scientists and religious thinkers who not only embrace evolutionary science but also view it as a fresh way to understand the Psalmist's sense of the divine presence in the depths of nature. I will call this the Engagement approach since it is open to an ongoing dialogue of science with religion, even to the point of tendering the bold suggestion that theology can read the universe more deeply after Darwin than before.[3] This approach acknowledges that evolutionary biology and recent cosmology have rattled our earlier perceptions of nature, as well as our understanding of human existence. And so we can no longer honestly turn away from the disturbing depths that Darwin's science has uncovered. Religious attention must focus directly on what the plows of geology, paleontology, biology, astrophysics and so on have turned up. The Engagement approach interprets the recent rumpling of nature's surface as an invitation to read it at a deeper level than ever before. After Darwin, theology and science, though quite different in their respective methods, can become partners in taking the long human quest for truth into deeper and darker territory than it had previously ventured.

The Engagement approach, then, hopes to undertake a more penetrating reading of the universe than either the Conflict or Separatist approaches. In fact, both the Conflict and the Separatist parties share the trait of systematically refusing to pierce beneath the surface of evolution. Both avoid what I have been calling the depth of nature. Although the Separatists claim to accept the conclusions of science, their theological appropriation of evolution is shallow at best. Evolution has not yet worked its way very deeply into their religious reflections, but instead remains only at the periphery if it is present at all.

Meanwhile those who see only an insoluble conflict between religious belief and the ideas of evolutionary science fail to embrace the opportunity that such clashes provide for resolution at a deeper level of understanding. I have already commented on the literalism of the creationist approach, and I intend to discuss Intelligent Design Theory in the following chapter. Here I shall look more closely at the approach I have been calling "evolutionary materialism" as one of the major representatives of the Conflict position. And within this camp I will turn my attention specifically to Richard Dawkins's impassioned evolutionist protests against the religious idea of divine providence. Following my portrayal of Dawkins's indictment of theism, I shall then turn to possible reactions by those in the Separatist and Engagement camps.

I. Evolutionary Materialism

As I noted earlier, a vocal contemporary representative of evolutionary materialism is the scientifically literate neo-Darwinian philosopher Daniel Dennett.

But Dennett's portrait of evolution follows almost slavishly that of the Oxford evolutionist Richard Dawkins, so we may focus for now on the latter. Dawkins argues that blind chance and natural selection, working over long periods of time, can *adequately* account for life's creativity, design and diversity all by themselves. As far as he is concerned, Darwin's is not only the most accurate reading of life we have ever had; it is also one that is so complete that it logically excludes any theological or "providential" explanation of life. Consequently, Dawkins insists, every intelligent and open-minded reader has to make a choice: either Darwin or God, but not both. Since the Darwinian reading is explanatorily adequate, theology must now be discarded as superfluous.[4]

The fundamental players in the game of life, according to Dawkins, are not individual organisms or populations of organisms, as some Darwinians have held. Rather they are the coded segments of DNA that we now refer to as genes. Evolution is really about "selfish" genes and the cunning ways and naive vehicles they devise to get themselves passed down through future generations. Genes play whatever tricks they can to secure their immortality. They even fashion for themselves elaborate organisms and diverse species to do the job of replicating and carrying copies of themselves so as to ensure their long-term existence. Sometimes this genetic compulsion to "survive" makes organisms resort to unseemly adaptive strategies, as when wasps lay their eggs inside of caterpillars so that the newly hatched larvae can devour the helpless creatures from within while the latter are still alive. Darwin himself cited this very example, and to him it indicated how far nature is from being a perfect divine design. But after Mendel and modern genetics, Dawkins believes, we are now in a position to say that it is selfish genes that run the whole show. The genes that make up the "river out of Eden" are the sort of agents that will do whatever they can to survive, no matter how much suffering this causes to their carriers. The entirety of Dawkins's ample body of comments on evolution and religion is premised on his conviction that life can be read most deeply at the level of natural selection and gene-survival.[5]

Accordingly, Dawkins says, Darwinian biology (now updated by genetics) has given atheism the most secure intellectual foundation it has ever had.[6] Today a significant number of other scientists and intellectuals share Dawkins's interpretation of evolution, but his reading is more heated than most others. One almost gets the impression from reading his books that his number-one priority is that of issuing a wake-up call to any of us who naively believe there is still room for a theological reading of life. Here I shall attempt to express as succinctly and directly as I can what he thinks of theology. The following are not his exact words but a condensation of what he wishes to get across to those of us whose minds have been shaped—or possibly warped—by the kind of religious sentiments we have seen in the author of Psalm 139.[7] This is what I hear Dawkins saying to anyone who still trusts in divine providence:

Darwin's theory of evolution by natural selection demolishes all lingering illusions that life and human existence are the content of an intelligent providential plan. No competent deity would ever have produced living beings in the way Darwin shows life to have come about. Darwinism contradicts every wish you religious believers ever had that the cosmos is guided and cared for by divine providence, or that a glorious destiny awaits it.

Most of you, including you theologians, are afraid to face squarely the religiously ruinous idea of evolution. Even when you think you understand it, you have not yet looked into it with any real depth of perception. Otherwise you would have abandoned the idea of a providentially governed cosmos long ago. Evolution is nothing more than a purely impersonal process engineered by the equally mindless mechanism of natural selection. The psalmist quoted earlier is simply ignorant. To achieve its "wondrous" results, evolution requires only random mutations, plus the deterministic laws of physics and natural selection, plus enormous spans of time. This three-part recipe is enough to make the idea of divine providence completely superfluous in the explanation of life's improbable achievements.

The discovery of deep time has been especially significant in showing how unnecessary a creative and providential God is in the creation of life's designs, including the human mind. Perhaps if the life-process had available only six thousand years or so to produce an organ as complex as the eye, you could be forgiven for appealing to religious doctrine. But, given enough time—and the several billion years that life has had should be enough—small incremental changes in organisms and the causal power of natural selection are quite enough to explain all of life's variety and complexity. Intelligent and informed people must therefore abandon all pre-scientific, religious ways of responding to questions such as how life came about, how it produced its marvelous designs, and why you and I are here.

If you theologians possessed the fortitude to look closely at evolution, you would see clearly that there is no room for divine causation to have ever played the slightest role in the evolutionary unfolding of life in this universe. Even the seemingly miraculous origin of life is the product of random events and impersonal physical laws. Therefore, those naive theologians and scientists who see no conflict between evolution and their religious beliefs are deluding themselves. If evolution has any message at all, it is that we live in a universe devoid of any providential governance, one with no explanation for its being here at all, and certainly one that never planned for our own existence from all eternity.

Once again, I want to make it clear that I am not speaking only to biblical literalists. After all, Darwin's great idea places in question all religious interpretations of the cosmos, not just Christian fundamentalism. Darwinian explanation is so powerful and complete that there is no room left for any religious or theological accounts of life alongside of it. Our new knowledge of the gene, in company with Darwin's bold idea of natural selection, allows us now to read life all the way down to its deepest depths. And the modern evolutionary synthesis demonstrates that there is no room whatsoever in these depths for any appeal to the idea of divine providence, a notion that is now therefore completely obsolete.

II. A "Separatist" Theological Response

There is little that is truly new or unexpected in Dawkins's attack on religion and theology. However, it is delivered with a directness that forces us to pay attention. How then might a theologian respond to Dawkins and those for whom he speaks? One way might be that of the Separatists:

Evolutionary science, though perhaps disturbing to a superficial piety, is no more threatening to theistic faith than is any other development in modern science. Science and theology, after all, are radically distinct ways of understanding, and they should be kept completely apart from each other. Science answers one set of questions, theology another. If we keep science and theology separate, there can be no conflict. The ugly disputes between Galileo and the Church, or Darwin and Christianity, could have been avoided if theologians had never intruded into the world of science and if people like Dawkins would refrain from making sweeping materialist claims as though they were in fact conclusions of science. Science, after all, is supposed to stay out of metaphysics.

Thus, Darwin's ideas, which for all we know may be quite accurate scientifically speaking, bear not even the slightest threat to our belief in divine providence. The alleged contradiction between Darwin and religious beliefs arises not from the scientific theory of evolution itself, but from the confusing of biblical accounts of creation with science in the case of the "creationists," and the equally misbegotten merging of evolution with philosophical materialism in the case of scientific writers like Dawkins. We have no argument with the purely scientific aspects of evolution. What we object to is the uncritical mixing of evolutionary science with non-scientific beliefs, a fusion that runs through almost all of Dawkins's books. What is dangerous is not so much Darwin's idea, but the way it gets captured by materialist ideologies that in themselves have nothing whatsoever to do with scientific truth.

Ironically, Dawkins does his part to keep alive the irritating anti-scientific re-actions of Intelligent Design Theory and creationism. These are attractive partly because evolutionists like Dawkins make it almost impossible for the unwary reader to distinguish real science from the materialist belief system in which he consistently embeds his interpretation of Darwin. He writes about life as though his readers have to embrace materialist ideology—and even explicit atheism—in order to accept with honor his account of evolution. And since no religious sense of God is compatible with materialism or atheism, Dawkins is making it logi-cally impossible for over ninety percent of the citizens in a country like the United States to accept evolutionary biology on his terms. This is hardly an agenda that is likely to promote the worthy cause of science education.

Dawkins, however, is not alone in wedding materialist ideology to biological science. Listen, for example, to Dawkins's evolutionist adversary Stephen Jay Gould, perhaps the most prolific recent interpreter of Darwinism:

> *. . . I believe that the stumbling block to [the acceptance of Darwin's theory] does not lie in any scientific difficulty, but rather in the philosophical content of Darwin's message—in its challenge to a set of entrenched Western attitudes that we are not yet ready to abandon. First, Darwin argues that evolution has no purpose. Individuals struggle to increase the representation of their genes in future generations, and that is all. . . . Second, Darwin maintained that evolution has no direction; it does not lead inevitably to higher things. Organisms become better adapted to their local en-vironments, and that is all. The "degeneracy" of a parasite is as perfect as the gait of a gazelle. Third, Darwin applied a consistent philosophy of materialism to his in-terpretation of nature. Matter is the ground of all existence; mind, spirit and God as well, are just words that express the wondrous results of neuronal complexity.*[8]

If you attend carefully to Gould's wording here, it is not difficult to see that what is so "dangerous" about Darwin is not the scientific information he and Dawkins deliver, but the ideology of materialism that has taken hold of this data, twisting it into an undifferentiated tangle of science and metaphysical beliefs about nature. It is the Separatist's conviction that Gould's and Dawkins's confla-tion of evolution with materialism is no less obscurantist than is scientific cre-ationism. Hence, in order to avoid any such confusion, we insist on sharply distinguishing science from all belief systems, whether religious or materialist. This means that evolutionary science cannot tell us anything significant about God that we did not already know from revelation, nor can our experience of God add much to our understanding of evolution. Evolution is a purely scientific theory that should not be taken hostage either by theism or materialism.

III. An "Engagement" Theological Proposal

I suspect that a good number of theologians have, at least implicitly, formulated a Separatist kind of response to evolutionary materialism. However, let
us now consider yet another type of theological response, that of Engagement. It might go something like this:[9]

*Although the sharp distinctions made by the Separatist are essential, the En-
gagement approach is convinced that evolution does make a difference theologically speaking. If we accept evolutionary science in an intellectually serious way,
it seems to us that we cannot have exactly the same thoughts about providence after Darwin as we had before. And so, we propose here another kind of theological
response, one in which we frankly confess that evolutionary biology demands a
reconfiguration—and in fact a deepening—of our sense of the infinitely caring
God whom many of us believe to be the world's creator, sustainer and ever faith-
ful liberator.*

*Unfortunately, it seems to us that most contemporary theology has still not
faced the fact that a Darwinian universe looks a lot different from the world-
pictures in which our religious traditions were born and nurtured. The world's
religions have still barely begun to feel the impact of evolutionary science. In
Christianity, perhaps a few theologians have taken a deliberate look at it, but, in
keeping with modern theology's general lack of interest in the natural world, the
topic of evolution generally remains outside the general concern of seminary and
academic theological education. When theologians talk about evolution at all
they typically edit out the most challenging features of the Darwinian and neo-
Darwinian pictures of life.*

*Theology's typical slighting of evolution is symptomatic of a lack of courage in
religious instruction and theological imagination. To us, it is the signal of a lost
opportunity for spiritual, theological and intellectual growth. We are convinced
that a serious encounter of theology with contemporary versions of evolutionary
science may not only enrich our understanding of the universe but also revitalize
our sense of divine providence. If theology is to flourish within contemporary
intellectual culture, our understanding of how God cares for the universe requires
fresh expression in evolutionary terms.*

*Skeptics like Dawkins, of course, will immediately ask how we can reconcile
the idea of an intelligent and beneficent providence with the randomness or contingency in life's evolution. Contingency, we would reply, is a fact of nature, but it
is one that can teach us much about the character of God, whose essence, as the
First Letter of John said long ago, is love. It is the nature of love, after all, to allow the beloved to exist without coercion. As we know even from our limited human interpersonal experience, genuine love never forces or compels. Love allows*

others sufficient scope to become themselves. So if there is truth in the biblical conviction that God really cares for this world as something other than God, then the universe must always have had some degree of autonomy, even during its long prehuman evolution. Otherwise, it would have been nothing more than an extension of God's own being, an appendage of deity. In that case, it could never have become genuinely other than God. There has to be room for contingency and chance in any universe held to be both distinct from and simultaneously loved by God. At the same time, the remorseless consistency of the laws of nature, including that of natural selection, is also essential for the relative autonomy with which the world is graciously endowed by its creator.

Moreover, if nature is truly differentiated from God, as it must be if we are to avoid pantheism, it has to have considerable temporal scope for wandering about experimentally. And once we allow that God's creative and providential activity includes a liberal posture of letting the world be, and not a manipulative controlling of it, we can hardly be surprised that the world's creation does not take place in one magical instant, or that every adaptation in evolution will be perfect. We should anticipate that evolution will take time—in calendrical terms, perhaps billions of years. Dawkins, along with the creationists, thinks that the gradualism of evolution is logically incompatible with the idea of divine providence. If God is a reality, Dawkins assumes, there should be special junctures where the hand of providence visibly interrupts the ordinary routines of nature. Dawkins cannot find any such punctuations of nature's gradualist regularity, and so he concludes that God must not be around.

However, a coherent theology may argue that God could not truly care for the universe unless the universe is allowed in some sense to be self-actualizing, though self-actualizing in a way that occurs within the boundary of relevant possibilities proposed to it by its creator. The enormous epochs of gradual evolutionary emergence, and the autonomous evolution of life by random variation and natural selection, are consistent with the idea of a God who loves the world enough to allow it to become distinct from its creative ground. We envision the entire history of cosmic evolution, including all of those features that seem to render it absurd when interpreted in terms of our human standards of time and right order, as the story of an emergent freedom capable of ever deeper intimacy with God. As theology reads beneath the surface of life and evolution, what it sees going on in the depths of nature is the gift of God's own self being poured out into the creation, and the emerging creation being taken into the life of God. And it can read all of this in the depths of nature while still allowing room for evolutionary explanations closer to the surface.

To Dawkins, however (as for Bertrand Russell earlier), the "wasteful" multi-millennial journey of evolution still counts against any realistic trust in providence.

Surely, if God were supremely intelligent and all-powerful, creation would never have taken so long and emerged so clumsily. A God who meets Dawkins's qualifications would have to be a more intelligent and efficient designer than Darwin allows us to believe in. But Dawkins's blueprint for an acceptable deity is that of a conjurer, or at best a distant architect, rather than an infinite love whose deepest concern is for the growth of the universe into genuine independence. On the other hand, a theology that understands God as liberating, suffering love rather than coercive power should already have anticipated that the cosmos would be given unimaginable temporal amplitude and, along with that, the opportunity to experiment with many different ways of existing.

The immensity of cosmic duration, together with the enormity of space, gives breadth and beauty as well as depth to creation. It provides the scope for a high degree of spontaneity and contingency in the origin of the first living cell, in the remarkable transformations in the life-story during the Cambrian period, and in such events as meteorite impacts that drastically alter the biosphere and open up new avenues for evolutionary experimentation. Nature's contingencies and evolution's randomness are not indicative of a divine impotence, but of a God caring and self-effacing enough to wait for the genuine emergence of what is truly other than God, with all the risk, tragedy and adventure this patience entails. A God who loves extravagance and diversity is able to rejoice in the evolving autonomy of a self-organizing universe. Such a God is also vulnerable enough to suffer along with life in its occasions of failure, struggle and loss.

Only a narrowly coercive deity would have collapsed what is in fact a long and dramatic story of creation into the dreary confines of a single originating instant. But instead of freezing nature into a state of finished perfection, a God of love gives the world ample scope to become a world distinct from its originator. This means that some of its evolutionary experiments may work and others may not. But in any case, we should not be surprised that a divine power rooted in the depths of an infinite love would not crudely stamp a prefabricated blueprint onto the creation. A divine providence that takes the form of self-humbling love would risk allowing the cosmos to exist and unfold in relative liberty. And so the universe would take on an evolutionary character not in spite of but because of God's care for it.

A theology that circumspectly ponders the reality of evolution will propose that divine providence influences the world in a persuasive rather than coercive way. It will not be alarmed that the life-story percolates with contingency. If God is love and not domineering force, the world would be allowed to evolve and to participate in the adventure of its own creation. If God were more directive or dictatorial, we would perhaps expect the universe to be finished all at once and remain eternally unchanged. If God were a controlling agency, the

Earth might have gone without the haunting organisms of the Cambrian explosion and later the bumbling dinosaurs and creepy reptiles, or the many other living creatures that seem so alien to us. Our divine magician would have constructed the world along the lines of our own human sense of perfect design. There would have been no struggle and no pain. Yet such a world would have lacked all the drama, diversity, adventure, intense beauty—and, of course, tragedy also—that evolution has brought with it. The world might have had a languorous harmony to it, and perhaps there would have been no suffering and evil. But such a bland cosmos would have featured none of the narrative grandeur that has occurred during the several billion years of life's unfolding. And it could not have allowed for the emergence of freedom.

When providence is conceived of—in a truly biblical spirit—as essentially promise, divine care means the opening of the world to an always new future. Today attention to biological evolution challenges theology to extend the sense of divine promise beyond the aspirations of Israel and the churches, beyond our human concern for the final outcome of human history, out into the universe itself. Awareness of evolution helps theology broaden the scope of divine promise as well as compassion. Theology today, therefore, needs to steep itself in, rather than flee in fear from, Darwin's imposing vision. Evolution helps us realize that God is much more interested in promoting freedom and arousing adventure in the world than in preserving the status quo or establishing impeccable design. Biblical faith has always been aware of God's concern for human liberation. But now evolutionary science invites us to connect our ideas of God to the larger story of life's arduous, ageless liberation from triviality.[10]

Certainly nature is filled with ambiguity. But, as Teilhard de Chardin reminds us, such ambiguity is inevitable in any world that remains unfinished. How could a process that has not yet been perfected be other than imperfect? Of course, faith longs for creation to reach fulfillment. But as long as the universe remains unfinished, its inhabitants are able to share in the momentous work of bringing it to completion, and they may trust that they abide continuously within the radiance of a new creation and an unprecedented, incalculable future.[11]

After Darwin, we may conjecture, our sense of divine providence has to take into account the fact that the natural world is no longer consistent with the innocent notions of perfect design entertained by the natural theology and design arguments characteristic of a pre-evolutionary frame of mind. Current evolutionary pictures of nature now provide us with the opportunity to go beyond our provincial insistence that nature should be better designed and more evenly ordered. The new evolutionary accounts of nature invite us to recapture the often obscured portrait of a self-humbling, suffering God who is anything but a divine controller or designer of the cosmos. Evolution points to a God who gives to all

creatures a significant role, and to humans a special (though inevitably limited)
partnership, in the task of creating the world.

Theological reflection, especially in an age where the idea of evolution has be-
come central to science, now demands that we entertain more seriously than ever
the notion of a God who, for the sake of relating fully to the world, refrains from
wielding the domineering kind of power that both skeptics and believers often
project onto their ideal of the absolute. We are not speaking here, however, of a
weak or powerless God incapable of redeeming this flawed universe, but of one
whose salvific and creative effectiveness is all the more prevailing because it is
rooted in a divine humility. A humble, utterly relational God, one who partici-
pates intimately in the evolutionary struggle of creation, may offend Dawkins's
sense of what should be the minimal requirements of a providential deity. But
theology allows us to envisage the story of the cosmos and of life as a whole—and
not necessarily just terrestrial life—as taken into God's own being, where it is fi-
nally preserved and redeemed from all that we humans may consider to be ab-
solute loss. The billions of years of evolutionary travail and innovation do not
occur outside the divine life.

In the minds of both skeptics and theists, providence has been too often con-
ceived of as "intelligent design." So we need to dig deeper than both Dawkins
and design arguments. An evolutionary theology stretches the picture of God's em-
pathy beyond design and beyond the human sphere so as to have it embrace all
the struggle, anguish and ambiguity as well as all of the order and enjoyment in
the entire emergent universe. A responsive providence enfolds and lovingly rescues
the whole of creation.[12]

Conclusion

In the words of St. Paul, of course, such a picture of God's hiddenness and
vulnerability may seem to be "foolishness" in comparison with our conventional sense of divine power and wisdom (1st Cor 1:25). And many will
find Darwinian evolution too problematic a notion to let it become so close
an ally of theology as the Engagement approach has just made it. But theology should already have prepared us long ago for evolution. As theologian
Karl Rahner reminds us, if God is infinite love giving itself to the finite
world, then the finite world cannot possibly receive this limitless graciousness in any single instant. In response to the outpouring of God's boundless
love, the universe would be invited to undergo a process of perpetual self-
transformation. In order to "adapt" to the divine infinity, the finite cosmos
would likely have to intensify, in an ongoing and open-ended way, its own
capacity to receive such a superabundance of generosity. In other words, it

might endure what we now understand scientifically as an arduous and dramatic evolution toward increasing complexity, life, consciousness and widening beauty. Ultimately it is because of the infusion of God's self-giving love that the universe is stirred into the movement of self-transcendence that we know as evolution.[13]

Viewed in this light, the evolution of the cosmos is more than merely compatible with a biblically and theologically informed notion of providence. Faith in a humble, promising God whose essence is self-giving love, a God who always opens up a new future for the world—it would not be too much to say—logically anticipates the evolution of life and the cosmos. In the final analysis, it would be simpler and more candid of theology to think about providence in terms of the picture of life that Darwin and contemporary evolutionary science have actually given us than in terms of an abstract, and generally lifeless, notion of a divine designer. But let us now examine more closely the intriguing question of God and design.

7

Deeper than Design

Intricate patterns in nature, especially the "design" in living beings, have always been a source of great wonder. What has impressed—and comforted—people is that the universe consists not only of murky episodes of disorder but also outlays of exquisite order. Our species has devised countless myths expressing the nearly universal intuition that order ultimately prevails over confusion. Indeed, the ultimate triumph of order over disorder is a fundamental teaching of most religions. Today, however, evolutionary biology may lead us to suspect that only a mixture of pure randomness and impersonal law underlies the spectacular world of life. The ultimate order that our myths depict may therefore be nothing more than the projection of our adaptive human brains and their need for pattern.[1] Yet the fact remains that our constructive brains themselves had to have been intricately "designed" by the universe, albeit through a Darwinian process that apparently had no such goal in mind. Whatever the way in which pattern emerges, we still confront the deeper wonder of a universe that bothers to enhance order at all, eventually manufacturing "mechanisms" as complex in their organization as the projective human brain.

The fact that the universe does not stay stuck in chaos or wallow perpetually in smug monotony becomes itself a legitimate object of wonder. How are we to account for nature's adventurous tendency to build more and more elaborate designs, especially in the sphere of life? The physical sciences will appropriately give their own answers—which should be pushed as far as they can go—and biology will attribute living design to natural selection. The collective sciences are certainly necessary to any full account, but do they take us deep enough? At some point, if we dig toward the deepest roots of design, as in all serious exploration, we inevitably arrive at a point where science must yield to metaphysics, that is, to some general vision of reality. Darwinian materialists can have no credible objection to our appealing to metaphysics at some point, since very early in their own reflections on life they have already turned from science to reliance on a worldview. Their general vision of reality consists of the controlling belief that essentially lifeless and mindless physical stuff is the ultimate foundation of everything. This is their metaphysics. Many evolutionists commit themselves to this materialist creed long before they embark on their "purely scientific" adventures. So the fact that theology would want to propose an alternative metaphysics as more suitable to the data of evolution does not as such seem entirely out of order.

It is both scientifically and theologically fatal, however, to take refuge in ultimate explanations too early in our attempts to understand the natural world. One of the great lessons theology has learned from modern science is to postpone such metaphysical gratification. To introduce ideas about God as the "cause" of natural phenomena at soft points in our scientific inquiries is intellectually inappropriate and theologically disastrous. It has been a wholesome development for theology, therefore, that it must now allow the sciences to carry their own explanations as far as they can possibly go, without pious interruptions. This new reserve means not that theological explanation is irrelevant but that, by granting science full scope at its own levels of inquiry, theology may now find its own depth. Theology is no longer obliged to do part-time duty in the same explanatory alcove as that occupied by the more proximate readings of nature proper to physical science. Contrary to the simplistic claim that science has rendered theological explanation marginal, science has instead permitted theology to gravitate toward its more natural setting—in the depths. So now theology no longer needs to diminish its proper compass by bending its attention to the minutiae of scientific inquiry. Instead it can devote full time to ultimate questions—questions such as why we should bother to do science or why there is any order in nature at all.

If there is providential significance in the historical emergence of scientific method, perhaps it is that science prolongs the mind's journey into the depths of nature, opening up plummetless ravines where we had previously expected to reach ultimate reality directly beneath the surface. Science's distancing of the divine from our immediate grasp is salutary for any religious awareness that takes seriously the notion of an infinite divine transcendence. It is essential to religious experience, after all, that ultimate reality be beyond our grasp. If we could grasp it, it would not be ultimate. And so, for this reason, theology need not be alarmed that Darwin's science has removed easy religious access to an ultimate explanation of design lurking immediately beneath living complexity. The path from surface design down to nature's ultimate depths turns out to be much longer and less direct than our myths of order had perhaps craved. But the Darwinian distancing of design from any unmediated divine engineering can have the effect of deepening, rather than banishing, the notion of divine creativity.

Postponing metaphysics, however, is a tough assignment, and both religious and cosmic literalism try to arrive at the ultimate foundations of nature too soon. They imagine they have reached the basement before the journey down the stairs has barely begun. One way of manifesting this metaphysical impatience is to paste the fact of life's complexity directly onto the cozy idea of divine intelligent design without first acknowledging and exploring nature's own self-organizing spontaneity. But another is to claim that design is "nothing but" the outcome of blind natural selection. If the former is a "science-stopper" because it makes a dubious theological appeal to a god-of-the-gaps when there is still room for more scientific elucidation, then the invocation of the idea of natural selection (or any other evolutionary category) as though it were an *ultimate* explanation of life's design and diversity is a "depth suppressor." Evolutionist materialism brings our search for ultimate explanations of life to a crashing halt at a point where most of the journey into nature's depth still lies ahead of us. By dressing the scientifically proper, but still relatively abstract, idea of natural selection in the apparel of metaphysical finality, some biologists are now leading their science to an unnecessarily premature climacteric.

Sterile "dreams of a final theory" are as conspicuous among Darwinian commentators today as among physicist-philosophers. And such fantasies of categorical closure are as likely to metamorphose into stale dogma as are the constructs of creationists. Science can have a lively future only if its practitioners enjoy an at least tacit awareness of the endless depths that lie beneath nature's surface. And so, if the premature appeal to theological metaphysics obscures the ranges that science can yet uncover, so also the current incapacity of evolutionary materialism to dig very deep into the metaphysical roots of life's organized complexity is an insult to the human mind's need for truly ultimate explanations.

Intelligent Design

Among those most sensitive to the cognitionally crippling implications of materialist evolutionism are the so-called advocates of Intelligent Design

Theory (IDT).[2] Through a flurry of articles and books, this small but vocal company of scholars argues that Darwinism is not enough to explain the seemingly miraculous fact of design in living organisms. As we look at the natural world around us, they insist, it is hard not to be amazed at the supernaturally complex ways in which the universe is organized, especially in the realm of living beings. Purely material forces, they say, could never account for such a stupendous display of engineering. Science has discovered not only DNA, but also numerous other cellular components that contain an unbelievable degree of design. Since the 1950s, biochemistry, aided by powerful new microscopes, has exposed the intricately ordered arrangements in the living cell with a detail previously unknown. Lacking our pinpoint microscopic technology, Darwin himself was unable to peer as penetratingly into living matter's organization as we are today. The cell for him was a black box, so he could not have noticed the "irreducible complexity" in cellular mechanisms, the "brittle" design, for which gradual evolution by natural selection allegedly cannot account.[3] IDT followers postulate, therefore, that we need to go deeper than Darwin to find an adequate explanation of life's designs. But here we need to ask whether IDT, for its part, takes us deep enough.

IDT's proposal is that we should read the astounding complexity in living beings as evidence of an underlying "intelligence." Citing especially the staggering complexity of the cell, IDT argues that it is both appropriate and necessary even for biologists—and not just metaphysicians or theologians—to invoke the idea of "intelligent design" if they are interested in getting to the real cause of living complexity. To IDT's critics, this proposal is fatal to science because it introduces an ultimate, metaphysical kind of explanation at a point in our probing of life where science itself still has plenty of room for deeper exploration of its own.[4] However, some proponents of IDT reply that "intelligent design" is not to be taken as a metaphysical explanation of life. Rather, it is a cause that belongs logically at the same level of scientific understanding as, say, the Darwinian notion of natural selection. "Intelligence" is not an explanation that theology alone is permitted to invoke but a causal reality that falls appropriately in the realm of scientific theorizing.

IDT advocates William Dembski and Michael Behe even deny that the idea of intelligent design refers directly to deity, and they claim that they are not reading the existence of God directly out of the text of life's design. Since the fact of design is an empirically available datum that Darwinians also observe and attempt to explain—although Darwinians do so in terms of natural selection—IDT argues that intelligent design is a much more proportionate, and more robust, *scientific* explanation than are lifeless and mindless Darwinian mechanisms. To IDT the problem is that blind natural selection (added to eons of time) is too empty a notion to account for something so exceptional as organic and cellular complexity. A better *scientific* explanation is "intelligent design."

Thus, IDT insists that the "inference to intelligent design" is not a theological but a purely scientific movement of the objectively disinterested human mind.[5] Intelligent design functions, so the theory goes, in an explanatory manner logically parallel to, though in competition with, Darwinian mechanisms. If scientists' minds would remain uncluttered by materialist biases, they would intuitively realize that the idea of natural selection is too vacuous to account for something so elaborate as cellular patterning, regardless of how much time evolution may have had to cobble bits of matter together into its marvelous contrivances. The intricate designs in the cell can only be explained by our invoking a commensurately marvelous agency, one that cannot be found among Darwinian categories.

What else, though, could the notion of "intelligent design" be pointing to if not the creator God of religion and theology? And if so, is not the "inference to intelligent design" a clear instance of what I referred to earlier as premature metaphysical gratification? It simply cannot be without interest to us here that the champions of IDT are themselves nearly always Christian— and occasionally Muslim or Jewish—theists. So it is hard to suppress the suspicion that they are appealing to ultimate theological explanations, and that they are doing so too early in what should be a very prolonged journey toward the depths of design.

Even more interesting for our purposes here is that, while professing a high degree of respect for biochemistry and molecular biology (as well as for new developments in physics and chemistry), IDT disciples typically remain overtly hostile to Darwinian accounts of life. Deep time and the narrative abyss of nature exposed by evolutionary biology lie, at least for the most part, beyond their focal interest.[6] At a time when an increasing number of scientists have concluded that evolution is *the* integrating concept in biology and other fields of natural and social science, IDT's staunch resistance to Darwinian biology clearly estranges its followers from the scientific community at large. The reason usually given for their aversion to Darwinism (or neo-Darwinism) is that it is not science at all, but instead simply an expression of philosophical materialism hiding behind the façade of empirically shaky data. And so, while they defend the hypothesis of intelligent design as a purely scientific idea, IDT proponents reject core concepts of contemporary science as spurious ideology. They argue—and I believe quite correctly—that the evolutionary materialists are even less willing to postpone metaphysical gratification than they are.[7] But we cannot ignore the judgment by most scientists today that IDT's appeal to intelligent design is scientifically illicit.

How to Read Design

It is not helpful, however, simply to dismiss IDT as the product of ignorance mixed with narrow religious biases. The advocates of IDT are no less intelligent than their Darwinian and theological adversaries. They are often themselves skilled and highly educated physicists, chemists, mathematicians or biochemists. They are neither stupid nor insane. Clearly the current dispute between biologists and IDT is not a matter of who has the highest IQ. Rather, once again, we have here something analogous to a reading problem. All parties to the discussion are looking at the same text—in this case, the impression of design in living cells and organisms. But one side reads this design at a level of depth that the others do not. This is not simply a case of one party's not being on the same page as the others. Rather, the several factions are all reading the same page (nature's design), but they connect their reading of that page to the larger book of life, the universe, and the inexhaustible depth of nature in drastically disparate ways.

Let us, then, take the obvious fact of "design" in living beings as a kind of "text" to be interpreted, focusing our attention on what all of us can acknowledge to be the adaptive character of that design. There are at least four distinct parties interested in reading this text: (1) evolutionary biologists, (2) evolutionary materialists, (3) IDT proponents and (4) evolutionary theists.[8] Evolutionary biologists (Group 1) are simply interested in laying out the historical, material or mechanical causes of living design, using such notions as variation, adaptation and selection. The evolutionary materialists (Group 2) are those who, by mixing physicalist metaphysics with evolutionary biology, take several Darwinian categories as the *ultimate* explanation of design. IDT disciples (Group 3), also fusing science with metaphysics, try to force the category of "intelligence" into the *scientific* arena of explanations, a set of disciplines that methodologically excludes notions of intelligence, intentionality or purposiveness.

Group 4, evolutionary theists, are those who consider Darwinian explanations to be appropriate to biology, but who firmly reject, as an instance of premature metaphysical gratification, the evolutionary materialist enshrinement of Darwinian categories as the deepest explanation of life's design. But no less emphatically, they object to IDT's insertion of the concept of "intelligence" into a (scientific) level of reading that methodologically precludes such intentional factors. Evolutionary theists do not deny that, *at a deeper level* of explanation than science itself can ever plumb, the appeal to divine intelligence is essential to a rich understanding of life. At some point, though not at a scientific level of understanding, theology is obliged to view the whole universe as a consequence of divine wisdom. Evolutionary theists embrace the notion of reading levels, explanatory pluralism or an extended hierarchy of explanation as essential to any fertile human understanding of a universe whose depth is inexhaustible. And this endorsement of layered models of explanation allows them to accept Darwinian accounts as quite appropriate at one level, while providing ample room for theological readings at a deeper one.

In this light, therefore, the so-called Darwin wars are really not so much conflicts between science and religion as they are disagreements about whether there is room for only one or perhaps multiple levels of explanation. And they are also disputes concerning where and when to introduce "ultimate" explanations. To those who have no sense of the distinction between scientific and metaphysical levels of explanation, the two inevitably become conflated, so that scientific explanation itself becomes in effect the ultimate explanation. The present book, however, argues that such a logical meltdown fails to do justice to either science or theology.

In their metaphysical impatience, both evolutionary materialists and IDT disciples compress what could be a rich hierarchy of explanations into a one-dimensional Flatland where scientific and ultimate levels either become indistinguishable, or else they are forced to compete for the single explanatory slot available. IDT, for example, tries to squeeze a non-scientific category of explanation (divine intelligence)—one that traditionally has had its home in metaphysics—into a scientific groove too narrowly hewed to accommodate worldviews. Even if the term "intelligent" in IDT is not intended to be directly theological, it is nonetheless a concept that belongs at a metaphysical rather than a scientific level of explanation.[9]

Meanwhile, however, evolutionary materialists bestow on Darwinian mechanisms the status of *ultimate* explanation of life's design, a procedure that turns out to be no less scientifically dubious than IDT's metaphysical ploys. There are countless instances of Darwinians moving noiselessly from evolutionary explanation into metaphysical doctrine, but two examples will suffice here. First, evolutionist Michael R. Rose slips Darwinism into the same patently metaphysical explanatory slot as that formerly occupied by theology. "Without Darwinism," he says, "biological science would need one or more deities to explain the marvelous contrivances of life. Physics and chemistry are not enough. And so without Darwinism, science would remain theistic, in whole or in part."[10] The unspoken but obvious assumption here is that Darwinism only does better what theology used to do—namely, provide an ultimate explanation of life. A second example is that of Gary Cziko's book *Without Miracles,* which seeks to show in great detail all the ways in which the idea of Darwinian "selection" has now *replaced* the notion of divine "providence" in explaining how living phenomena work.[11] Instead of viewing selection and providence as two radically distinct levels in a richly layered set of explanations, Cziko merely substitutes one concept for the other—keeping intact the assumption that all explanation must be one-dimensionally collapsed. Instances of such condensation abound in evolutionist literature.

Evolutionary theism, on the other hand, allows room for both scientific and metaphysical levels of explanation. Unlike IDT and evolutionary materialism, it assumes that there is an inexhaustible depth to nature, and that this depth permits a plurality of readings as well as interminable scientific probing. My argument, then, is that the first and fourth groups, evolutionary biology and evolutionary theism, can form a fruitful partnership. However, both Groups 2 and 3 are unsuited not only to each other—as we already know from the current spats between IDT advocates and the proponents of evolutionary materialism—but also to evolutionary biology as such (Group 1).

This latter point may sound peculiar, especially to those like Michael R. Rose, Stephen Jay Gould, Michael Ruse, William Provine, E. O. Wilson, Richard Dawkins and many others who apparently find it impossible to separate Darwinian biology from a metaphysically materialist setting.[12] However, it is crucial to the argument of this entire book that evolutionary biology neither requires a materialist metaphysics nor provides ultimate explanations. The claim that evolution entails materialism is a statement of faith, and it is one that, due to its metaphysical impatience, logically subverts rather than energizes the enterprise of open-ended scientific exploration. By proclaiming that the foundational layer of all life is a combination of dead matter and atomic or mechanical causes, it not only leaves out most of what is truly essential to life but also discourages ongoing scientific inquiry into other possible physical factors that, alongside of and complementary to Darwinian factors, can give us an ever richer understanding of life. Already, in fact, a number of post-Darwinian biologists and philosophers, without necessarily opposing standard evolutionary biology, are exploring such prospects.[13] But the evolutionary materialists, out of a sense of devotion to their monocausal metaphysical commitments, typically repudiate any such reaching toward more nuanced understandings of life.

There can be no objection, of course, to placing science within a metaphysical setting. This is unavoidable. But in order to prevent any amalgamating of science with belief it should be done carefully, self-consciously and, above all, patiently. For the sake of science itself, our beliefs about the ultimate nature of reality should not be alloyed in a hasty way with scientific explanations. Otherwise, before long our metaphysics will be doing the work of science. Such substitution of metaphysics for science is patently obvious in both IDT and evolutionist materialism. Evolutionary theism, on the other hand, renounces metaphysical impatience, locating ultimate explanation in the distant depths, dodging in principle any temptation to confuse the work of God with the workings of nature. In its careful distinguishing of the divine creative depths of nature from the surface continuum of natural causes, evolutionary theism also logically excludes any placing of theological explanations into competition with Darwinian accounts.

By distancing the divine from easy supernaturalist intrusions into the surface levels of nature, evolutionary theism opens wide a space for pure, uninterrupted scientific inquiry that neither Group 2 nor Group 3 is forbearing enough to tolerate. Instead of closing off the native openness of human inquiry by coming to rest in materialist abstractions (misplaced concreteness) or in premature appeals to "intelligent design" (misplaced ultimacy), evolutionary theism gives ample room to ongoing scientific progress in the understanding of life. A theistic trust in reality's ultimate intelligibility, when placed alongside the religious intuition of nature's infinite depths, provides a most favorable setting for open-minded scientific research.

Beneath Design

With our four positions staked out, then, let us return to the question of how they read design. About the naked fact of "adaptive design" in living phenomena there can be no reasonable dispute among our four parties. Even evolutionary materialists are willing to agree that a bird's wing is "designed" for flight, or the heart for pumping blood, or cilia for locomotion. Here the designer, of course, is blind natural selection, but the outcome of its labor is an intricately adaptive, though not inevitably perfect, "fit" of living organisms to their environments; and so, such traits merit the label "design." The question, therefore, is not about the fact of design as such but about how to explain it. What lies beneath the surface of living design?

IDT (Group 3) takes the intricate structure of design to be the consequence of an apparently unmediated underlying "intelligence." The assumption is that something analogous to the human intellect must have engineered what to all appearances is as intricate as anything devised by human mechanical ingenuity. "Intelligence" means, at the very least, a causal factor distinct from both the absurdity of sheer randomness and the blindness of selection. Since what is purely random and impersonal is also inherently unintelligent, Darwinian processes allegedly cannot account for the intelligible order in nature. Moreover, embedded in the complexity of the cell, and especially in the specific sequence of bases in an organism's nuclear DNA, is an informational arrangement that naturally points to an intelligent cause.[14]

Darwinian materialists (Group 2), however, claim that this "intelligence" is only veneer, and that beneath the admittedly improbable design in our text there lies a rich compost of factors explainable ultimately by the notions of mindless physical stuff, chance events, invariant natural laws and enormous amounts of time. These ingredients are unintelligent, but they are nevertheless sufficient to account for the evolution of functional design in biological phenomena, including the wonder of human intelligence itself. Indeed our own intelligence itself is just one more instance of the adaptive evolutionary "fit" between organism and environment.[15] IDT would reply to this that attributing the creation of cellular and organic design simply and solely to a mindless neo-Darwinian process cannot explain what strikes intelligent beings as so utterly mind-like in its engineering. But the evolutionary materialists would insist that great stretches of time can accomplish what shorter periods cannot. Mindless selection of a hit-and-miss string of blind variations can *gradually* produce our text, including mind itself.

The Darwinian reading (Group 1), for its part, wants nothing to do with IDT as a scientific explanation of life. It does not deny the obvious fact of complex order, but it reads the text of living design in a way that dispenses methodologically with any appeal to intelligence as a causal factor. In fact, its deliberate refusal to allow ideas like mind, intention, subjectivity or purpose to play any part in the evolutionary explanation of nature, including accounts of life and the human mind, is not peculiar to Darwinism but is generally taken to be an essential feature of modern science as such. To violate science's methodological exclusion of mind, intelligence, subjectivity, purpose, personality, intentionality or divine providence from *scientific* explanation is incompatible with the way science reads anything whatsoever. Therefore, such metaphysical factors should no more appear in evolutionary biology than in chemistry or physics. As I mentioned above, evolutionary theism (Group 4) is quite willing, for theological reasons, to go along with this methodological exclusion of categories like intelligence from scientific discourse; and for that very reason it coexists comfortably with evolutionary biology.

To IDT, however, science's methodological exclusion of intelligence is unacceptable. Perhaps highly periodic forms of order that make up entities like crystals do not require intelligence as a proximate factor. But the aperiodic informational sequencing (specified complexity) in a DNA molecule calls for an exceptional kind of explanation.[16] Good science, IDT insists, should not leave out any genuinely causal factors when it attempts to explain natural phenomena. And logic dictates that specified informational design calls for something at least proportionately intelligent as its cause. If science still refuses to make intelligent design part of its explanatory apparatus, then we need to reform scientific method until it is properly armed to do battle for the whole of truth.

All along, however, the Darwinian materialists (Group 2) keep reminding us that for most of our human history—until roughly the middle of the last century—humans were unable to read beneath the facade of life's design into the unimaginable depth of *time* during which a combination of blind chance and mindless laws of nature could have brought living "design" into existence without any need for providential stimuli.[17] Only by leaving out the ideas of intelligence and purpose in nature are we now finally able, they say, to look into the gaping abyss of mindlessness beneath life's designs. The evolutionary sciences, including geology and cosmology, have now fitted us with spectacles that have removed our myopia. Until we put them on, we were unable to see the impersonal, long, clumsy and wasteful journey of matter and life buried beneath the surface of our text.

For their part, the evolutionary theists (Group 4) consider both Groups 2 and 3 to be still too nearsighted themselves. Evolutionary theists are fully appreciative of Group 1's methodological disposing of intelligent design as a properly scientific explanation. But they emphasize that both evolutionary materialism and IDT share a metaphysical impatience that arrives at *final* explanations too soon and therefore cuts off the road to deeper scientific understanding of life. From the perspective of evolutionary theism, both parties have raced too quickly toward allegedly ultimate explanations. As Paul Tillich would advise, there can be no depth without the way to the depth, and no deep truth without undertaking the long and difficult struggle for truth. Yet both Groups 2 and 3 attempt to reach the depths without having actually journeyed there. The difficulty is that in its own kind of literalism, each of these antagonists attempts what I earlier called a hybrid reading. It forces scientific information *prematurely* onto a metaphysical template. Each side in the contemporary debate assumes that there can be only one level of reading or explanation, namely its own, and then tries to map onto this reading a content that is natively incommensurate with it.

Even though a religious understanding of life's design may justify our appealing—at some level—to the notion of divine intelligence, IDT inappropriately introduces this idea at the level of scientific explanation, where such a meta-physical appeal is methodologically out of place. In order to make intelligent design an acceptable scientific idea, IDT in effect tries to expand the method-ological boundaries of science beyond their conventional placement. While try-ing to be more encompassing than traditional scientific method, however, IDT ironically ends up ignoring the valuable information that evolutionary science has been gathering during the last century and a half.

At the same time, Darwinian materialists (Group 2) refuse to allow intel-ligence to be a causal factor at *any* level of human understanding of life. Why invoke something as complex as intelligence to explain life, including intelligent life, when a completely mindless process of selection can fully account even for our adaptive cerebral design?[18] Isn't the appeal to intelli-gence a violation of Occam's razor? The simple Darwinian formula seems so *exhaustively* explanatory that the idea of intelligence must be dropped as utterly superfluous—even for those kinds of inquiry that traditionally fall outside the boundaries of scientific exploration. Indeed, any other kind of inquiry—such as the theological—is dogmatically excluded as unable to ex-plain anything whatsoever. According to the evolutionary materialists, theo-logical explanation, therefore, is always in *competition* with science, and therefore must be suppressed.[19] Thus, as Cziko's treatise *Without Miracles* so clearly exemplifies, because only one explanatory slot is available, we must choose time and again *between* Darwin and divine providence. The impres-sion that theology exists in a perpetually competitive relationship with science is, of course, only exacerbated by the fact that IDT insists on mak-ing intelligent design (which inevitably sounds like theology) an alternative *scientific* explanation.

Evolutionary theism, on the other hand, disallows any competition of sci-ence with theology since it endorses science's methodological exclusion of theological categories. But while the scientist is perfectly justified in exclud-ing the idea of intelligent design from any properly *scientific* understanding of life, it does not follow that every scientific explanation of life's design is ei-ther deep or adequate. Indeed, it is not self-evident that science can ever give us the deepest possible understanding of anything. If its practitioners claim that it can, then they have gone beyond science into the murky swamp of be-lief. They *believe* that to understand life we must read it only at the scientific, and for many this means an exclusively Darwinian, level of understanding.

Both IDT and Darwinian materialism shrink what could be an extensively storied hierarchy of explanations of life down to one level. This single level is construed differently in each case, but both sides refuse to entertain the idea of a plurality of complementary explanations. For both groups, there exists only one explanatory slot, and so the decision to follow one kind of explanation inevitably excludes the other. Without the explanatory pluralism that accompanies a hierarchy of distinct reading levels, it becomes necessary to choose between two highly conflated versions of Flatland. In their common aversion to a multiplicity of distinct reading levels, both IDT and evolutionary materialism are willing to settle for a world devoid of depth, taking refuge in their respective versions of literalism. Ultimately, both approaches lead to a shallow understanding of nature. I will now show, in more depth, why I think this is the case.

Beneath Evolutionary Materialism

Suppose you subscribe to evolutionary materialism. This means that you embrace the tenet that all facets of life can have a purely and *exclusively* naturalist explanation. More specifically, this means that Darwinian selection is the ultimate explanation of living phenomena. Since your own brain is part of nature, it too must be the product of adaptive selection. Cziko admits that it "may seem mysteriously ironic" that purposeless natural selection leads to an organism capable of framing purposeful designs. But, he goes on, "the irony fades when one considers the great survival and reproductive advantages of organisms that are able consistently to achieve goals essential to their survival and reproduction despite an unpredictable, uncaring, and often hostile environment."[20] Or if you lean toward Stephen Jay Gould's interpretation of evolution you may give a more significant causal role to contingent or accidental events in natural history in accounting for the factors that led to the existence of your brain and its intellectual abilities. In either case, or perhaps by appealing to a combination of adaptation and contingency, you are logically obliged to conclude that your own mind, like all other products of evolution, is fully intelligible in terms of causes (blind selection and chance) that are—by your self-definition as an evolutionary materialist—themselves completely devoid of mind and intelligence. Let us assume in what follows that you are closer to Dawkins and Cziko than to Gould, though essentially the same point could be made in both instances.

The question I have for you, then, is this: Given the avowedly exhaustive explanation of your intelligence in terms of purely unintelligent causes, why should I, or anybody else including you, take seriously the claims that this *purely adaptive* instrument is now making? Why should I assume that this adaptive instrument (your mind) is able to discover *truth*?[21] Obviously, you want me to accept your mind's evolutionary explanation of intelligence as *true*, and not merely as functionally adaptive. But how can I accept this as true if, at the same time, your own intelligence may simply be engaging in one more adaptive—and that means possibly deceptive—exercise? How can I tell when you're just being adaptive and when you're telling me the truth? Some of your friends among the evolutionary psychologists have even argued that the mind is adaptive because it is a great deceiver, never to be trusted, since its real objective is adaptation rather than arriving at truth (although they obviously want me to accept at least that truth as something more than mere adaptation).[22]

In other words, there is a blatant contradiction between an *exclusively* selectionist explanation of mind, on the one hand, and the implicit trust you place in your own mind's capacity to arrive at the naked truth, on the other.[23] Clearly, in asking me to accept the *truth* of evolutionary materialism's selectionist explanation of human intelligence, you have tacitly introduced something extraneous to your pure Darwinism. Therefore, adaptationist explanations of mind, accurate though they may be at a certain level of scientific explanation, must be insufficient—that is, if you want me to take you seriously. Your Darwinism, in other words, has not taken you deep enough to deal with the question of the truth of Darwinism itself.

You have implied that the mind is capable of knowing *truth as such* and of distinguishing truth from mere illusion. Otherwise, why would you be trying to convince me that Darwin is right and that both IDT and evolutionary theism are wrong? You have a desire to know what is objectively true, and the quiet presence of this pure desire to know the truth now requires that you go deeper than Darwin if you expect other people to take your own ideas seriously.[24] One of your evolutionary materialist heroes, Daniel Dennett, has made the claim that Darwinism is a "universal acid" that cuts through everything. But I cannot help noting that even for Dennett the acid does not cut through that assertion itself.[25] Otherwise Dennett could not possibly expect us to take seriously either his claim that Darwinism is a universal acid or the nearly 600-page argument supporting this declaration.

The point is, there is a quiet and gracious element in your intellect's actual performance that, mercifully, neither you, nor Dennett, nor Darwin's acid can ever dissolve, and this is quite simply the trust you have in your own mind to bring you closer to *what is.* Your evolutionist materialism is not enough to justify this trust, since that belief system is obliged to explain away your trust as nothing more than evolutionary adaptation. If your own intellectual performance is mere adaptation, then how can you trust it to give you truth, especially since adaptations can easily be deceptions?

So in all candor you need to look for a metaphysics (an understanding of reality) more consistent with the native confidence that *you cannot help* placing in your own intelligence. Evolutionist materialism cannot be the world-view you need here, since it gives you so many reasons *not* to trust either that reality is ultimately intelligible or that the pursuit of truth is anything more than a survival function. Your materialist creed tells you that the ultimate origin of your mind is utter mindlessness and that the deepest you will ever penetrate in your search for understanding is to the blank physical stuff out of which life and mind have awakened for a brief moment. Everything about that brand of metaphysics explicitly subverts the trust that you *actually* have in your mind's capacity to discover truth. I'm only asking that you not deny in your philosophical beliefs what you affirm in your every act of knowing.[26]

If you find yourself protesting what I have just said, it is not because of anything your evolutionist materialism has taught you. Rather, it is because you cannot help trusting your own critical abilities. The upshot, then, is this: *The trust you have in your own capacity for truth does not match the universe that your evolutionist materialism believes in.* Your mind itself will never form a comfortably "adaptive fit" with the worldview articulated by the priesthood that regulates contemporary materialist metaphysics. The solution to this mismatch, however, is not to suppress the trust you have in your own intelligence by defending a view of reality logically unable to contain it. Rather, you must look for a vision of the real, an alternative metaphysics, that fits more tightly the intelligence—including your own intelligence—that has emerged in evolution.

The most efficient way I can convince you that evolutionary materialism's "ultimate" explanation of intelligence—in terms solely of mindless causes—does not go deep enough, therefore, is simply to ask you to reflect in a sustained way on three points. First, look at the undeniable trust that undergirds your own search for truth. As long as you try to account for this trust as nothing more than an adaptive evolutionary contrivance, and not something inherently capable of finding truth, you will be sabotaging every judgment your intellect makes. In actual fact, however, you cannot completely subvert the trust you place in your mind. Notice, for example, that right now you are striving to understand what I'm saying, trying to dig beneath my words to the meaning they are expressing, and above all how vigilantly you are on the lookout to see where I've gone wrong in my argument here. You could not undertake this critical activity without trusting in your own intellect's capacity to arrive at *what is.*

Second, note also that this intelligence of yours is as much a part of nature as are rocks, trees and rodents. If you are an evolutionary materialist, you cannot disagree with this, nor can anyone who accepts evolutionary biology. Your intelligence and the trust that underlies it are woven intricately into an evolving universe. Your mental activity, as Whitehead rightly emphasizes, is not something that takes place outside of the natural world.[27] But if your intellection is part of nature, then this tells you something important about the nature of the universe itself.

Third, then, think about what kind of universe it must be that gives rise in its evolution to an intelligence that cannot help trusting that truth is worth seeking. Does your native trust in this world's intelligibility—and in your own mind's capacity to grasp this intelligibility—"fit" well into the ultimately absurd and mindless universe articulated by your evolutionary materialism? Or instead does it not fit much more satisfactorily a universe that, in its depths, bears an endless intelligibility, a universe that invites you to search deeper and deeper for truth, and that beckons you with a promise that such a pursuit is worthwhile?

No doubt you will make your own choice, but for my own part, only the latter, or something close to it, is *logically* consistent with what I know to be undeniably true about human intelligence. If I seriously thought that the world were not inexhaustibly deep, or that its depth were not infinitely intelligible, the trust that grounds my search for understanding and knowledge would wither and perish. Logically speaking, the mind's capacity for truth, a capacity in which even materialists fervently trust, can never form an adaptive fit with, nor for that matter ever have been selected by, a universe that inherently betrays this trust. However, an intelligence that naturally pursues understanding and truth, an intelligence that can "survive" only if truth is inexhaustibly deep and attainable incrementally, can, at least in principle, form a tight adaptive fit with an environment that is inexhaustibly deep and endlessly intelligible. This is the mind's environment as construed by what I have been calling evolutionary theism. And so, of the four approaches discussed earlier, only the combination of 1 and 4 corresponds with both scientific evidence and the inevitable trust that underlies human intelligence.

Deeper Than Intelligent Design

If you are inclined to accept IDT, two critical remarks are also in order. First, you will have no difficulty agreeing that the universe as it is portrayed by evolutionist materialism does not match up well with the fact of human intelligence. But does the world as it is pictured by IDT correspond proportionately with your own mind's need for an *inexhaustible depth* of exploration? By invoking the idea of intelligent design at a point in scientific inquiry where the road to understanding may be just beginning, are you not suppressing the adventurous human journey into the wilderness of reality's depth? Your metaphysical impatience places you much closer to your materialist assailants than you may have noticed.

It is important, moreover, for you to distinguish more carefully among your opponents: Group 1 (evolutionary biology) is not the same as Group 2 (evolutionary materialists). This is a distinction that IDT seldom if ever seems to notice. I have been arguing that there is a different dynamic operative in each group. Whereas Group 1 rigorously sticks to a method, Group 2 slips into metaphysics. Group 1 is concerned quite rightly to defend the purity of scientific method from contamination by the kind of explanations that IDT is proposing. Group 2, on the other hand, opposes IDT not so much to protect science as to refute a belief system inconsistent with materialist ideology. Evidence for the latter's ideological interest lies in the fact that evolutionary materialists typically make no differentiation between Groups 3 and 4.[28] As far as the evolutionary materialists are concerned, evolutionary theism and IDT are equally unacceptable since both claim that materialism is inadequate to account for life.

However, the appropriate response to this confusion is not to change the definition of science, as IDT is trying to do, so as to slide non-scientific explanations onto the same reading level as that of natural science. Rather, the answer is to acknowledge that the universe and life are so inexhaustibly deep that their intelligibility requires a proportionately layered hierarchy of explanations or reading levels. And since there is no obvious reason to exclude metaphysical and theological explanations from being essential levels in this rich hierarchy, there is no need for you impatiently to slip the category of "intelligence" into the explanatory slot that science is supposed to occupy. Instead, my advice is to save the idea of "intelligence" (or wisdom) to be used as a metaphor at deeper levels of explanation than those proper to scientific abstraction. When we refer to the dimension of inexhaustible depth, only metaphorical language is appropriate anyway. Let "intelligence" become a category at the levels of theological or metaphysical explanation, but not at those of natural science. Allow science to leave out any appeal to intelligence altogether, and in that way you will not force science to take on the burden of being a worldview.[29] By stretching the definition of natural science toward an all-encompassing explanatory competence, your IDT reveals that, no less than your materialist opponents, pushers of intelligent design permit only one explanatory slot. They too have little use for an extended hierarchy of distinct levels of explanation that might allow us to differentiate science clearly from metaphysics and theology.

My second remark, however, is that the depth of the universe is not adequately represented by the metaphor of "intelligence," nor is the alleged intelligence underlying the life-world appropriately represented by the notion of "design." Life is too rich and mysterious to be captured by the notion of "intelligent design." In living processes there is the constant presence of novelty along with design. And there is a creative as well as tragic depth in nature that we can intimate only through the symbolic language of poetry and religion. The explanatory role of theology, then, is to formalize the intuitions of this depth that first erupt in metaphor and religious symbol. Such explanation, at least to those who have become aware of nature's subterranean depth, in no way displaces science but instead leads us toward levels of being that science alone cannot reach.

8

Religion and
Deep Darwinism

D id Darwin get it right? Most scientifically educated people today would
say yes. Darwinian science tells us at least part of the story of life. We
may disagree on just how far contemporary neo-Darwinian biological explanations can really take us toward an adequate explanation of living phenomena. But most of us will agree that they certainly take us a long way.

Today, however, many biologists and a growing number of social theorists,
anthropologists and philosophers think Darwin got it so completely right
that any alternative accounts of life are essentially vacuous. The leap from
"Darwin got it right" to "Darwin tells the whole story" has proven increasingly irresistible. Numerous scientific careers are now being dedicated to the
proposition that the modest nineteenth-century naturalist's ideas are powerful enough to make complete sense of almost anything in the realm of living
and thinking beings. Darwinian explanation can even give us an unsurpassably foundational understanding of human ethics[1] and religion.[2]

Here let us consider—more deliberately than we have done up to this
point—what religion looks like when viewed from a Darwinian perspective.[3]
For a long time evolutionary biology stayed away from religion. Its proponents were typically reluctant to apply their science's insights to something so
apparently *sui generis* as the experience of the sacred. But the inherent drive

of science is to look for purely natural explanations. Science is compelled, in fact, to approach its subject matter without bringing any supposed nonnatural causes into its account of phenomena. Why not look at religion naturalistically also?

The new science of evolutionary psychology, a derivative of sociobiology, proposes to "naturalize" our understanding of religion completely by way of neo-Darwinian explanation. This means that *cultural* accounts of behavior will no longer play the fundamental role. But it also means that any *theological* appeal to the idea of God or the sacred will no longer be necessary to account for religious life and thought either. Why look for supernatural explanations of religion if we can find purely natural ones? And we can now explain "the persistence of the gods," so goes this confident new program, without assuming the hidden influence on human consciousness of any ontologically real divine presence.

Evolutionary psychology starts with two claims: first, that human behavioral patterns and cognitional responses are *inherited*, no less so than our anatomy or physiology; and, second, that inheritance in humans, as in all other species, is a matter of genes seeking to get themselves passed on to future generations. Genes, however, exist not only in individual organisms but in their kin as well, and so fitness (the probability of reproducing) means not individual but *inclusive* fitness. This broadly genetic reinterpretation of Darwinian evolution was worked out by George Williams (in the United States) and William Hamilton and John Maynard Smith (in the United Kingdom) during the 1960s.[4] In the 1970s, Robert Trivers and Richard Alexander argued that the notion of Darwinian selection works best when the units of selection are taken to be genes rather than organisms or populations.[5] Thus, as Alexander writes: "genes are the most persistent of all living units, hence on all counts the most likely units of selection. One may say that genes evolved to survive by reproducing, and they have evolved to reproduce by creating and guiding the conduct and fate of all the units above them."[6]

Darwinian psychology claims that the ways in which the human brain responds to the world were designed by evolution during the Pleistocene (starting 1.5 to 2 million years ago) specifically for a hunter-and-gatherer type of existence. The brain comprises distinct systems designed to cope with specific problems related to survival prior to and during the Paleolithic period. Thus, according to Leda Cosmides and John Tooby, the brain is less like a general-purpose computer than a Swiss army knife.[7] Its various components are designed for separate tasks. People today carry around the same kind of brain that our Paleolithic ancestors had; and because this organ was shaped by adaptive evolutionary processes in different circumstances from those we face today, it is not difficult to understand why contemporary humans have so much trouble adapting to the new environments that subsequent cultural developments have brought about.

To evolutionary psychologists, one of the more puzzling responses this human brain has made to the world is its tendency to create illusions of the sacred and other "counterintuitive" religious ideas, often garnished with strange rituals and bizarre beliefs. Why has religion accompanied us so persistently, perhaps even from the very beginning of Cro-Magnon humanity? Most representatives of the present generation of Darwinian anthropologists now agree that religion is an irritatingly obsolete but stubbornly ineradicable human tendency. Our religious orientation seems to be so deeply rooted and so pervasive that it cannot be understood simply as a cultural invention. Religion must be connected more closely to the specific kind of brains we have, to cerebral systems that served the cause of survival during the course of human evolution. Thus, the ultimate explanation of religion has to do with gene survival. Genes need vehicles that will allow them to replicate faithfully and prodigiously. And it now appears that vehicles equipped with a tendency to be religious were among the most suitable to human gene survival. How, then, could we hope to explain religion more fundamentally than in a purely naturalistic evolutionary way?

A recent example of this kind of approach is Pascal Boyer's confidently titled book *Religion Explained: The Evolutionary Origins of Religious Thought*.[8] Apparently modeling his title, as well as his philosophical assumptions, on Daniel Dennett's materialist manifesto *Consciousness Explained*, Boyer, by training a cultural anthropologist, understands the religious attachment to gods to be the consequence of our Pleistocene ancestors developing brains that aided our survival only by acquiring certain adaptive skills. The brain, Boyer argues, has no specifically religious instinct. Religion itself, he says, is "airy nothing" that persists only because it is parasitic on several cognitive systems that originally evolved as purely survival mechanisms. One of these systems is that of predator detection. Our evolutionary heritage is "that of organisms that must deal with both predator and prey."[9] Organisms that are not good at detecting predators obviously cannot adapt and are therefore unworthy vehicles for gene survival. Those that are good at detecting predators are the ones that survive and pass on genes that give us the predator-detecting cerebral properties we have today.

A brain endowed with the capacity to detect unseen predators is one that can function readily as a host for parasitic religious ideas. It is only a small step, after all, from being vigilant for hidden predators to looking for hidden *agencies* of all kinds. Natural selection caused our brains to develop in such a way that they would eventually look for supernatural explanations that remain out of sight. From a survival strategy fashioned by ancestral genes, human brains have inherited the disposition that leads us even now to persist in our creation of gods. Although our situation today is different from that of hunters and gatherers, it is ultimately the remote Pleistocene project of gene survival that explains, in an ultimate and purely naturalistic way, just why we still tend to be religious.[10]

This Darwinian explanation seeks to demonstrate that we are a religious species not because we have ever encountered God, or been grasped by any divine revelation, but simply because our ancestors were genetically endowed with an adaptive propensity to create illusions of the sacred. These illusions—fortunately for them and us—helped our species adapt to an inherently hostile universe. Religious imagining reinforced the genetic endowment that gave rise to ideas about the gods in the first place. So the *ultimate* explanation of religion and its persistence, at least when viewed from the new Darwinian perspective, has more to do with what our genes need in order to survive than with cultural conditioning or an alleged encounter with transcendent reality.

The working assumption here is that any behavioral characteristic that enhances the prospect of gene survival may be said to be "adaptive." Genes that make a snow rabbit white, for example, heighten the chances that the whitest snow rabbits and their genes will be the ones selected for survival. Likewise, genes that molded humans into religious animals long ago, in coordination, of course, with genes for other adaptive traits, have made it possible for us to survive and eventually become the dominant species on Earth. All of the characteristics we associate with religion—its rituals, doctrines, stories, institutions and theologies—are fully understandable, then, if we read them as having had an adaptive function.

A usually unspoken but clearly operative postulate in this new Darwinian interpretation is a quite modern one: In an unfriendly cosmos, religion kept our ancestors from having to look into the abyss of the world's impersonality. By constructing mythic visions of eternal cosmic order, religions provided illusory but effective shields against the terrors of existence. And by favoring our species with the fictitious phantasm of a purposeful universe, religions gave our human predecessors a reason to keep on living, to bear offspring and thus keep their genes from perishing.

The Darwinian exegesis of religion implies all of this, but adds the authority of biology to the vagaries of psychology. The "biology of religion," while still in its infancy, has begun to gather momentum in academia. It has been advocated in one form or another by such authorities as classicist Walter Burkert, psychologist Robert Hinde, philosopher Daniel Dennett, anthropologist Pascal Boyer, linguistics expert Steven Pinker, philosopher of religion

Loyal Rue and many others.[11] What all of these interpreters—writing out of diverse disciplines—agree upon is that with Darwin's (and E. O. Wilson's) help, we can now provide a deeper naturalistic explanation of our ageless and persistent longing for gods than ever before.

After many thousands of years of religious ignorance, during which time we *thought* that our worship was responding to the genuine otherness of a divine presence, Darwinian anthropologists now inform us—with more scientific confidence than Marx, Nietzsche or even Freud could marshal—that there is a purely natural explanation for our religious dispositions. Biology provides not only a necessary but also a sufficient explanation of the stubborn persistence of religion. Although we had supposed all along that our religious fervor was responding to the sacred as something eminently real, the new Darwinians now instruct us that *at bottom* our religions are purely fictitious ways of ensuring reproductive success.

Darwinian psychologists and anthropologists, we should observe, are not the moralistic accusers of religion that many earlier critics of religion had been. Indeed, they are rather sympathetic toward benighted religious believers. They realize, after all, that adaptive human brains prone to creating religious illusions have in the long run had the positive effect of promoting the cause of our species' gene survival. Although they agree that in our devotion to religious objects we have really been living a "lie," it is a benign and adaptive lie, one that has served well the cause of life.[12] The biologists of religion are aware that they themselves would not be here to explain religion for us were it not for the guileful way in which religion made their own ancestors function as unknowing vehicles for gene survival. Even though it was human weakness and ignorance that allowed our ancestors to invent patterns of religious meaning, something important has been gained through all of the centuries of their naiveté—our own existence!

The neo-Darwinian debunking of religion, of course, is not the first instance of the post-Enlightenment claim that religion is "nothing but" this or that. During the modern period, a number of other candidates have sought the office of Ultimate Explanation of religion. Religion has been explained—or explained away—as the projection of infantile desires, the reflection of societal ideals or the longing for pattern and meaning.[13] Rationalism and science have allegedly demystified spiritual longing, showing it to be a product of human weakness, fear, resentment, repressed sexuality—in general, of an inability to face "reality." But evolutionary psychologists, without necessarily rejecting the earlier theories, are convinced that by dint of Darwinism, we have at last hit upon *the* final and fundamental reason for religion.

Darwinian biology, in its genetically revised versions, apparently has allowed us to dig deeper than ever before into the roots of our spiritual inclinations. During the time that our primate ancestors were becoming hunters and gatherers, our genetic program had already taken on essentially the same specific sequencing it has today. This genomic arrangement determined not only our physical features but our behavioral traits as well. As the result of natural selection, our ancestors' genetic constitution made their brains and anxiety-prone nervous systems fertile soil for the implantation of a kind of religious conjecturing that in turn has abetted the cause of gene survival. And because our gene sequencing is essentially the same today as it was 100,000 or more years ago, can there be any wonder that religions are still around?

Boyer typifies the growing resignation among anthropologists and other scientists to the prospect that religion will not be easily uprooted, contrary to the earlier expectations of many culturally oriented studies. As long as social science had assumed that human behavior is shaped primarily by cultural contingencies, rather than by a persistent mental substrate rooted in biology, there was a hope that social and cultural shifts, especially the future flourishing of science, might rid human life of the nuisance of religion. Puzzled that his fellow humans have not yet outgrown religion, Boyer is now resigned to be an observer and *explainer* of the remarkable persistence of religion. And he claims to have discovered in evolutionary biology the scientific—and ultimately physicalist—explanation of religion for which previous critics of religion had been searching, largely without success.[14]

Earlier, many cultural anthropologists had mistakenly thought that science would so radically transform human culture that the filmy religious illusions characteristic of a pre-rationalist era would spontaneously evaporate under the blazing sun of science. Moreover, since human ideas had seemed so closely tied to the shifting winds of history, economics and politics, the conjecture had been that when these all underwent alteration, their religious superstructures would simply dissipate. But religions still persist, and gods won't go away. So we need a better method of explaining this endurance than we got from the standard social science that accounts for human behavior primarily in terms of culture.[15] Boyer, whose book's title is indicative of the confidence he places in purely Darwinian explanation, offers evolution as the definitive explanation of religion.

In a more tentative way, the classicist Walter Burkert's erudite Gifford Lectures, *Creation of the Sacred,* had already argued that something "beyond" culture and beyond individual civilizations is needed to account for the *universalia* of religion and its stubborn refusal to disappear.[16] And since for

Burkert what lies "beyond culture" cannot possibly be the sacred itself—as religious people have irrationally thought—an adequate explanation must look for religion's ultimate explanation in the realm of the only other domain available "beyond culture." That domain could only be nature itself.[17] By virtue of Darwinian science, Burkert claimed, we are in a much better position than ever before to understand just why religion continues to exist and in some places even thrive. Darwinian analysis allows anthropology to conclude that religion, beneath its complex surface manifestations, was *ultimately* invented by our genes as an adaptive contrivance. Religion is fictitious to the core but extraordinarily effective as far as the survival of the genes that invented it is concerned. In Burkert's understanding, once again, the gods persist because of our genes' need to persist.

The proximate explanation of religion lies of course in specific regions or systems of the human brain; but because the properties of the brain are themselves to be understood as essentially adaptive, the ultimate explanation of our piety lies in segments of DNA. The story, of course, is a bit more complicated than this, as even most of the new biologists of religion will allow. Genes are interwoven with cultural expressions that vary from place to place and from time to time. There is "coevolution" of genes and culture. Our genes do not directly control our religious ideas. However, they do determine that we will have the kinds of brains and nervous systems that lead us to engage in prayer, mythmaking, sacrifice, worship and adherence to sacred codes. In the final analysis, we dance to our genes' music, even when we are convinced that our religions are responses to the "totally other" world encountering us from a sacred beyond.

The Whole Story?

If neo-Darwinian evolutionary psychology is giving us an *adequate* explanation of religion, if it is telling us the *whole story*, then of course we would now have to concede that our religious ideas are cognitively empty. They are pure fictions, and lovers of truth should be willing to give them up—as apparently the new Darwinian debunkers of religion have done themselves.

However, it is interesting to watch how the Darwinian anthropologists deal with the notion of truth. While they claim to be in possession of the final truth about religion, they are not terribly disturbed, as were earlier critics of religion, that most of humanity still wallows in the essentially false comforts of religion. There is a new tolerance of religious illusions, an indulgence that critics like Sigmund Freud, Karl Marx, Friedrich Nietzsche, Bertrand Russell, Jean-Paul Sartre, W. K. Clifford or Jacques Monod would have found highly objectionable on moral grounds. Why do the new Darwinian critics treat religion so much more gently, even if still condescendingly? Is it perhaps because a gene-focused Darwinian unmasking of religion is obliged to conclude that if our ancestors had adhered to a modern scientific ethic of knowledge, we would not be here to point out their naiveté? If Paleolithic humans had been in a position to face the "truth" head-on, or if they had idealized "objectivity" in the way Darwinian scientists themselves are supposed to, would they and their genes ever have survived?

Lacking our scientific and technological ways of coping, our ancestors could not have adapted to the natural world without the illusions of religion—at least if we follow the logic of our Darwinian critics. Happily for us, nature endowed our species in its infancy and adolescence with a glorious capacity for self-deception. The human ancestral inability to face the truth has been one of our most adaptive and even endearing features! Thus our Darwinian critics are now in the interesting position of having to embrace the objectivist (naturalist) ideal of knowing as far as their own work and educational vocation is concerned, while at the same time implicitly rejoicing that our ancestors did not share this ideal themselves.

Some of the new Darwinians would even go so far as to encourage the persistence of religious illusions into the future for the sake of gene survival. Influenced heavily by E. O. Wilson and Darwinian anthropology, for example, the philosopher Loyal Rue has recently argued that our own survival and thriving as a species is in great measure the consequence of a genetically based capacity for lying and self-deception. From a biological perspective, the propensity for "guile" can be viewed as a kind of saving "grace."[18] Among animals, nature tends to select deceivers, while those incapable of deception do not survive and reproduce. Likewise, "the role of deception in human adaptive strategies has been so important that we may suspect it to be essential to our survival."[19]

According to Rue, the rationally and scientifically awakened human mind must now embrace *nihilism* as the only "truth" that faithfully reflects the real world. But, thank goodness, we have been endowed by evolution with a capacity, especially in our religions, to spin noble lies that allow us to deny this truth and keep it out of view! Humans happily have evolved the cerebral equipment to cover over the "real" world with colorful and inspiring "lies" that give meaning to our lives and the universe.[20] The capacity for deception and self-deception must be nourished, not eliminated, if we hope to survive as a species. Earlier, Otto Rank and his disciple Ernest Becker—in opposition to Freud—had maintained that in order to maintain our psychic equilibrium, we humans have to create "vital lies" by which to live. Otherwise, we will fall into psychic illness. Apparently, it is just those who are courageous enough to look at reality nakedly and without illusions who will be most prone to psychosis. The healthy-minded among us should give thanks for our species' capacity to evade truths that would surely sicken us if we looked straight at them.[21]

Thus, the new Darwinian anthropologists are not the only interpreters of religion to have worshipped privately at the shrine of naturalistic objectivism while publicly tolerating a less severe devotionalism for the herd of humanity on the other. Condoning fiction for the fortuneless masses is the accommodating posture of the new brand of critique. The truly enlightened and courageous among us will now take pride in realizing that we have at last—especially with Darwin's help—looked into the emptiness of the cosmos without blinking. Now that we know that we had been tricked into our false states of belief by the crafty evolutionary mechanism of gene survival, perhaps we can look for more realistic reasons to go on with our own lives. Meanwhile, though, we should be tolerant of, and in Rue's opinion even encourage, a more general persistence in vital lies that will propel the human gene pool into the indefinite future.

Deeper than "Deep Darwinism"

Let us give the name "Deep Darwinism" to the evolutionist proposals we have just reviewed. Its proponents claim that we can gain no more profound understanding of all manifestations of life, including human ethics and religion, than those provided by the Darwinian ideas of reproductive fitness and selection. Deep Darwinism contends that we can account for nothing in the life-world, including religion, more objectively and foundationally than in terms of evolutionary adaptation.[22] Although many of us will initially balk at such a claim, an increasing number of books and academic careers are now dedicated to promulgating it.

The Deep Darwinians will admit that religious people themselves are convinced that symbols and stories about the sacred put us in the presence of what is ultimately Real. But the salient evolutionary "discovery" is that all religious ideas, no matter how seemingly realistic, are in fact fictitious because they ultimately serve the powerful mechanism of gene survival. This non sequitur is usually inexplicit, but it lurks in the background of almost all evolutionary accounts of religion. Holmes Rolston, III, calls this the "if functional, therefore untrue" fallacy, a logical blunder that seems to be at least a tacit feature of many of the new biological discussions of religion.[23] And there are other logical peculiarities in the new Darwinian criticism, as my discussion of Michael Polanyi's philosophical reflections on the nature of life and human knowing will be able to show a bit later.

I should say at once, however, that there is nothing inherently problematic about an evolutionary or even a genes'-eye perspective on life or any of life's manifestations, including religion. Just as there is nothing questionable in our approaching the living cell by way of a molecular perspective—or anything physical through an atomic analysis—there is no reason to complain when scientists look at religion through the lenses of evolutionary biology or genetics. Something useful about the story of religion may be learned through our focusing on the complex natural history and genetic occurrences that underlie the kind of minds that are able to engage in religious worship. A biological approach may very well have something very important to teach us about religion.

The real issue here, however, is the claim (sometimes tacit but often explicit) by Deep Darwinians that an evolutionary account gives us the *ultimate* explanation of religion, thus making all theological explanations superfluous. Typically, evolutionary psychologists profess to have naturalized religion not just as a methodological strategy, but in so radical a way that theological explanation will be either inconsequential at best, or completely unnecessary at worst. Once again, to "naturalize" religion means to give a purely natural, in this case biological and ultimately physicalist, explanation for ideas or beliefs that were formerly thought to have been inspired by revelatory experience or by independent cultural factors. To "naturalize" means, in this instance, to ask what we can make of religion not only by leaving out cultural accounts but also by ignoring what religious people themselves would identify as its ultimate explanation. If we can explain religion without such superfluous ideas as God, revelation or the sacred, we will finally have cut through to what human spiritual longing is *really* all about.

In one way or another, the naturalizing of religion has been going on ever since the birth of science, and in a more diffuse way even from the time of Greek and biblical antiquity. Scientific method, moreover, is *supposed* to seek a natural explanation of everything, and so even religion is grist for the mill. But science is a method, not a metaphysics. And so it is not science itself, but only the philosophical belief that science's naturalizing method gives a fundamental, ultimate, adequate and exhaustive explanation, that energizes so much Darwinian discussion of religion today. As we have seen in previous chapters, the slide from method to metaphysics is not at all uncommon among Darwinians. And nowhere that I know of has the attempt to understand religion been carried out with more confidence that an *exclusively* "natural" explanation of it has finally been reached than in recent writings influenced by evolutionary psychology.[24]

What is just as problematic, however, is that the Darwinian naturalizing of religion not only professes to show that the reality of the divine is not a necessary part of the explanation of religion; just as remarkably, it has also made the human subject itself only incidental to a radical explanation of the persistence of the gods. Although they are implicitly aware of the intermediary role our brain mechanisms, subjective thoughts, emotions and desires play in the making of religion, the biologists of religion now formally dispense with the complicity of human subjectivity or "personality" as far as any truly *fundamental* account of religion is concerned. The human subject, if there is such a thing at all, is not a significant factor in the new Darwinian understanding of religion. Ultimate explanation lies at the level of our genes. For some unspecified reason—so goes the argument—genes have an inherent need to survive into the next generation. Following their command, human organisms and brains assemble in such a way as to carry out the genes' relentless pursuit of immortality. The point is, our own seemingly *personal* longings for, and theological justifications of, the sacred are really quite unimportant as far as any cardinal insights into religion are concerned.

Almost every other attempt in modern and recent times to explain religion—or explain it away—has grounded the genesis and persistence of religion much more immediately in human subjectivity itself. The theories of Freud, Frazer, Durkheim, Nietzsche and even Marx have all made at least some allowance that the human person's own feelings and desires are central factors in the creation of the gods.[25] But the deep Darwinians are much less willing to grant personal agency any really constitutive role. The genesis and persistence of the gods must be attributed ultimately to the drive or longing of our genes to survive. Our own personal desires, if we can attribute any significant initiative to them at all, are in the service of a much deeper kind of natural striving. It is in the "beyond" of life's genetic domain, therefore, and not in the supernatural or cultural realms, that we will find the deepest roots of our spiritual appetites.[26]

Other physicalist theories, Freud's for example, also made nature, understood as impersonal "matter," the remote explanation of religion. But after bowing to his materialist creed, Freud virtually ignored it and in fact made his theory of religion rest implicitly on the mysterious desiring at the heart of the human subject.[27] The material basis of mind remained in the background while Freud focused on human passion as more essential to the dynamics of religion. In the case of deep Darwinism, however, the theory of religion is much less concerned with what persons want than with what genes want.

Notice, however, that the idea of a subject or "personality" does not disappear at all in this interpretation. The Deep Darwinians try to *objectify* life, human beings and religions as radically as they can. In accordance with modern naturalistic assumptions, the whole idea of subjectivity remains for them formally taboo.[28] But, in point of fact, the banished subjectivity is simply displaced from human centers onto impersonal genetic units and processes. The Deep Darwinians cannot avoid attributing to the level of allegedly impersonal genes a clearly centered and personal interest, a *striving* or a "commitment" to achieving a goal—that of survival. And in spite of qualifying comments that they are not attributing personal agency or intentionality to genes in a literal sense, their inability to avoid use of terms like "striving," "cooperation," "success" and "failure" in the struggle by genes to survive, can make sense only if genes are being understood in terms of what the philosopher Michael Polanyi calls the *logic of achievement*.[29] In this case, the logic of achievement has strayed far from its original home in living centers and personal human subjects and taken up residence in segments of DNA.

According to Polanyi, it is the "logic of achievement" that allows us to recognize living beings as truly alive. Organisms are said to be "alive" only because they are capable of some kind of achievement. We sense in all living beings something akin to our own striving personhood, and it is this intuition that allows us spontaneously to differentiate them from lifeless objects and processes. We humans, including Deep Darwinians, naturally have an immediate awareness of being striving centers ourselves. Our talent for "trying" is what makes us alive, and the fact that our endeavoring emerges from an intentional center is what makes us "persons." To be alive as human beings is to have the capacity to extend ourselves toward various kinds of goals. And this kind of undertaking is something we tacitly and analogously understand to be a feature of all other living beings as well.

In more direct terms, it is their striving to achieve something—whatever it may be—that distinguishes living from nonliving entities or processes. And it is our immediate apprehension of our own striving that allows us to recognize other beings as living. Whether it be an amoeba going in search of nourishment, a tiger pursuing its prey or a human person searching for meaning, these living beings all share the trait of striving and therefore of being able either to succeed or fail in their respective endeavors. And so we attribute "life" to them.[30] Contemporary gene-enchanted Darwinism, however, has exiled living beings, including human subjects, from their natural home in the sphere governed by the logic of achievement. Simultaneously, it has projected the deracinated attribute of centered striving onto atomic genetic units that both physical science and common sense are normally obliged to consider incapable of any kind of commitments or personal agency whatsoever.

This fiction is important to Deep Darwinians, however, since it allows them to wrest the roots of religion away from human subjects and to understand such an inclination as the helpless offshoot of an allegedly "deeper" kind of striving that goes on among units of heredity in the psychologically distant realm of DNA. Burkert's dimension "beyond culture" in terms of which biology may now "explain" religion in an ultimate way, and without having to focus on either religious subjectivity or the question of the reality of God, is the purely physical realm of nucleotides. In Deep Darwinism, the genetic dimension of our being has taken center stage as the foundationally energizing source of the striving that renders our species religious.

If we could be assured that the idea of "genes striving to survive" was simply a convenient way of speaking, and one not to be taken too literally, then we might have reason to be less concerned about this dramatic displacement. However, the new Darwinian projection of subjectivity onto our genes is more than an innocent literary device. Matt Ridley's lucid summary of the new evolutionary thinking clearly demonstrates that much more is going on in Deep Darwinian discourse than linguistic playfulness. He observes that, a generation ago, most biologists would have been quite reluctant to personalize genes, instead viewing them as unconscious and inanimate. But then he goes on to say that

> . . . in the last few years the revolution begun by [George] Williams, [William] Hamilton, and others has caused more and more biologists to think of genes as analogous to *active and cunning individuals*. Not that genes are conscious or driven by future goals—no serious biologist believes that—but the extraordinary purely logical fact is that evolution works by natural selection, and natural selection means the enhanced survival of genes *that enhance their own survival.* Therefore, a gene is by definition the descendant of a gene that was *good at getting into future generations.* A gene that *does things* that enhance its own survival may be said, *teleologically,* to be doing them because they enhance its survival. *Cooperating* to build a body is as effective a *survival strategy* for genes as cooperating to run a town is a successful social strategy for human beings.[31]

In this quote, I have italicized the words that exemplify the logic of achievement. Ridley's book *The Red Queen* repeatedly attributes to genes activities and intentions that we formerly had associated only with centered (personal) striving. Genes are said to "cooperate," and their main achievement is "survival."

"A gene has only one criterion by which posterity judges it: whether it becomes an ancestor of other genes. To a large extent it must *achieve* that at the expense of other genes."[32] It is a mix of cooperation and competition among striving and achieving genes that, according to Ridley, accounts for the evolutionary invention of gender-based behavior. Sex, he says, is the outcome of genes devising *strategies* to avoid their demise at the hand of parasites.[33] In a similar way, according to evolutionary psychology, our genes give rise to religious instincts in human vehicles so as to help the genes *succeed* in their own effort toward self-perpetuation.

If genes are "strategizing" and "striving" to survive, then of course they can also "fail" in such endeavors. The point is, we are apparently to understand lifeless and mindless strands of DNA in accordance with the logic of achievement. But the logic of achievement—implying the possibility of success and failure—as Polanyi has consistently attempted (often without success) to get across, is simply inapplicable to impersonal processes. Striving, succeeding and failing are attributes logically attributable only to living subjects and personal centers. Indeed it is only because they strive (for a goal), and are therefore subject to failure, that we can recognize living beings as "alive" at all. In the brave new biology, however, life and striving are no longer identifying marks of organisms, let alone human persons. The latter are simply passive mechanisms or "vehicles" of a more substratal kind of striving.[34] Centered striving is now the defining attribute not of human subjects but of genetic monads, or perhaps arrays of monads, that can be "cooperative" or "selfish" and can either succeed or fail.

The Deep Darwinians have taken what most cultures and "folk psychologies" call "personhood" and projected it onto the world of genes. This displacement of tabooed subjectivity onto our genes may seem rather inconsequential until we notice that, in order to understand religion "objectively" or naturalistically, Deep Darwinism must first divest it of almost everything religious people have themselves always thought essential to it. A major fact about religion, after all, is that religious persons are themselves engaged in a most intense kind of striving. Even the Deep Darwinians would not be able to identify religious phenomena as distinctively "religious" without their own tacit recognition that religious *persons* follow the logic of achievement. But the new biology of religion prefers not to take this most elementary fact into account.

Whatever else religions may be, after all, they are instances of *life* striving to reach a goal. At the very heart of religion there is aspiration, hoping, struggling to overcome obstacles. Religious symbols, rites, doctrines, codes of behavior and institutional self-organization are all manifestations of life—intelligent life—endeavoring, and therefore risking failure, in pursuit of a particular kind of goal. Religions clearly fall within the range of phenomena that can only be known by a tacit awareness of the logic of achievement operative in their devotees.

What are religious persons striving for? At the very least, according to theologian John Bowker, they are seeking pathways through the most stubborn limits on human life.[35] This fact places religion in a line of inheritance that goes all the way back to the most primitive forms of metabolism. Religions are ways by which intelligent living persons, usually as part of a social group, try to make their way through the most intractable obstacles to the continuity of life. Ordinary human ingenuity, after all, can take us only so far before it runs up against fate, suffering, the threat of meaninglessness, and eventually death. Unlike other human enterprises, the focus of religion, as Bowker sees it, is on how to negotiate these "impossible" barriers to the continuity of life.

Religious persons and groups *strive* to find a path through the most difficult obstacles to the continuation of human life. In Bowker's words, religions are a kind of "route-finding."[36] In diverse mythic, practical and ritualistic ways, religious persons *aim* toward an ultimate "Rightness," an infinite Compassion or simply an incomprehensible dimension of depth that in some unspecifiable way provides a "route" through the most intractable roadblocks to ultimate liberation and fulfillment. Whatever judgments we may initially make about the objectivity of the many religious representations of ultimate reality, it can hardly be denied that religion is an intense manifestation of *life* in its characteristic mode of striving.[37]

As I mentioned earlier, it is only because even Deep Darwinians recognize—tacitly and personally—the fact of religious striving and "route finding" that they are enabled to identify and name religions in the first place. There is no evidence, however, that this tacit knowledge has ever been explicitly integrated consciously into their theories of religion as anything more than incidental. In fact, in their formal theoretical "explanations" of religion they ignore as inconsequential the personal striving that allows them to take note of religion at all, relocating all relevant endeavor in the impersonal chemical constituents of genetic processing.

This displacement of "striving" from human persons onto an impersonal flow of genes is a matter of considerable irony. While explicitly *striving* to avoid the embarrassingly "unscientific" use of anthropomorphic projections characteristic of naive religious people, our Deep Darwinians lavishly indulge their own proclivity for the very same kind of projection—in this instance onto the "beyond" of impersonal nature. Thus, they end up attributing to mindless genes the very human subjectivity that they first subtracted from *us* in order to view our religiousness "objectively" or "naturalistically." Scarcely anything could be more "anthropomorphic" and unobjective than this substitution. For in *subjectifying* our genes, the scientists have put themselves in a situation where *objective* knowledge of the coveted realm "beyond culture" remains logically inaccessible after all. If genes are centered *subjects,* capable of striving, then the inevitably objectifying method of scientific knowing could never penetrate to their inner reality. The quest for objective knowledge ends in the aporia of DNA's own supposed subjectivity. Few modernist attempts to depersonalize human knowing have illustrated more clearly the impossibility of our ever ridding ourselves of the reality of subjectivity.

Meanwhile, the Deep Darwinians themselves keep striving. For what? Perhaps for truth? Perhaps to liberate religious subjects from the false conviction that their beliefs have anything to do with what is ultimately real? Whatever their objective, the Deep Darwinians are in any case *striving*. Like our hunter-gatherer ancestors, their own predator-detecting cognitive systems are striving to detect some hidden agency to explain the puzzling (and one may suspect threatening and even anxiety-producing) persistence of religion. And like all striving, theirs also confronts the possibility of failure. In fact, if Polanyi is correct, their attempts to give an ultimate explanation of why gods persist are rooted in the persistent failure of modern thought to welcome subjectivity into the sphere of true being, and personality into the heart of knowing.

Conclusion

Once again, then, we must go deeper than Darwin. I am not claiming, however, that objectivist Darwinian explanations of religion are entirely devoid of illuminating merit. I believe—as I have made clear in the preceding chapters—that neo-Darwinism, including evolutionary psychology, may be one layer in a whole hierarchy of explanations needed to account for religion. But, for all we know, an important layer of a truly fertile explanation of religion may be the one that religious persons themselves have given, namely, that "the sacred" has in some way (sacramentally, mystically, silently) broken into their awareness.

Acknowledging the reality and power of the divine would not rule out an explanatory pluralism that gives ample room to Darwinian accounts alongside others. An open-minded theological method can appropriate whatever light evolutionary biology has to shed on religion. In fact, we may assume that a human response to the sacred would in some way promote the cause of gene survival, and that our genetic endowment disposes us to be religious.

If religion had not been genetically adaptive, at least in a general way, we would not be here. And if our genes had been configured in some completely different way—for example, like an alligator's—we would not be religious. All of this goes without saying.

What is questionable are two claims commonly made by our Deep Darwinians. The first is that genes themselves can be personal centers of striving and, therefore, by themselves subject to success or failure. Even the premises of materialist evolutionism, according to which all activity in the world is ultimately mechanistic and devoid of final causation, forbids the idea that genes could be centers of striving. Thus it is all the more intriguing that the Deep Darwinians understand genes in terms of the logic of achievement. The same must be said, incidentally, of the atomic cultural units that some evolutionists now refer to as "memes." Memes, according to Richard Dawkins, the inventor of the idea, are virus-like bits of information such as tunes, ideas, catchphrases or fashions that allegedly make their way from one mind to another.[38] Like genes, they are said to be self-replicating, and, consistent with Dawkins's understanding of genes, they are held to have a life of their own. That is, they are portrayed as centers of striving, much as we associate with living organisms. Memetics, like genetics, however, does not belong to the sphere of the logic of achievement, although this is where its advocates typically place it.

The second questionable assumption of the Deep Darwinians is that once we have (naturalistically) detected the hidden genetic stratum that allegedly underlies the persistence of the gods, we have arrived at the ultimate explanation of religion and in doing so divested all religious teachings of any plausible claims to truth. What is problematic here is both the "if functional then untrue" fallacy and the arbitrary substitution of a single-level (physicalist) approach for a rich hierarchy of explanations.

Finally, we may note, the Deep Darwinians' own unmasking of religion ends up unmasking itself. They too start out looking for a hidden agency, one that will "explain" religion. Their own agency-seeking systems, adaptations that arose by selection for predator detection thousands of years ago, lead them, no less than their religious ancestors, to look for what lies *hidden* beyond appearances. And they end up locating the agency that gives rise to religion in a fictitious realm of subjectivity (that of the selfish gene), which, when we come right down to it, would be no less inaccessible to objectifying comprehension than are the explanations given by religious persons.

9

Truth After Darwin

Not every skeptic who has made the Darwinian turn is so cavalier about the question of truth as are the Deep Darwinians we encountered in the previous chapter. We find a throwback to an older and more rigorous school of critics of religion in Frederick Crews, who recently published a titillating two-installment article on God and Darwin in *The New York Review of Books*.[1] Crews, an emeritus professor of English at the University of California at Berkeley, is best known in American intellectual life for his relentless pounding of Freud, whom he has not hesitated to call a fraud. What he has never questioned, however, is Freud's materialist metaphysics. Although he chastises the father of psychoanalysis for failing to live up to the "empirical attitude" essential to good science,[2] he clearly shares with his adversary the unshakable belief that beneath life, consciousness and culture, there lies only a mindless, meaningless whorl of purely physical stuff.

For Crews, the tragically indifferent universe that Freud presupposes and that Darwin has further exposed is the ultimate truth to which we must now resign ourselves. Any proposed consonance of science with religion after Darwin is ludicrous. In his essay on God and evolution, Crews has made his own philosophical leanings clearer than ever. Cozying up to the most radically materialist contemporary interpretations of Darwin—those of Richard Dawkins and Daniel Dennett—he has demonstrated that, at least on the question of the nature of ultimate "reality" and the relationship of science to religion, he is not far removed from Freud after all.

Crews announces his new romance with Darwinian biology by commenting on eleven recent books dealing with God and evolutionary biology, including one of my own.[3] Zealous to protect pure Darwinian truth from defilement at the hands of creationists and devotees of Intelligent Design Theory (IDT), as well as from the "evasions" practiced by evolutionary theists, Crews mockingly entitles his essay "Saving Us from Darwin." As it turns out, it is Darwin who saves Crews, providing him at last with what he takes to be an empirically satisfactory grounding for the robust impeachment of religion that we can no longer expect to get from Freud, Marx, Nietzsche and the rest.

Crews's commentary on the question of Darwin and God is witty and, if one is willing to put up with the expected dose of hyperbole, more than occasionally incisive. It is not hard to agree with him, for example, that "anti-Darwinian fervor has as much to do with moral anxiety as with articles of revealed truth." "Creationists," he reflects, "are sure that the social order will dissolve unless our children are taught that the human race was planted here by God with instructions for proper conduct. Crime, licentiousness, blasphemy, unchecked greed, narcotic stupefaction, abortion, the weakening of family bonds—all are blamed on Darwin, whose supposed message is that we are animals to whom everything is permitted. This is the 'fatal glass of beer' approach to explaining decadence. Take one biology course that leaves Darwin unchallenged, it seems, and you're on your way to nihilism, Eminem, and drive-by shootings."[4]

Likewise, Crews rightly rebukes conservative publications such as *First Things, Commentary* and *The New Criterion* for shiftily ignoring the overwhelming and convergent evidence for evolution. Whenever Darwinian science appears to challenge the benign cosmological assumptions underlying rightward-leaning journalism, it is much easier to announce that Darwin is wrong than to reexamine the assumptions themselves. Crews finds it remarkable, for example, that Richard John Neuhaus, the editor of *First Things,* gives such a ringing endorsement of Darwin's main current opponent as this: "In all the vast literature on Darwinism, evolution, creation, and theism, one will likely not find a treatment so calm, comprehensive and compellingly persuasive as Phillip Johnson's" (quoted on the dust jacket of Johnson's latest attack on evolutionary biology, *The Wedge of Truth*).[5]

Crews may not be so willing, however, to acknowledge that his own annoyance with Neuhaus is no less ideologically motivated than the anti-Darwinism he so mercilessly attacks in *The New York Review of Books.* Throughout his article, he brandishes an understanding of evolution indistinguishable from the "philosophical materialism" that he acknowledges to be the real reason for both conservative refutations and theological "evasions" of Darwinism. We need only look at Crews's own words to realize how completely he enfolds his own understanding of evolutionary science within an avowedly physicalist belief system. He asserts, for instance, that Daniel Dennett has "trenchantly shown" that Darwin's thought leads logically to "a satisfyingly materialistic reduction of mind and soul" and that evolutionary theory entails a "naturalistic account of life's beginning."[6] Many of us are quite certain that materialism and naturalism are really metaphysics or worldviews, not science; but for Crews, they are stitched seamlessly into biology. If you wish to drink of Darwinian science, you have to swallow the bitter pill of naturalist materialism, along with the godless cosmos that comes along with it.

But isn't this exactly what Phillip Johnson, William Dembski, Michael Behe and others from the ID community have been telling us about Darwin all along—although, of course, they advise us not to take the poison? Crews rightly upbraids the ID literature for sneaking metaphysics into logical spaces appropriate only to science. But his own version of Darwinism does not differ in any substantive way from that of his religiously aroused opponents. Like the creationists and IDers, he understands evolution to be inseparable from the nonscientific *belief* that matter is all there is and that the universe is inherently pointless. These, it goes without saying, are assumptions logically antithetical to theism of any stripe. And then Crews wonders why his opponents can be so foolish as to repudiate Darwin's great revolution.

For Crews, the real "truth" in Darwinism is at bottom clearly nothing other than materialism and its attendant notion of a purposeless universe. Pascal Boyer would agree with all of this, and Loyal Rue would insist on adding the label "nihilism" just to be perfectly clear on what he thinks evolution really entails.[7] But while Boyer and Rue appreciate the adaptive value of illusions that shield us from the horrible truth, Crews—sounding once again remarkably like Freud—wants us to grow up and face the indifferent world like adults.

If the evolutionary psychologists are correct, however, then Crews is advocating a non-adaptive posture, one not destined to leave many survivors. It is not certain that he catches the irony, though, since he endorses without reservation the kind of explanation of religion we saw earlier in Boyer and other biologists of religion. Darwin, he claims, has now given us "a more plausible framework than divine action for guessing how the human brain could have acquired consciousness and facilitated cultural productions, not excepting religion itself. It is this march toward successfully explaining the

higher by the lower that renders Darwinian science a threat to theological
dogma of all but the blandest kind."[8]

Notice here that, in accounting for religion, Crews, in the same manner as
many other Darwinians we have already encountered, would force us to
choose *between* evolutionary and theological explanations. Evolution and
theology have to battle for the single explanatory slot available. We must follow either Darwin or the theologians, but not both. There is not a shade of
acknowledgment here that, in principle, a complex phenomenon like religion may be open to what I have been referring to as a hierarchy of explanations, in which incommensurable levels of reading may coexist and
complement, rather than contradict, one another. So if the creationists and
IDT advocates deserve our reproach for making us choose unnecessarily between a natural evolutionary process and God's creativity, then Crews is
scarcely less of a literalist when he presents us with the same simplistic set of
options.

Disappointingly, then, Crews has failed to carry the important contemporary discussion of Darwin and God any farther than where Dawkins, Dennett, Boyer, IDT proponents and creationists had already left it. He
completely abandons his wonted critical aggressiveness when it comes to the
utterly unscientific way in which his evolutionist mentors, especially Richard
Dawkins and Daniel Dennett, have themselves taken Darwin's grand picture
of life hostage to the most obsolescent of modernity's myths. Slavishly aping
his heroes, he understands Darwinism to be inseparable from "naturalism,"
clearly understanding this term to imply the very same materialist "godlessness" that offends Phillip Johnson and delights Dawkins and Dennett. The
closer one looks at this mixing of materialism and evolution, the more one
wants to save Darwin from Crews and his cultural icons.

Many biologists, philosophers and theologians have had little difficulty
distinguishing evolutionary biology from metaphysical materialism, but
Crews will condone no such nuance. Not surprisingly, he considers all attempts to reconcile theology with evolutionary biology as "evasions" of what
he now knows to be the "truth." Those who have argued that evolutionary
biology, in the conventionally accepted neo-Darwinian sense, is quite consonant with biblical theism are among the guilty "evaders." Yet Crews's unshakable belief that Darwinism is inescapably materialistic renders him
intractable to any proposal that evolutionary science may be logically compatible with an alternative metaphysics. In *God After Darwin*, I argued that
evolution is religiously not only tolerable but even exciting. Crews, however,
simply dumps all theistic interpretations of evolution on the same mound
with creationism and IDT, and then labels it all "evasion."[9]

Darwinian Evaders of Truth

Since Crews carelessly attributes to me positions that in fact I take pains to distinguish from my own, I cannot but wonder how closely he has read the other books on his list. For our purposes here, however, it is not necessary to dwell on such imperfections. It is of more interest simply to notice what is going on in the mind of our Darwinian critic himself, especially since he is by no means alone in marrying biology to philosophical materialism.

What exactly does Crews mean by "truth" when he says that theistic interpretations of evolution are evasions of it? He is emphatically not one of the so-called postmodern relativists, and he has spoken previously of his devotion to the "empirical attitude" as the only way to get in touch with the real.[10] One can only assume, then, that his criterion of truth is not significantly different from the one articulated by the despised Freud himself: Truth is what we arrive at by following the "reality principle." And to educated people, embracing the reality principle means, above all, following the empirical spirit of science. But Crews, in effect, goes far beyond a perfectly justifiable endorsement of the empirical attitude. He leads us back to a now aging, though still extant, scientism as the cradle of his sense of the real.

The only book on his list to which Crews gives unqualified approval is Robert Pennock's *Tower of Babel*, an important critique of anti-Darwinism, but one that I believe misleadingly conflates creationism with Intelligent Design Theory. Even though Crews himself acknowledges that IDT defenders like William Dembski and Michael Behe are not biblical literalists, he fails to reprove Pennock's fusion of the two distinct versions of anti-Darwinism. However, from the perspective of philosophical materialism (a stance that Crews probably thinks Pennock is defending), all expressions of theistic belief have the same benighted quality. Indeed, any dissent at all from standard physicalist metaphysics—a dissent essential to religion and theology—renders one an enemy of the "empirical attitude" appropriate to science. In the Darwin wars, it seems, Crews turns up in Freud's corner once again.

Since for him contemporary biology entails materialist naturalism, Crews insists that evolutionary scientists and philosophers should be uncompromising with this "truth." Contrary to Loyal Rue's counsel that we settle into our illusions, he wants us to face head on, and without the comforts of religion, the desolate world that Darwin has laid out before us. Yet, to his chagrin, not even some of our most celebrated Darwinians are willing to heed this call to courage. Especially vexing are the late paleontologist Stephen Jay Gould and the Darwinian philosopher Michael Ruse. Both are non-theists, and both—correctly according to Crews—have previously claimed that Darwinism implies materialism. Yet their recent books display a disappointing failure of nerve.[11] Neither of these respected evolutionists wants to press the decision between Darwin and God so imposingly upon us as do Crews and the creationists. Ruse, for example, allows that a Darwinian *can* be a Christian (since, after all, there have been a good number of them). And Gould argues that science and religious belief can get along quite well if they just stay in their respective corners. On the question of God and evolution, Gould is happy to report that even he and Pope John Paul II can sit down comfortably together.

Crews, sounding more and more like Richard Dawkins, is not going to be party to such a cowardly compromise. He quotes from Gould's *Rocks of Ages:* "Science gets the age of rocks, and religion the rock of ages; science studies how the heavens go, religion how to go to heaven. I join nearly all people of goodwill in wishing to see two old and cherished institutions, our two rocks of ages—science and religion—coexisting in peace." But then Crews recalls derisively what Gould had said in another context: "I think that notion that we are all in the bosom of Abraham [is] enormously comforting. But I do think it's just a story we tell ourselves."[12] In other words, for Gould, it is appropriate to believe in God, but all reasonable people should know, especially after Darwin, that such belief is nothing more than fiction.

It is this condoning of illusion that so aggravates Crews. Gould does not go as far as Loyal Rue in making the case for actively nourishing adaptive fictions that will deceitfully abet the cause of our genetic immortality. But the softer compromises that he and Ruse are willing to make with "truth" are still too much for Crews to stomach. In support of his disapproval, Crews even cites Cornell evolutionist William Provine's oft-cited declaration that in order to accept both Christian faith and Darwinian biology, "you have to check your brains at the church-house door."[13]

Theology and Truth After Darwin

As much as we might appreciate Ruse and Gould's mannerly overtures to religion, I believe that Crews is justified in pointing out the slippage in their logic. In order to appease all parties, these celebrated evolutionists, having previously made no secret of their own conviction that Darwinism goes best with materialism, clearly sacrifice what Crews refers to as "considerations of truth" by cavalierly allowing the rest of us to go on believing in God. It is entirely reasonable for Crews to remind us, on the contrary, that a materialist view of the world is incompatible with each and every brand of theism. Here there can be no compromise.

However, on what basis can Crews himself claim that materialism is the ultimate truth underlying Darwinism? Indeed, what exactly does Crews mean by truth? As in any worthwhile discussion, issues of epistemology (How do we know what is real?) and metaphysics (What do we mean by the real?) must eventually come to the surface in the Darwin wars. As far as Crews is concerned, the "empirical attitude" of science is the only way we can get cognitionally to what is truly real. And the bottommost reality that science finds, especially after Darwin, is an inherently meaningless universe. Only those who are courageous enough to embrace this ultimately pointless world are also in a position to claim that they really grasp the "truth" of Darwin's theory.

Logically speaking, however, Crews's belief that the "empirical attitude" of scientific method alone can lead us to truth does not fall within the realm of scientific discourse, nor is it conceivably susceptible to empirical demonstration. Crews's starting point is really not different from that of all other academic devotees of scientism. And his directives for getting to the ultimate truth about the universe are no less faith-filled than those on which theology is based. After all, by itself science can give no decisive reasons for either asserting or denying that the universe is pointless, even though its findings are not irrelevant to our deliberations on this question. Pronouncements about the ultimate nature of things, about what is really real, or about the fundamental criteria of truth, emerge from mysterious regions of human consciousness that no science can ever pretend to plumb. They are not part of science as such, but faith claims. The assertion that scientific method is the only way to truth is itself one that flows not from science but from a deep human need to form webs of belief in which to embed our understanding of things. And the question always remains whether any of these webs take us deep enough in the direction of the truly real.

As far as the understanding of life is concerned, Crews would reply that Darwinian science has now taken us as deep as we need to go. After following Darwin down into the depths, we shall find no room down there, Crews believes, for any truly illuminating theological reading of life. But how does Crews—or for that matter Boyer, Rue, Dennett or Dawkins—know this to be the case? To declare that theology is superfluous as far as an adequate understanding of life and evolution is concerned would require a kind of surveillance that science as such cannot command. It is not within the range of *any* scientific readings of nature to hold forth on such issues as the ultimate nature of the real, on what lies in the ultimate depths of being and therefore on whether theology is an evasion of truth. Such claims belong to metaphysics, not science. Clearly, once again, the Darwin wars are not so much clashes of science with religion, but of one kind of metaphysics with another.

Metaphysical commitments, of course, are unavoidable. We all carry around with us an implicit sense of what is really real, for we cannot even use the verb "to be" without an at least vague sense of *what is*. So the primary question Crews raises for us is whether the most enlightening metaphysical setting for science, and for making sense of evolution, is the modern materialist creed. I have been proposing throughout this book that materialist belief fails to take us deep enough into contact with the *real truth* of Darwinism. The mechanistic metaphysics to which Crews is so suppliant actually mummifies the luxuriant life-world that evolutionary discoveries have themselves dug up from nature's depth. To grasp the real "truth" of evolution, we now have to peel away the encrusted physicalist literalism that screens us from the narrative flow of life. The dramatic epic that hardworking biologists, geologists, paleontologists, geneticists, embryologists, anatomists and so on have hit upon dies and decomposes under the flickering lamp of a now aging mechanism. Life's richness deserves a better home than the frozen physicalist frame that Crews and his heroes have erected for it.

Once we dig beneath the shallow world of Crews's cosmic literalism we shall find ample logical space for making sense of evolution in terms of a *metaphysics of promise*. Rather than absolutizing an essentially lifeless realm of "matter" as this has been abstracted by modern physics, a metaphysics of promise, more cognizant than materialism of the obvious fact of life's *striving*, takes into account the realm of the *future*, the arena "up ahead" into which the life-story propels itself. The future, not the dead past, is the foundation upon which the world leans "as its sole support."[14] Hidden beyond our grasp, in the depths of the future that forever faithfully takes us and our world into itself, there resides the really real, in other words what biblical religion knows as "God." Theologically speaking, a promising God who opens up the world to the future is the *ultimate* explanation of evolution.

Such a metaphysics, like all other visions of the really real, is not subject to proof by science. But, then again, neither is Crews's materialism. Crews, however, moves comfortably among scientists who make blatantly philosophical judgments and then pass these off to the public as though they were purely scientific conclusions rather than composites of science and metaphysics. Crews himself has naively been drawn into this kind of confusion by his idols, Richard Dawkins and Daniel Dennett, both of whom have consistently alloyed evolutionary biology with materialist metaphysics. It is only on the basis of this kind of mix-up that Crews can issue his dogmatic declaration that theological visions of evolution are mere "evasions."

Hence, if classical theology appears to have fallen short of the reality of evolution, so also, at least to those whose sense of the real is shaped by a metaphyics of promise, has the materialist vision of the world that cramps Crews's own reading of Darwin. Materialist metaphysics, after all, cannot seriously claim to be proportionate to the opulence of evolution. Yet for many, if not most, scientifically informed thinkers today, there is still no alternative to an obdurate physicalism as the conceptual setting for evolutionary biology. As Crews's essay exemplifies, much of the intellectual world still tries to clarify the story of life against the backdrop of what theologian Paul Tillich, referring to materialism, rightly called an "ontology of death."15

The problem with scientific materialism, as Alfred North Whitehead long ago pointed out, is that it is simply incapable of doing justice to what we all actually *experience* as the rich reality of actual life. It seeks to purchase intellectual clarity by leaving out the novelty, striving, cooperativeness, relationality and indeterminacy characteristic of living beings and processes. I would add that it also abstracts from life's inherent openness to the future. By thinking of evolution in mechanistic and atomistic terms, materialist interpretations typically muffle our intuitive sense of life's striving toward the incalculable not-yet. Almost by definition, scientific materialism leaves out almost everything that our inherited wisdom and ethics mean by "life." Darwin's own portrait of nature, on the other hand, is at least redolent of real life—with all of its drama, endeavor, tragedy and creativity. His own grand story of living processes, when not drowned in the deadening swamp of materialism, can add depth and richness to our religious intimations of ultimate reality. Darwinian science is not inherently opposed to the divine—even though Darwin had his own misgivings about God.

Crews simplistically assumes, along with other evolutionary materialists, creationists and IDT disciples, that if there were a place for God in our thought, it would be in the role of a direct designer of life's complexity. And since neo-Darwinism has shown that design in organisms can be economically explained by natural selection working on minute random genetic changes over long periods of time, there is no longer any role for a divine designer to play. Therefore, it seems to Crews, evolutionary biology has exposed once and for all the utter godlessness of the cosmos. Once again, however, he does not say why an evolutionary account of complex design in life would exclude a theological explanation of life at a deeper level than science can articulate. He shows no awareness of the power of layered explanation or explanatory pluralism, even though science itself employs it often.

From all that one can tell by reading his theological comments, Crews's own notion of divine creativity lies roughly at the same level as the creationist and IDT interpretations that also envisage divine action as competing with natural processes for the one available explanatory slot. As far as Crews is concerned, divine creativity is an *alternative* to natural causation rather than a gracious wellspring of all natural spontaneity. The truly great theologians and philosophers have never thought of God's action in the world as somehow *rivaling* natural causation, but Crews sees only a competitive relationship between the two. For a theologian like Paul Tillich, God is the ultimate depth and ground of all causes, rather than one cause among others in the finite chain of world events. For Crews and his mentors, on the other hand, the literalism of creationism is the epitome of theological profundity. The *true* explanation of life, therefore, has to be *either* natural selection or God, since it cannot possibly be both.

From Augustine and Aquinas to recent religious thinkers such as William Temple and Pierre Teilhard de Chardin, God is seen not so much as directly engineering this life-endowed world as arousing the world to self-creativity. But this way of thinking about God almost never shows up in the public debates between creationists and evolutionary materialists. As for Crews, his own theological education appears to consist solely of what he has picked up in his visits to the camps of creationism and IDT. Consequently, it has not occurred to him that for the universe to be a repository of meaning, we do not think of God as stamping various forms of design forcefully or permanently onto the world-fabric. The cosmos, after all, is not just an "order" but a still unfinished process. Science shows clearly that the universe is still emerging into being, brimming with potential for incalculable future outcomes. The world, in theological terms, is still being created. In an unfinished universe, the horizon of an unprecedented future stretches magnanimously ahead, and God may be thought of—again in biblical terms—as the world's ultimate future. Such a God is not captured well by the idea of an "Intelligent Designer," a notion with which Crews is as happy to caricature the Creator as are (implicitly at least) Dembski, Johnson and Behe.

Conclusion

I have chosen to focus on Crews in this chapter in order to show how thoroughly the mind of one of America's most esteemed academics, critics and intellectuals has succumbed to the highly questionable impression that Darwin's great idea takes us as far as we can ever expect to go into the depths of nature and life. Crews is a true believer in the complete adequacy of Darwinian science to explain not only life but also religion. And, of course, in explaining religion, he also believes that Darwin explains it away. His essay on Darwin and God appears in one of our premier critical periodicals, and we can assume that many intelligent readers take seriously the opinions expressed there. Obviously, materialist evolutionism is one of the most significant of all current readings of life; and so there can be no objection to the fact of its being featured prominently in such outlets as *The New York Review of Books*. My intention here, however, has not been to criticize Crews's attraction to Darwinian *science,* whose accounts are in themselves reliable, exciting and deep. Rather, my purpose has been only that of demonstrating how easily such accounts can, in the mind of a true believer, become a final truth that rivals anything we find in the world of religious literalism.

In Crews's case, the true believer not only has embraced science but has also entered into the murkier realm of myth by assuming in effect that Darwin has given us something like a "final theory" of life. Reading Crews gives one the impression that human inquiry into the depths of nature may now come to rest finally on the bedrock of natural selection, leaving everything else as mere commentary. For all we know, however, Darwinian materialism is not as deep as we can go. Perhaps the final "truth" beneath evolution is a world open to the coming of God. From a biblical perspective, God must be thought of, after all, as the inexhaustible—but also sometimes disquieting— wellspring of novelty, and not merely as an imagined source of fixed order. If we follow some classic biblical texts, God is the one who "makes all things new." And as the new arrives, the old has to give way. A promise-making God, resident at a deeper level of the world's being than science itself can ever fathom, opens the life-story to a future that forever outreaches our own human sense of good order. The point is that Darwinian evolution, without undergoing any editing, can easily find a home on such theological terrain. A biblical understanding of God as one who comes toward the world from out of the future is not only compatible with evolution; it also logically anticipates the kind of life-world that Darwinian biology is now lavishly setting before us. Beyond both scientific materialism and "intelligent design," there lies a vision of God fully open to the findings of evolutionary science as well as to our longing for truth.

IO

Darwin
and the Deities

The same questions abide, age after age. What's going on in the universe?
Is there any point to it all? Why are we here? Is there any purpose to our
lives? How should we live? Does God exist? Where did the universe come
from? Why does anything exist at all? Why is there so much suffering? Why
do we die? Do we live on after death? How can we find release from suffering
and sadness? What can we hope for?

Let us call these the *big questions*. They are the ones that never go away. We
may momentarily distract ourselves from them, but they loiter on beneath
the surface of our lives. In some of us, they remain dormant for years, but ex-
treme circumstances, such as bitter personal defeat and needless suffering,
the prospect of our own death or the death of another, may force us to face
them head on, at least occasionally. And even in moments of great joy, we
may be moved to wonder about the meaning of our lives and of the universe,
why we are here, what we should do with our lives, how to make our fleeting
moments of happiness last forever.

It is the main business of religion to answer the big questions. And this is
why, even when we try to distance ourselves from it, we remain intrigued by
religion. Religion responds to the preoccupations that spring up when life
comes up against barriers beyond which ordinary—including scientific—

ways of coping cannot take us. For our purposes here, therefore, religions may be understood very simply as pathways through the ultimate limits on our lives.[1] These limits, as Paul Tillich points out, include not only death, but also the encounter with fate, guilt, doubt, the sense of being unloved or unaccepted, and especially the threat of meaninglessness—anything that stands between us and lasting peace or happiness.[2]

Religion proposes passage through the most intransigent roadblocks that we meet in life. It is puzzling, though, that there are so many religions and so many different routes available. And it is no less curious that, even within the history of each religious tradition, a new generation can outgrow the maps to salvation that seemed to work before. In the wide world of religious route finding, nothing ever seems completely settled.[3] A particular cluster of religious ideas or symbols, such as we find in the history of Egypt, for example, may remain relatively undisturbed for centuries or millennia, but a long view will chart considerable change and eventual obsolescence even in the most durable of creeds. Enormous variety pervades our spiritual traditions, across generations and around the globe. Why is this the case?

We might expect, as did Sigmund Freud, that the biggest of our questions should receive the clearest of answers, but this does not happen.[4] The more important our questions, the vaguer the responses. Because of religion's diversity and fuzziness of formulation, some modern thinkers have concluded that the whole spiritual enterprise is empty gesturing. If we cannot achieve clarity and agreement in answering the most pressing of our questions, then why should we take our religions seriously, especially in an age of science?

Moreover, one would expect that if religions dealt with what is most important, they would be more resistant to obsolescence. Instead of lasting forever, most of the deities our ancestors worshipped have by now "gone down the chute," as H. L. Mencken put it. When Mencken conducted his "burial service" for the gods, he called out by name hundreds of deities now lost in the haze of history, but none of them answered his roll call: Reseph, Anath, Ashtoreth, Baal, Astarte, Hadad, El, Nergal, Nebo, Ninib, Melek, Ahija, Isis, Ptah, Anubis, Addu, etc.; deities with names like Bile, Ler, Arianrod, Morrigu, Saturn, Cronos, Odin, Venus, Anu, etc. "Where is their graveyard?" Mencken asked. The gods numbered in the thousands, he observed, but they have now vanished.

What lingering mourner waters their mounds? . . . Men laboured for generations to build vast temples to them—temples with stones as large as hay-wagons. The business of interpreting their whims occupied thousands of priests, wizards, archdeacons, evangelists, haruspices, bishops, archbishops. To doubt them was to die, usually at the stake. Armies took to the fields to defend them against infidels: villages were burned, women and children were butchered, cattle were driven off. . . . They were gods of the highest standing and dignity—gods of civilized peoples—worshipped and believed in by millions. All were theoretically omnipotent, omniscient and immortal. And all are dead.[5]

To skeptics like Mencken, the story of the births and deaths of gods is proof of the utter silliness of religion. Religion's symbolic diversity throughout history is clear evidence of its unreliability. If religion were a trustworthy enterprise, it would have had more consistency, but to lovers of logic it seems to be a hopeless muddle. Mencken, not unlike the biologists of religion we met in Chapter 8, raises once again the fascinating question of how to explain the sense of God (or of the gods) that most people have had. To the Deep Darwinians, the answer is simple: Not God, but *we*, or more fundamentally our genes, are the ultimate explanation of the sense of God.[6] According to the new Darwinian version of the "projection theory," all human impressions of divine reality are products of a purely natural yearning. We humans fancy that God is real only because our wishes for an everlasting and saving reality are so powerful; and our wishes are so powerful because our genes dictate it for the sake of their survival. The human sense of God—ultimately rooted in the adaptive striving of our genes—stems from evolution's creating brains that in turn produce almost palpable images of deity, phantasms that seem so real to us only because we wish for them so fervently. The point is that the God-idea is itself nothing more than an adaptive fiction. The origin of the idea of God lies not in God or revelation, but in us and our genes.[7]

The religious person, of course, has to believe that *God* (or however the Absolute is named) is the source of the sense of God. Otherwise, religion won't work. To the serious devotee, God is really there. The overwhelming impression is that there *is* an ultimate reality, a "totally other" sacred presence whose self-disclosure, sacramentally mediated by way of ordinary objects, awakens the devout to worship. Theologically speaking, it is our being grasped by the divine, not our own imaginings, that fundamentally explains religion. To the Deep Darwinians, our genes may be the ultimate source of our sense of God, but, to religious believers, God is the ultimate source of the sense of God.

Obviously, these two positions are mutually exclusive. There can be only one *ultimate* explanation of religion. It is not inconceivable, however, that both scientific and theological accounts of religion can exist side by side without competing with each other. Almost everything else in our experience admits of a plurality of explanatory approaches, so why not religion also? Does a Darwinian account necessarily exclude a theological explanation? To Frederick Crews and the Deep Darwinians, as we have already seen, it does. Religion must be *either* the product of purely natural causes *or* the consequence of revelation from God. If one starts out with this forced option, then once Darwinism shows that religion is the product of evolution, it follows that any theological explanation is superfluous. If the sense of God comes from our genes, then it must not come from God.

In this either/or thinking, however, the evolutionary materialists show themselves to be no less literalist than creationists and Intelligent Design proponents in assuming that only one reading level is possible for so complex a phenomenon as religion.[8] A deeper understanding of religion will show that we do not have to choose between the two alternatives, Darwinism and theology. One "explanation" does not necessarily rule out the other. Once again we may appeal here to the notion of layered explanation or explanatory pluralism. That is, we may understand religion *both* as evolutionary adaptation *and* as response to God. We may plausibly hypothesize that the sense of God comes both from evolutionary causes and simultaneously from a divine depth that grasps hold of us. Looking at the very same historical mishmash of deities that led Mencken to conclude that religion is sheer fabrication, or that persuaded Freud, Feuerbach, Marx, Nietzsche and the new biologists of religion to dismiss our spiritual imaginings as pure illusion, we may approach religion by way of complementary levels of understanding. While properly "naturalizing" religion at a scientific level of explanation, we may without contradiction understand it theologically as the consequence of our being drawn toward the illimitable dimension of depth that we have been calling God.

To clarify this point, let us look at religions as something like information systems.[9] If there is indeed an ultimate divine dimension of depth, its presence to human awareness would in some sense be analogous to informational input (though not necessarily purely verbal). If God does exist, it would not be surprising that the divine depth would insinuate itself into human consciousness by a kind of informational feedback. An example of such feedback, as I pointed out in Chapter 3, is the sense we have at times of being grasped by the depth beneath the surface of our lives. We cannot focus on this depth, but we can experience it and allow ourselves to be drawn down into it, even against our first wishes. It is hard to deny its reality, even though it is cognitionally elusive. We sense its summons, after all, whenever we allow our minds to undertake the search for truth. And we feel its presence whenever we are drawn irresistibly toward goodness and beauty as well.

Religions may then be thought of as information systems awakened in an especially vivid way to the ultimate depths of the universe. If so, the historical instability of religions highlighted so colorfully by Mencken's burial service for the gods becomes theologically intelligible. Since the inexhaustible depth of being cannot be captured in any single lucid representation, we should expect that religious consciousness would experiment with a rich plurality of symbols. In its attempts to approximate what always escapes adequate representation, religion will inevitably be both diverse and unclear. It will understandably try out any number of imaginative models of ultimate reality. Viewed in this light, the eventual twilight of various gods would be just as likely as their dawning. Perhaps, then, the *ultimate* explanation of the births *and deaths* of gods is the infinite depth of being that we have been referring to as God.

Let us probe this possibility by considering an elementary aspect of information systems, the notion of negative feedback. Negative feedback is information about the variance between a system's actual state and an ideal state. For example, through negative feedback, a heating system informs the thermostat to adjust itself when the temperature falls below a set point, allowing the heat to come back on until the idealized temperature is reached. Registering the discrepancy between an actual and an ideal state is a feature of many information systems. It may be useful then to envisage religions as adaptive evolutionary information systems capable of registering the enormous distance between our concrete symbols and the inexhaustible depth they symbolize. In addition to all the genetic and evolutionary causes that Darwinians are conditioned to look for, religions are simultaneously information systems attempting to adjust to the negative feedback emanating from the inexhaustible depth toward which they are oriented, but to the bottom of which they can never conclusively arrive. Because of its own boundlessness, an *infinite* depth could never be adequately represented by any particular set of symbolic portrayals. There would always and forever be a distance between the ultimate depth of the universe on the one hand, and the finite religious systems that seek to model and codify it on the other.

Viewed in terms of an informational analogy, therefore, it would be inappropriate to expect that religions could ever come to rest in quiet equilibrium, especially if they profess to be responding faithfully to an inexhaustible depth. Religions, precisely in order to function as religions, must carry with them the impression of an infinite gulf between their symbolic depictions and the divine depth itself. This impression would be manifested at times in a reluctance on the part of some religions to take particular images of deity with unreserved seriousness. The eventual death of various gods, then, is not inevitably a signal of religion's silliness but perhaps an indication of the inexhaustible depth to which religions seek to adapt—without ever completely succeeding. Religions, understood as evolutionary information systems striving to adapt (always inconclusively) to an infinite depth, would possess, by virtue of a kind of negative feedback, an iconoclastic impulse that at least occasionally urges us to discard all our god-images as inappropriate.

Here it is important to remember that some of our religious traditions quite explicitly profess that *no* images of God are ever satisfactory. Therefore, the births and burials of gods would be exactly what we should expect as part of the ageless and never-ending quest for the infinite depth in whose elusive ambience religions attempt, more or less successfully, to implant their devotees. An informational modeling of religious systems may even allow us to make sense of two apparently contradictory aspects of religion. The first is religion's *sacramental* tendency, and the second is its recurrently *apophatic* inclination, that is, its tending at times to retreat into complete silence in the presence of the divine depth.

Let us look more closely at the sacramental and silent sides of religion. Religions usually speak about the unspeakable depth of reality by using concrete symbols or "sacraments." A sacrament, broadly speaking, is any object or event through which religious awareness is awakened to the "sacred" or the divine. Informational feedback from the infinite would lead religions to grope toward it by way of vivid symbols grounded in our ordinary experience of nature and human life. These symbols or sacraments constitute the "positive" language of religion. But in its more mystical moments, a wholesome religion records a kind of negative feedback. This is information about the infinite discrepancy between our actual symbols and the unfathomable depth that they attempt to portray. In the face of this negative feedback, religious people and communities may fall back at times into a state of complete silence. Thus is born the *via negativa,* the negative way of religion, which is to be distinguished from the *via positiva,* the positive way of analogy and sacrament. The way of silence is born out of an awareness of the unbridgeable distance between our symbolic imaginings and ultimate reality itself.

Such an awareness led Lao-tzu in China during the sixth century B.C.E. to declare in the *Tao Te Ching* that the Tao (ultimate reality) of which one speaks is not the real Tao. It is negative feedback that moved the late Indian *Upanishads* to declare that God is "not this, not that" *(neti, neti).* Perhaps it is also negative feedback that led the Buddha to renounce all theological speculation and the prophet Amos to declare to the Israelites (in the eighth century B.C.E.) that God despised their crude religious modes of worship. It accounts for Islam's removal of sacred images from its religious art. And it explains why, in the world of Christianity, Quakers can exist alongside Catholics. The history of religion presents us with a ceaseless contest between silence and sacramentalism. We may note, as examples, conflicts between the Buddha and the elaborate sacramentalism of popular Hinduism, between the Hebrew prophets and priests, between the iconoclasts and the image-centered devotionalists in early Christian history and the more recent arguments between Reformers and Roman Catholics.

Interpreting religions as instances of evolving information systems adapting to the universe's inexhaustible depth may help us understand better the constant tensions within religion. Informational feedback from the depth would stimulate ever new religious efforts toward sacramentalizing ultimate mystery. But then, at least in the case of some sensitive individuals and traditions, there may occur an extraordinary "feedback" that reduces devotees to the posture of complete silence in the presence of the divine. In some cases, it may even lead to an iconoclastic repudiation of all sacramental religion.

Following a suggestion of John Bowker, we may use a very simple analogy to make this point even clearer.[10] When a young man falls in love with a young woman, it is not unusual that the early phases of the romantic involvement will carry illusory expectations. The young man will project features onto his beloved that will not accurately represent the full reality of the young woman's personality. Through informational feedback (again not necessarily verbal), she will inform her suitor that his illusions do not portray her true being accurately. And so, if the relationship is to stabilize at a deeper level, he must revise his illusions, though he may never completely abandon them. A romantic relationship often involves ongoing revisions and approximations followed by more disillusionment and attempts at closer characterization.

Now, as Bowker points out, even though our young man's romantic illusions may be epistemologically suspect, they are nonetheless significant developmental stages in his eventually arriving at a more realistic knowledge of his beloved. Without the early illusory projections onto his beloved, any deeper encounter may never have occurred at all. Likewise, the story of humanity's religious infatuation with the divine is likely to go through periods of infantile or adolescent projection. And it is quite possible that Darwinian explanations may at least partially illuminate this blatantly "natural" aspect of religion. But in the case of religion, we cannot rule out the possibility that deeper readings than the Darwinian are essential for richer understanding of so complex a phenomenon.

As early humans embarked upon the long quest for the divine depths, they employed a sacramentalism that today we might consider crude and magical. The primal phases of the human religious journey may contain layers of childish wishing. Religions, for that matter, may always be accompanied by at least some degree of infantilism. But while the philosopher of religion is rightly intolerant of religious illusions, an informational-evolutionary perspective can be a bit more lenient. The illusions of religion may be developmental stages in the human process of adapting to the ultimate depth that we are calling God. The deepest of truths cannot be completely appropriated instantaneously, or even during a whole lifetime. Religions may be adapting incrementally—and more or less successfully—to ultimate reality, even while simultaneously adapting to their proximate terrestrial environments. Were we to suppress completely our wishing for God, or remove the adaptive genetic substrate of our religious aspirations, we might even cut ourselves off from any realistic encounter with the divine.

We may conclude, then, that if, in the cosmic depths, there does reside the inexhaustible transcendent dimension that we have been calling "God," it would indeed be quite surprising if historians failed to find a great deal of projection and illusion in the actual story of religious life. It would also be astonishing if Darwinians did not find in us a "genetic disposition" to create adaptive religious images, ideas and rites. Both the evolutionary constitution of religion and the creative variety of religious projections are consistent with the hypothesis that there is *in fact* an infinite depth whose informational input arouses the desire for it while at the same time also permitting a flight from it. In response to their being grasped by depth, religions would stagger only unsurely toward the evasive but always inviting and promising divine mystery. Although religions are inevitably projective, they are also systems capable of recording realistically a unique kind of information that explains both their persistence and their instability.[11] Like all other evolutionary phenomena, religions are never perfectly adapted or adaptive.

In accordance with our evolutionary information systems model of religion, negative feedback from a transcendent source of information would then be enough to explain the "scandal" of religion's lack of symbolic consistency throughout the ages. To skeptics like Mencken, the births and deaths of countless deities, the contradictions among the religions, the ironically perishable nature of our symbolic depictions of an allegedly eternal absolute—all of these seem to constitute evidence that religions are groundless. If there were any real substance to religious claims, the skeptic insists, they should all be logically compatible with one another as well as resistant to change. But, instead, we find irreconcilable conflicts and endless flux. If religions were trustworthy registries of an ultimate dimension of depth, they should be more durable and mutually consistent. Instead, they all seem subject to decay and death. The evolutionary information systems perspective, however, allows us to conclude that the births and deaths of gods recounted by Mencken are just what we should expect if indeed the universe is grounded in the inexhaustible dimension of depth that religions refer to by the name "God" or by countless other designations of ultimacy.

Thus, the projection theory and the Darwinian naturalizing of religion make a valid point by insisting that imaginative and creative humans—and, deeper than that, our selfish genes—are the source of the "sense of God." However, an explanatory pluralism does not exclude the possibility that our sense of God is at the same time *ultimately* the result of our being grasped by the revelatory input of information emanating from the divine itself.

Religion in an Unfinished Universe

Mencken's defunct deities at one time had the power to give meaning to the cosmos and significance to people's lives. But now almost all of them have "gone down the chute." Answers to scientific questions, on the other hand, come packaged in clear formulations to which all kinds of people, from many cultural backgrounds, can give common assent. If humans can achieve a high degree of clarity and consensus when answering relatively trivial questions in science, should we expect anything less when it comes to the big questions, those that religions address? Why should we pay any attention to the babble of conflicting religious voices if they cannot respond as unambiguously to the most worrisome of our questions as science does to our less urgent and more mundane curiosities?

Religious traditions, it is true, sometimes answer our ultimate questions with carefully formulated creeds consisting of core teachings that remain verbally stable down through the ages. But even in the midst of doctrinal stability there will be different ways of understanding the core beliefs, depending on historical and cultural circumstances. To save the fundamental religious teachings from irrelevance and obsolescence "theologians" offer fresh interpretations of their meaning. Even then, of course, disputes continue about whether new interpretations are consistent with beliefs central to a creed. When these disputes become severe, schisms may occur, leading to separate denominations and sometimes entirely new religious systems.

For over three centuries, one of the main questions facing the various religious traditions has been that of whether their creeds can survive at all in view of what the natural sciences tell us about the universe. Today, the same concerns arise especially because of neo-Darwinian biology. To those familiar with evolution, the modern intellectual world can easily seem to be on the brink of saying a final good-bye to the entire pantheon of Mencken's deities.

However, instead of divesting past or present religions of any substance whatsoever, evolution actually allows us to discover a deeper meaning in all our wild gesturing toward the sacred. The idea of evolution, when taken in combination with that of information, can even help us make sense of the fact that religions need to undergo constant revision in order to remain alive.

The key point is that evolutionary biology, now supported and widened by cosmology, has made us realize that we live in an *unfinished* universe. Both living species and religious systems are part of a universe that is still coming into being. The fact that the cosmos is even now perhaps in the early phases of its full emergence helps us understand why, religiously speaking, we remain always somewhat in the dark, why our answers to the biggest of our questions will always be frustratingly opaque, why we must walk by faith rather than by sight, but also why it makes so much more sense to hope than to yield to despair.[12]

The physical universe is a work in progress, still responding informationally to the depth that underlies it all. And religions, firmly embedded within nature itself, are continuous with this evolutionary-informational responsiveness. Religions, as the Deep Darwinians have already told us, are part of the wider story of life adapting itself to a challenging environment. But what exactly is the environment of religious adaptation, and how far does it extend? Throughout this book, I have been arguing that the ultimate environment of religious understanding (and also of the scientific quest) is an inexhaustible dimension of depth, a dimension that in some degree grasps hold of all of us and to which we have all responded, even if only by taking flight from it.

It is especially in the act of asking the big questions laid out in this chapter's opening paragraph that humans begin consciously to experience the monumental presence of a fathomless depth pulling us away from the surface of our lives. Immediate evidence of this allurement may be noted once again in the discomfort you are possibly feeling toward what I have just said. Your own desire to understand and criticize my claims is awakened by a depth that has already begun to take you captive, a depth into which you are drawn, and from whose attracting force you may also prefer (at times) to escape. To this infinite depth, as I have suggested with Paul Tillich, no other word in our language is more suitable than that of "God." Understood in both informational and evolutionary terms, therefore, religions are the most explicit ways humans have of *adapting* to the infinitely elusive "feedback" from infinite depth. And it is precisely because this depth is *inexhaustible* that our religions can never fully adapt to it. This depth, therefore, is the ultimate explanation not only of the births but also the deaths of Mencken's deities.

In a wider than human sense, the whole cosmic process may be understood, theologically speaking, as the story of creation "adapting" to its infinite depth. This process of adaptation, however, can by definition never reach a static point of completion. Hence the enormous amount of time involved in cosmic, biological, cultural and religious evolution should come as no surprise, theologically speaking. Moreover, theology after Darwin may now suggest that the universe, understood as an adaptive process itself, evolves at all only because in the remote reaches of its endless depth, there beckons something like a *promise*. It is here that providence resides and beckons. Providence is not manipulative of nature, but instead a reservoir of possibilities gently proffered to the world throughout its creative advance. This nonintrusive realm of endless possibility is, I believe, identical with the deepest kind of care conceivable, that is, with what theology calls providence (from the word "provide"). Evolution does not destroy but confirms the religious intuition that there is everlasting care at the bottom of things. And the fact that it takes time—to us humans an unfathomable amount of it—for the possible to become actual is no reason for despair.

We are inclined, of course, to ask why providence would wait so long for the world to be finished, but as theologian Jürgen Moltmann has rightly noted, patience and waiting may be the profoundest expressions of care.[13] Those concerned about the plausibility of the idea of providence after Darwin might reflect on these words:

> God acts in the history of nature and human beings through his patient and silent presence, by way of which he gives those he has created space to unfold, time to develop, and power for their own movement. We look in vain for God in the history of nature or in human history if what we are looking for are special divine interventions. Is it not much more that God waits and awaits, that—as process theology rightly says—he "experiences" the history of the world and human beings, that he is "patient and of great goodness" as Psalm 103:8 puts it? . . . "Waiting" is never disinterested passivity, but the highest form of interest in the other. Waiting means expecting, expecting means inviting, inviting means attracting, alluring and enticing. By doing this, the waiting and awaiting keeps an open space for the other, gives the other time, and creates possibilities of life for the other.[14]

And so, as evolution is adapting to God, God is awaiting the world. Evolution is both adaptation and anticipation. For our part, we humans experience this adaptive anticipation in the current of trust that bears us along. But the implicit trust that allows us to be taken captive by depth can be activated only by a kind of informational feedback from something redemptive and promising lurking in the depths of the cosmos. In an unfinished universe, of course, this trust is always partially mixed with distrust, a distrust rooted in our mistaking the often fractured surface of nature for what lies in the depths. Nature, as Darwin reminds us, is not paradise. It is filled with beauty, but also with violence and death. We cannot deny the ambiguities that compel many noble souls to despair of there being any "point" or purpose to it all. But even without dispelling ambiguity, it is possible to appreciate the universe as the carrier of a great promise—a promise whose fulfillment can be only vaguely visualized in metaphor, symbol and myth. It is in carrying a promise, I have been suggesting, that the evolving cosmos finds its fundamental meaning.

If I were to ask, along with Steven Weinberg, what to make of the idea of an "interested" God in an age of evolution, it is the God of promise, not a deistic designer, that I would be thinking about. It is the promise-making God of Abraham, the liberating God of Moses, the justice-loving God of the prophets and the passionately interested "Abba" of Jesus. This is the God who is still coming, and who therefore is not yet in every sense clearly present. It is the God who is still to be disclosed and who is often concealed ambiguously in the gods who have "gone down the chute." It is the God who is in some sense absent but who may nonetheless abide with the world most intimately in the mode of promise.

This is the understanding of God that I want to take with me as I look into Darwin's world. I do not want to look at nature for evidence of an engineer. There is too much disorder for that kind of focus. Instead, I want to reflect on evolutionary science with a mind and heart molded by a sense that nature is seeded deep in its fertile subsoil with limitless possibility. Although the cosmos does not exhibit any finished order or perfection, it is not unreasonable to trust that it is still opening toward a meaningful future. Even in its present ambiguity, we may read the universe as a context for universal hope.

Science and Religion As Evolutionary Adaptations

Finally, the notion of adaptation implied in Darwin's theory of natural selection can help us better understand the relationship of science to religion in an age of evolutionary awareness.[15] Whatever else they may be, science and religion both belong to the larger story of cultural evolution on planet Earth. As is the case with biological evolution, some cultural attempts at adaptation to reality succeed, while others lose out in the struggle for existence.

Dawkins, Crews and Dennett, of course, would claim that science and religion are locked in a competitive struggle, one in which science is now proving more capable of adapting human consciousness to the cosmic depths than is religion, and that consequently religion is destined for extinction. However, it is significant that science has not yet succeeded, nor apparently ever will succeed, in completely adapting the human mind to reality's depth. Although a few scientists suspect an imminent closure of the scientific quest, it is neither historically nor epistemologically wise, nor even logically plausible, to commit oneself to such a suffocating belief. Almost by definition, science is always obliged to seek out new ways of falsifying its current hypotheses, or to search for more fruitful research programs. The very integrity of science perpetually depends upon an at least tacit belief that an always wider and deeper intelligibility lies beyond the frontiers of current cognitional achievement. The entire scientific enterprise demands a trust that the real world in some way perpetually transcends what the human mind has grasped so far. Science too is borne along on the waves of promise.

Viewed broadly, science is the story of the modern human intellect struggling to correspond to a "reality" that in some way always lies beyond it. Whenever scientific "hypotheses" fail to fit this "reality," they are discarded, and only those that more or less "fit" the real world are selected for transmission to future generations. As it turns out, however, none of our scientific hypotheses are ever perfect "fits," so scientists must persist in their search for deeper and wider correspondence. It is only a tacit faith commitment to reality's not yet fully comprehended intelligibility that can explain the energy and devotion with which science tries to adapt our minds to the cosmos. To the extent then that religion and theology confirm the scientist's faith that reality is endlessly intelligible, they promote the evolutionary adaptation of human consciousness to its world. In this sense, religion in no way conflicts with, but instead enthusiastically sponsors, the scientific and evolutionary adventure of discovery.[16]

The history of religion, like that of science, is a long series of partially successful but mostly inadequate attempts on the part of humans to adapt to the fathomless depths of the cosmos. Religion tries to adapt humans to the world's depth through various symbols, myths and creeds. But the infinite elusiveness of this depth forever evades exhaustive depiction. And so, the religious quest, like that of science, is always frustratingly incomplete. Thus we humans, much more than animals and plants, often feel a sharp sense of dislocation and lack of correspondence to our world. This is because we are made to adapt not just to actuality, but even more to *possibility*, that is, to promise. We are, in other words, genetically wired for a world forever open to the future.

II

Deeper Than Death

O ur universe, as we have recently learned, is a story, not a state. But what
is the story about, and where is it going? Obviously, we humans cannot
give a clear answer to questions like this. Even our religions discourage the
thought that we can ever find out, at least with any clarity, what the "point"
of it all might be. God's appearance to Job out of the whirlwind is an eternal
reminder of the paltriness of all human perspective. Nevertheless, religions
do not greet the question of cosmic purpose with total silence. Silence at
some point will be necessary, but a refusal to inquire about the meaning of
things, including the meaning of the universe, is to suppress an instinct essential to human vitality.[1]

An inclination at least to *search* for meaning smolders at the very core of
our being, as even the most religiously skeptical Darwinians will agree. Our
longing for meaning is one of the traits that distinguishes us clearly from
other species of living beings. We humans are most fully alive, it seems, when
we endeavor to make sense of things, scientific inquiry itself being one route
to accomplishing this objective. And human vitality requires a tacit trust that
the universe's intelligibility runs deep, deeper even than science can reach.
Humans, including scientists, cannot endure the idea that all inquiry leads
eventually to a dead-end, or that the world's comprehensibility will eventually be spent.

It is the role of science to explore nature's intelligibility, but it is the indispensable function of religion to protect the sense of this intelligibility's

inexhaustible depth. Religion, understood as an ultimate concern for depth, keeps before us a sense of reality's endless horizons. And religion fortifies the trust that our excursions into nature's abyss will neither terminate nor be undertaken in vain. By grasping hold of us and inviting us to surrender our lives to it, the inexhaustible depth can grace our existence with meaning even while we struggle to find it. Although we can never clearly focus on ultimate meaning, we can allow ourselves to be carried away by it. The depth forever eludes us, but our inclining toward it already gives direction to our lives and backbone to our commitments.

The term "depth," as we have been using it, stands not only for "meaning" or "purpose" but, even more importantly, for "truth" as well. The depth beneath the surface of nature can give us meaning only if it is also the place where we expect to encounter *what is*. All our longing for meaning must finally be judged by reality itself. If we discovered somehow that our religious ideas are pure fiction, bearing no correspondence to something objectively real, they would, at least to all lovers of truth, fail to give us meaning also. If, in the ultimate depths of nature, beneath the abstractions of science, we were to unearth at the very bottom layer of being—as evolutionary materialism claims Darwin has done—an aimless, impersonal materiality, we would then have to concede the accuracy of cosmic pessimism. But we would have to acknowledge the ultimate futility of all scientific exploration as well, since our intelligence will then have met an impenetrable obstruction—the absolutely unintelligible. Such a finale would mock mercilessly all our efforts to understand the universe.

However, any claim to have fully plumbed the depth of nature, or any swaggering that we are about to do so, is both shallow and self-contradictory. Only cosmic literalists will claim to have read the world all the way down, and what they take for ultimate depth sooner or later turns out to be merely surface. Today's literalists, as I noted in Chapter 2, are so entranced by quantum events, chemical alphabets, genetic codes and Darwinian grammar that they may not even feel the narrative undercurrent that carries life, and indeed the entire universe, along. It seems more modest, therefore, to wager, along with the great wisdom traditions, that reality's depth is inexhaustible. It is this trust, after all, that alone can open up an always fresh frontier to science on the far side of every new discovery.

I have been proposing that beneath the surface of nature we now find ourselves drawn down—though not without resisting—into a narrative depth that we had not been mindful of until quite recently. Sustained reflection on the penetrating discoveries of evolutionary biology and contemporary cosmology now allows a new level of depth to tug at our surface awareness. And reflection on the universe's narrative momentum stirs us to reflect more seriously on where the cosmic succession of events may be carrying us. In a most startling way, Darwin awakened us to narrative depths of nature that had been invisible throughout most of human history.[2] And we are still reeling from his panoramic display of the epic of life and its long struggle prior to human emergence. Many people, as we have already seen, shrink back in disgust or horror at the extravagantly "wasteful" and impersonal episodes in evolution. But Darwin himself was more impressed than depressed by what he beheld, remarking at the end of his *Origin of Species* that "there is grandeur in this view of life." Considerable suffering attends the evolutionary epic but so also does immeasurable richness. In all of its ambiguity, the story bodies forth profligate beauty.

Behind the Veil

However, we cannot help asking whether all the beauty in the story is enough to redeem the loss. Evolution gives rise to a stupendous display of diversity, uncountable kinds of life and multiple modes of experience, including human consciousness. But, simultaneously, the evolutionary story is one of perpetual perishing. Nothing in the universe is forever, and those things that bear the most beauty, especially the many varieties of life, seem to last least long of all. The life-story goes on and on, leaving to death all the organisms that had any experience of that life. How then can we think of the universe as a place of promise and purpose if in the end everything in the story pales off into oblivion?

Life, it is clear, is not an unmixed good, especially since it is all subject to death. Alfred North Whitehead rightly observes that the fact of evil in the world comes down, in the end, to the plain and simple fact that things perish.[3] Perishing entails the loss of what is inherently valuable. In every death, a center or cluster of experience dissolves. So unless somewhere there is permanence, and unless this permanence is able to redeem all perishing, evil ultimately wins out over goodness, and the world in the end is absurd. For the universe to be purposeful, there has to be a redressing of all loss. The stream of perishing must flow toward something that saves it all from final nothingness. Deeper than evolution, if evolution is to escape final absurdity, there must be something that gathers up, and holds in eternal memory, the great cosmic epic.

But how could this be? Religions are intriguing to us in great measure because most of them claim that beyond the façade of perishability something or someone saves all things from complete oblivion.[4] Their visions of eternity provide solace to millions of humans as we face our own deaths and experience the passing of our loved ones. Religions often even anticipate personal, subjective survival beyond death. But in an age of science, it has become more difficult than ever to believe in such a prospect. In addition to materialist interpretations that deny the existence of souls and conscious immortality, today's Darwinian anthropologists interpret all religious trust in the afterlife as merely adaptive fiction. Hope in a destiny beyond death, they tell us, is simply a way of coping with our grief and, deeper than this, ensuring the survival of our genes.

The English poet Alfred Lord Tennyson's grief-filled poem "In Memoriam" expresses movingly the agonizing uncertainty that accompanies all hope for the beyond in an age of science:

> *Oh yet we trust that somehow good*
> *Will be the final goal of ill,*
> *To pangs of nature, sins of will,*
> *Defects of doubt, and taints of blood;*
> *That nothing walks with aimless feet;*
> *That not one life shall be destroyed,*
> *Or cast as rubbish to the void,*
> *When God hath made the pile complete:*
> *That not a worm is cloven in vain;*
> *That not a moth with vain desire*
> *Is shrivelled in a fruitless fire,*
> *Or but subserves another's gain.*
> *Behold we know not anything;*
> *I can but trust that good shall fall*
> *At last—far off—at last, to all,*
> *And every winter change to spring.*
> *So runs my dream: but what am I?*
> *An infant crying in the night:*
> *An infant crying for the light:*
> *And with no language but a cry.*
> *O life as futile, then, as frail!*
> *O for thy voice to soothe and bless!*
> *What hope of answer, or redress?*
> *Behind the veil, behind the veil.*[5]

But where Tennyson left room for at least the possibility of a positive response to the pain of loss, Algernon Charles Swinburne seemed quite sure that perishing is final:

We thank with brief thanksgiving
Whatever Gods may be
That no life lives forever;
That dead men rise up never;
That even the weariest river
Winds somewhere safe to sea.[6]

It seems to many highly educated people today that science now favors the more pessimistic of our two poets. A kind of cosmic despair has increasingly wormed its way into the high expressions of Western culture. A good amount of nineteenth- and twentieth-century art, literature and philosophy illustrates lavishly Matthew Arnold's sense that the sea of faith that once encircled us has now withdrawn "down the naked shingles of the world," again as the result of science.[7] Several generations of intellectuals have now nourished their doubts about final meaning on morsels of reputed "scientific evidence." Natural science has apparently clinched the conjecture that only final gloom and absolute perishing lie "behind the veil."

Still, a theology attuned to reality's depth may justifiably remain confident, even after Darwin, that the obvious perishing in world process is not the final word, and that a vein of permanence abides behind the veil of all cosmic becoming and loss. How such a prospect is conceivable we shall consider momentarily. For now let us not lose sight of the overwhelming religious conviction that an unshakable ground and depth endures throughout all transitions, something that lasts even while everything else apparently fades. And this permanence, to those who are sensitive to it, is able to rescue everything from absolute expiration. Religion, as Whitehead has put it,

> is the vision of something which stands beyond, behind, and within, the passing flux of immediate things; something which is real, and yet waiting to be realized; something which is a remote possibility, and yet the greatest of present facts; something that gives meaning to all that passes, and yet eludes apprehension; something whose possession is the final good, and yet is beyond all reach; something which is the ultimate ideal, and the hopeless quest.[8]

But is it reasonable to believe that there is indeed something that stands so steadfastly beyond, behind and within the flow of perishing moments? Let me begin a response to this question by reflecting on a couplet by Tennyson's friend, the poet Arthur Hugh Clough:

It fortifies my soul to know,
That though I perish truth is so.[9]

Extending this poet's intuition a bit further, I may say that although I perish, and everything in cosmic evolution and human history also perishes, the *fact* that things have happened is imperishable. For example, the dinosaurs have all perished, but the *fact* of their having existed has not perished. The proposition that dinosaurs once walked the Earth is as true today as it was millions of years ago. And millions of years from now it will still be true that dinosaurs existed. Let me go even further: Trillions of years from now, when the Big Bang universe has died of cold and all life has vanished for good, it will still be true that dinosaurs lived for millions of years during terrestrial history. Nothing will ever obliterate the *truth* that dinosaurs existed.[10]

But *where* will this be perpetually true? What is it that keeps all truths from annihilation? Where, in other words, is truth imperishably registered? What is it that makes it true that "though I perish, truth is so"? And in the future, what will make it true *then,* and in each new future, that dinosaurs and you and I lived? Or if you are now doubting that there is any truth at all, what will make it forever true that you had such doubts about truth? What is it, in other words, that upholds all truths and preserves facts from ever becoming nonfactual?

Deeper than evolution, beneath all becoming, perishing and death, there resides a rock-solid registry that prevents the erasure of all facts from the indelible record of having happened. Although we cannot focus on it, you and I assume the reality of this registry every time we utter a proposition or even ask a question. Evolutionists and historians assume, whenever they delve into the past, that there is something about reality that fixes forever the facticity of things. Otherwise, there would be no point to historical inquiry, even if the latter always involves a great deal of interpretation. There is a sealant that freezes in perpetuity what has occurred, so that, through our archeological efforts, we can at least try to approximate the objective past. Something judges and measures the truth or falsity of all our propositions—including the one I have just stated. There is indeed something "behind the veil," something deeper than all death and all perishing. We have been calling it the dimension of depth. Some religions call it "God."

For the past to be imperishable, however, events that have already happened must in some sense still be resident in each new "now." Henri Bergson, the great French philosopher, notes that duration is not simply a matter of one instant *replacing* another. "If it were," he goes on, "there would never be anything but the present—no prolonging of the past into the actual, no evolution, no concrete duration. Duration is the continuous progress of the past which gnaws into the future and which swells as it advances. And as the past grows without ceasing, so also there is no limit to its preservation." The past never evaporates but instead accumulates. Moreover, the past is preserved "in its entirety." In the case of human experience, the past "follows us at every instant; all that we have felt, thought and willed from our earliest infancy is there, leaning over the present which is about to join it, pressing against the portals of consciousness that would fain leave it outside."[11] If Bergson is right, it seems safe to assume also that the whole of life's evolution and the entire cosmic story are similarly ingredients in each present cosmic instant. Every past event in the cosmic drama still resounds in each new moment of the world's unfolding.

Whitehead, even more subtly than Bergson, shows how the cosmic past can endure in each new present. Physical reality in an evolving universe is made up, he observes, of moments, events or occasions, not chunks of spatialized stuff.[12] It is an illusory abstraction to assume, as old-fashioned materialists do, that the fundamental units of nature are particles of lifeless matter. If nature is a process of becoming, then its reality is temporal; and time, logically speaking, is composed of happenings, not atoms. What we think of as mechanisms or bits of matter are not concretely real, but at best useful scientific abstractions. If nature is in evolution, then its fundamentally temporal character can be broken down concretely only into events, not materialized monads.[13]

This point is decisive, because if nature is made up of transient events, paradoxically their very perishability is what allows the past to accumulate. The perishing of previous events permits the past to "grow without ceasing." And even though each discrete moment itself perishes, it becomes a constituent in subsequent moments, contributing itself to a series that adds up into something that lasts. As Bergson has just reminded us, time is not a matter of subsequent moments replacing previous ones. If that were the case, there could be no past for us to refer to at all. In order for me to be able to talk about the past, the moments previous to this one could not have utterly vanished as new present moments occurred. Rather, past events, unlike diffused material particles, can cohere or add up in such a way as never to be wiped out. As events perish into the past, the past amassment enters into the present, and each new event inherits or synthesizes the whole series of past occasions. Each present moment assimilates not only the immediate past, but in a vague way the remotest temporal sequence of events in the cosmic story.

Thus, nothing in the stream of universal and biological evolution is ever totally lost. By leaning over and gnawing into the present, to use Bergson's terms, each event receives what Whitehead calls an "objective immortality."[14] Although, spatially speaking, an object may vanish from the scene, temporally the universe keeps on harvesting the past. In perishing, each cosmic event is deposited in the next, and that into the next, etc., so that the entire past persists everlastingly. Indeed, it is only the abiding presence of the past in each "now" that allows for the fact of causation in nature and that gives any coherence to the cosmos. The objective immortality, by which each perished event gets deposited in subsequent events, is the reason why I can refer to the past as influencing the present.[15] It is the reason why I can say that "though I perish, truth is so."

Can We Be Saved?

Religiously speaking, however, the objective immortality of the past in each present is not enough to redress Tennyson's anxiety. Two other conditions must be fulfilled. First, there must be an *ultimate* repository of all perished events in the transient universe, a treasury that holds them in "memory" everlastingly. If the evolving cosmos is to evade final nothingness, there must be something that receives the whole story into itself and experiences it all with unfading immediacy. There must be an eternal reality that synthesizes and preserves forever the *totality* of the world's becoming. And if this repository is not to perish along with the universe, it must in some sense exist *independently* of the passing stream of occurrences. The religious intuition of God points us toward such a reality, as does our notion of the depth of nature. Nature's depth, I must now make clear, is not identical with the whole of transient nature itself. The divine depth runs infinitely deeper than nature and evolution. While receiving into itself and preserving everlastingly the sequence of events that make up the universe, the divine depth also infinitely transcends the universe. Otherwise, there would be nothing to keep the universe from perishing ultimately. Only an everlasting reality could truly redress the fact of loss.

Second, if Tennyson's hope is a realistic one, there must be some way in which the centers of striving that we call living beings would have the opportunity to attain a fulfillment proportionate to their striving. What this would mean for other species of life it is impossible to say. But for humans, it would entail—at the very least—that beyond our own deaths the pursuit of meaning, truth, goodness and beauty that orients our specifically human lives would be open to a conscious, experiential fulfillment. I say "beyond our deaths" because no matter how much meaning, truth, goodness and beauty we may have encountered during our brief life spans, each of us dies an unfinished fragment. And even if we can claim a good deal of personal satisfaction in our own lives, we remain attached to an unfinished universe. As long as the universe is unfinished, so also is each one of us. Because of the intricate way each organism and each human person is tied into the cosmic story—a story still not fully told—no living being can attain a satisfying fulfillment independently of the cosmos. Our personal redemption awaits the salvation of the whole.

Belief in a personal destiny beyond death has many different meanings in the world's religions. In the Abrahamic traditions, however, this destiny is often thought of as bodily resurrection. Even the metaphor of resurrection allows for a diversity of interpretations, but theologically speaking, "resurrection of the body" must mean that in some way the entire sequence of events in each person's life-story is taken everlastingly into the compassionate love of God. Yet, after Darwin, Einstein, Hubble and Hawking, we now know that each human story is inseparable from the evolution of life on Earth and the larger cosmic narrative of an expanding universe. We now realize that, in telling our own stories, we can no longer leave out the captivating preamble that geology, evolutionary biology and astrophysics have jointly assembled. Nor can we divorce our life stories from whatever future chapters the universe will add to what has been. Human life, biological evolution and cosmic process now constitute one continuous unfolding, and so nothing in the telling of the cosmic story can be completely alien to the telling of the story of our own lives. There is also every possibility that, in the cosmic sweep of things, our human epic will be succeeded by endless future creations and perishings that we can now know nothing about.

Consequently, in the same act of gathering the separate moments of each human life into the divine depths, and endowing them with the coherence of "new creation," a trustworthy God concerned with our own bodily resurrection would also assimilate and redeem the whole cosmic drama. For this reason, humans cannot remain indifferent here and now to the question of generic cosmic destiny. And any theology that deliberately shuts its eyes to the intimate connection of our own existence to that of the larger evolutionary and cosmic totality would be insufferably trifling. Moreover, since in humans the universe has awakened to consciousness, and evolution has now become conscious of itself, it is inconceivable that any truly cosmic redemption would tolerate the suffocation of the very consciousness to which the universe has been straining so mightily to give birth.

Although we may concede the plausibility of some kind of objective immortality, we still remain troubled by the obvious loss of immediacy of enjoyment that characterizes all experience, ours included. Is there any sense, therefore, in which immediacy does not fade? "The process of time," White-head admits, "veils the past below distinctive feeling." As novelty streams into the world, the present gets pushed into the past, where it gets lost and eventually forgotten, at least to human awareness. As each new present appears, the past becomes more obscure, and this fading of the present into the dim past constitutes the "ultimate evil in the temporal world." "The most general formulation of the religious problem," our philosopher continues, "is the question whether the process of the temporal world passes into the formation of other actualities, bound together in an order in which novelty does not mean loss."[16]

Whitehead considers this question to be perhaps the most important one that philosophy and religion have to deal with: "The world," he says, "is haunted by terror at the loss of the past, with its familiarities and its loved ones. It seeks escape from time in its character of 'perpetually perishing.'"[17] So is there some way in which immediacy does not fade but abides everlastingly? The religious notion of God, once again, points us toward such a reality in the depths beneath all death.

The loss of immediacy is what evokes our most anguished concern. Paul Tillich believes that, beneath our human anxiety about death, there lies a more fundamental concern about our being forgotten forever. Our experience of how the present gets pushed into the past and then becomes further veiled by each new present makes us wonder if we also shall not be eternally forgotten. What makes us anxious about our having to die, in other words, is not simply the prospect of our ceasing to exist. In the depths of our dread of nothingness there lies the "anxiety of being eternally forgotten."[18] What we find most difficult to bear is the idea of a complete oblivion wherein no traces of our ever having lived will remain. Tillich contends that humans have never been able to bear the thought that our having lived could become so veiled by the past that it would become completely lost to all memory. For this reason, we have devised a variety of ways to ensure that we will be remembered.

> The Greeks spoke of glory as the conquest of being forgotten. Today, the same thing is called "historical significance." If one can, one builds memorial foundations. It is consoling to think that we might be remembered for a certain time beyond death not only by those who loved us or hated us or admired us, but also by those who never knew us except now by name. Some names are remembered for centuries. Hope is expressed in the poet's proud assertion that "the traces of his earthly days cannot vanish in eons." But those traces, which

unquestionably exist in the physical world, are not we ourselves, and they don't bear our name. They do not keep us from being forgotten.[19]

So we keep on asking whether there is anything that can indeed keep us from being forgotten. Does the past remain perpetually buried behind the veil of perishing and death?[20] Unless something somewhere has *immediate* access to the past now gone from us, there can be no gladdening response to Tennyson's grief. Nor can there be any lasting significance to the cosmos or our lives unless the events that compose them are imprinted permanently on what lies deeper than all death. Unless our experiences are somehow preserved in their immediacy, our anxiety about death remains without redress. Then the cosmic pessimists will have had the last word.

If the evolutionary materialists we have been discussing in previous chapters are correct, Tennyson's and Whitehead's and all other religious longing for permanence is futile. Few philosophers have expressed more directly and truthfully the dismal implications of materialist metaphysics than has William James:

> That is the sting of it, that in the vast driftings of the cosmic weather, though many a jewelled shore appears, and many an enchanted cloud-bank floats away, long lingering ere it be dissolved—even as our world now lingers for our joy— yet when these transient products are gone, nothing, absolutely *nothing* remains, to represent those particular qualities, those elements of preciousness which they may have enshrined. Dead and gone are they, gone utterly from the very sphere and room of being. Without an echo; without a memory; without an influence on aught that may come after, to make it care for similar ideals. This utter final wreck and tragedy is of the essence of scientific materialism as at present understood.[21]

It is not inconceivable, however, that, behind the veil that shrouds the past from us, the very same registry that fixes and preserves the past in objective immortality also retains each cosmic present with an immediacy of feeling and memory that does not fade. Certainly, the religious intuition of many people has been that the immediacy of our experience enters into God's life without the paling that we humans experience in our own temporal perishing. What is impossible for us, religious faith proclaims, is possible with God. If, as Jesus believed, the very hairs of our head are numbered, or, if the Psalmist is right that all of our tears are deposited in God's flask (Ps 56:8), then somehow every event in cosmic process is salvaged and preserved eternally in God in full immediacy. Paul Tillich expresses this religious intuition as follows:

> Nothing in the universe is unknown, nothing real is ultimately forgotten. The atom that moves in an immeasurable path today and the atom that moved in an immeasurable path billions of years ago are rooted in the eternal ground. There is no absolute, no completely forgotten past, because the past, like the future, is rooted in the divine life. Nothing is completely pushed into the past. Nothing real is absolutely lost and forgotten. We are together with everything real in the divine life.[22]

Whitehead would add that in God the immediacy of all events and experiences never fades. God is the underlying permanence that preserves fully everything that occurs in the entire cosmic process.[23] And even though each momentary event may eventually drift far from our own present awareness, it resides in God in full immediacy. We cannot prove this point, of course, but we fail to do justice to religious experience if we interpret its hope or trust in divine redemption simply as pure adaptation rather than also as an intuition of what lies in the depth beneath all evolution and all perishing. Earlier I noted that Bergson and Whitehead, in a purely philosophical way, have clearly demonstrated that there must be something in the nature of things that keeps the past from absolute perishing. Otherwise we could not refer to the past at all. Religions may not be unreasonable, therefore, in weaving onto this general human intuition of permanence their additional impression that the depth beneath all perishing bears the stamp of everlasting care and promise.

Additionally, as it considers the large question of the possible "point" or purpose of the universe, theology may now reasonably conjecture that this same divine care takes into itself all of the suffering, discord, tragedy and enjoyment in biological evolution and cosmic unfolding, as well as in human history. If the permanence beneath process is endowed with the character of care, as theology is entitled to assume, it is not beyond reason to trust that this eternal care could also transform local cosmic contradictions into a wider harmony of contrasts, that is, into an unfathomable depth of beauty, and that our own destiny beyond death admits of conscious enjoyment of this beauty as well.

Theology, which takes as its point of departure the religious experience of a community of believers, may infer that God's own experience salvages whatever from our own perspective may seem to be "utter final wreck and tragedy." God, Whitehead speculates, "saves the world as it passes into the immediacy of his own experience."[24] In a world conceived of as a temporal process, each experience adds something new by way of contrast, and it is, therefore, eternally rescued by its "relation to the completed whole."[25] Thus, in its orientation toward an endless breadth of beauty, the universe may be endowed with an ever burgeoning meaning as well.[26]

In God's assimilation of the events that make up our personal lives, biological evolution and cosmic process, things that appear irredeemable from our narrow perspective may contribute to the limitless depth and breadth of God's own life. Theology may then trust that local clashes, dead ends or absurdities may be transformed eventually into contrasts that contribute intensity and beauty to the "wider vision." In God's registry of the world's becoming, each occurrence is preserved. And so there is no sound reason for us to reject the possibility that this redemption includes not only the survival but also an expansion beyond death of the consciousness that evolution has already produced in us. Religious hope for some extended and transformed mode of subjective survival beyond death is not at all inconsistent with the undeniable fact of objective immortality.

At any rate, we need not simply brush aside as naive the poet's hope for a permanence behind the veil of perishing. There is, at the very least, something eternal about truth. This is a point, as I have argued, that cannot be coherently denied. And it may well be also that everything that touches on truth, especially the human spirit of inquiry, partakes of what never perishes. If we find that a portion of our own awareness is attracted to *what is,* is it not because we are *already in the grasp of truth?* And in allowing ourselves to be grasped by truth, are we not also, as Plato observed centuries ago, somehow already in the realm of the imperishable "good"? And, along with us, the entire universe?

Conclusion

Still, we cannot help asking why that which allegedly delivers all beings from impermanence has to be itself so dim to us now, so thin in its present availability. Why does "the final good" or "the ultimate ideal" or the "greatest of present facts" have to be beyond all reach? Why does "that which gives meaning to all that passes" have to elude apprehension? Science cannot make any sense of the religious vision of what lies hidden "beyond, behind, and within" the flux of phenomena, since it always bases its ideas and predictions on available evidence. However, I would like to propose once again that the paradoxes of religion, though off-limits to science, fit especially well the current evolutionary picture of an unfinished universe. The unavailability or hiddenness of God is in some sense, I think, a function of the fact that the universe we live in is still coming into being.[27]

Religious hope, though quite distinct from science, fits comfortably our newly acquired scientific awareness that we humans are part of an immense cosmos still in the making. If our universe were currently a completed and finalized creation, we could rightly demand the end to all ambiguity. Transparency, we might then insist, should replace at once our current "seeing through a glass darkly." But as long as the world remains in process, we cannot reasonably expect to make out clearly what it is all about, or what lies beyond, behind and within it. So it is not surprising that what Whitehead calls the greatest of present facts (by which, of course, he means God) must still be, at least in some sense, beyond our grasp. In an unfinished universe, God can be "evident" to us at present only in the mode of promise rather than finalized presence. And any intuition we may have of a divine permanence that stands beyond, behind, within—or beneath—the passing flux of immediate things could be apprehended only by a consciousness that is willing to suspend its longing for clarity and allow itself to be flooded with patient and long-suffering hope. "For in hope we were saved. Now hope that sees for itself is not hope. For who hopes for what one sees? But if we hope for what we do not see, we wait with endurance."[28] And, as Paul Tillich would add, "We are stronger when we wait than when we possess."[29]

12

A Deeper Theology

The world's religions, at least during the period of their emergence, knew nothing about Big Bang cosmology, deep time or biological evolution. Generally speaking, they have still not caught up with these ideas. Even in the scientific West, the findings of evolutionary biology and cosmology continue to lurk only at the fringes of contemporary theological awareness. The sensibilities of most believers in God, including theologians, have been fashioned in an imaginative context defined either by ancient cosmographies or, if philosophically tutored, by equally timeworn ontologies that are static, vertical and hierarchical. Religious understandings of ultimate reality, thoughts about the meaning of human existence, intuitions about what is ultimately good and what the good life is, and ideas of what is evil or unethical—all of these at least originally took up residence in a human awareness still innocent of the implications of deep cosmic time and largely unaware of the prospect that the universe may still be only at the dawn of its journey through time.

How, then, are we to think about God, if at all, in a manner proportionate to the new scientific understanding of biological evolution and cosmic process? A good many scientists have given up on such a project, settling into their impressions that the immense universe of contemporary natural science has by now vastly outgrown the one-planet deity of our terrestrial religions. Theology, meanwhile, is just beginning to reconsider the idea of God in a way that would render it consonant with the scale of evolution.

The famous Jesuit geologist and paleontologist Pierre Teilhard de Chardin (1881–1955) was far ahead of professional theologians in perceiving evolution's demand for a revitalized understanding of God. Our new awareness of nature's immensities—in the domains of space, time and organized physical complexity—provides us, he thought, with the exciting opportunity to enlarge our sense of God far beyond that of any previous age. Moreover, as Teilhard also emphasized, the new scientific picture of the universe has not only amplified our sense of cosmic immensity; it has also altered our whole understanding of the sort of thing the universe is. Science has now shown quite clearly that the cosmos is a story. Nature is narrative to the core. As I noted earlier, the physicist Carl Friedrich von Weizsäcker argues in *The History of Nature* that the greatest scientific discovery of the twentieth century was that the universe is historical.[1] And Teilhard was one of the first scientists in the last century to have fully realized this fact. The cosmos, he often repeated, is not a fixed body of things, but a genesis—a still unfolding drama rather than merely a frozen agglomeration of spatially related objects. The world is still coming into being.[2]

It is now of utmost importance, therefore, that religious thought reshape its ideas of nature, human existence and reality as a whole in a manner commensurate with the idea of a cosmos still emerging in the remarkable ways that science is recording. Above all, evolution requires a revolution in our thoughts about God. But "who," Teilhard asked, "will at last give evolution *its own* God?"[3] Although Teilhard himself was a profoundly religious thinker, he was not a professional theologian, and so his own efforts to construe a "God for evolution" stopped short of the systematic development his intuitions demanded. The project of shaping theology in a manner fully apprised of evolution still remains to be done. It may be instructive, therefore, to look into a great theological system such as that of Paul Tillich as a possible resource for a contemporary theology of evolution. After giving a brief sketch of Teilhard's central ideas immediately below, I will scan several facets of Tillich's theology to see if it may prove capable of giving us "a God for evolution."

Teilhard's Main Ideas

For Teilhard, the whole universe is in evolution, and there is a clear direction to the cosmic story. The Jesuit scientist consciously extended the term "evolution" beyond its biological meaning and applied it to the whole cosmic process. In spite of the obvious meandering or "branching" character of biological evolution, he observed, the universe as a whole has clearly moved in the direction of ever increasing "organized complexity." The cosmic process has gone through the pre-atomic, atomic, molecular, unicellular, multicellular, vertebrate, primate and human phases of evolution. During this journey, the universe has manifested a measurable growth in instances of organized complexity.

What gives significance to this story is that during the course of cosmic evolution, in direct proportion to the growth in organized physical complexity, there has been a gradual increase in "consciousness." In accordance with the "law of complexity-consciousness," as matter has become more complex in its organization, consciousness and eventually (in humans at least) self-awareness have emerged. The "inside" of things has become more and more intensified, more centered and more liberated from habitual physical routine. And there is no reason to suspect that the cosmic journey toward complexity, having reached the level of human consciousness, will now inevitably come to a halt. Indeed, our own hominized planet is now developing a "noosphere" (a new geological stratum consisting of tightening webs of mind, culture, economics, politics, science, information and technology), thus moving evolution in the direction of a new level of complexity-consciousness. In spite of the protests of some biologists to the contrary, a cosmological perspective shows that there is a net overall advance or "progress" in evolution. Teilhard abstractly refers to the ultimate goal of this advance as "Omega."[4]

Omega is "God." Nothing less than a transcendent force, radically distinct from, but also intimately incarnate in, matter could ultimately explain evolutionary emergence. For Teilhard, it is the attraction of God-Omega that *ultimately* accounts for the world's restless tendency to move beyond any specific level of development toward ontologically richer modes of being. In the world's religions, the universe's "search for a center" finally becomes conscious. At a deep level of explanation—deeper than science itself can ever reach—evolution can be said to occur because as God draws near to the world, the world explodes "upwards into God."[5] If we read deeper beneath the surface of the world that science has uncovered, we may understand both humanity's long religious journey, and the whole epic of evolution prior to it, as one long cosmic search for an integrating and renewing Center. This quest recurrently gathers the past into a new present and carries the whole stream of creation toward the God who creates the world from "up ahead." Since Teilhard was completely comfortable with what we have been calling layered explanation or explanatory pluralism, he had no difficulty saying all of this at a religious level of interpretation without fearing that he was intruding into the work that natural science carries on autonomously at its own rather abstract levels of inquiry.[6]

Teilhard also thought in cosmic terms about the Christ of his own creed, deliberately following the cosmic Christology of St. Paul and some later Christian writers. As a Christian thinker, he pictured the whole vast universe as converging on and coming to a head in the Christ of the Parousia, the one who is to come. Redemption, for Teilhard as for St. Paul, coincides with the new creation of the whole universe in Christ.[7]

As his thought matured, Teilhard increasingly complained that traditional theology, insofar as it is focused on *esse* (the idea of *being*), is unable as such to contextualize the dramatic new sense of a world still in the process of becoming. Moreover, theology has conceived of God too much in terms of the notion of a Prime Mover impelling things from the past *(a retro)*. Evolution demands that we think of God as drawing the world from up ahead *(ab ante)*, attracting it forward into the future. Creation is a process of gathering the multiple strands of cosmic evolution into an ultimate unity located not so much up above as up ahead: *creatio est uniri* (creation means "being brought into unity"). For Teilhard, as for the New Testament author of Revelation, God is both Alpha and Omega. But after Darwin and the new cosmology, we must say that God is less Alpha than Omega: "Only a God who is functionally and totally 'Omega' can satisfy us," Teilhard exclaims. But he persists with his question and now ours as well: "where shall we find such a God?"[8]

Tillich and Teilhard

Half a century after Teilhard's death, we have yet to answer this question satisfactorily. For the most part, theologians still think and write almost as though Darwin, Einstein and Hubble never existed. Their attention is fixed on questions about the meaning of human existence, human history, social justice, hermeneutics, gender issues or the individual's spiritual journey. These are all worthy of attention, of course, but except for a smattering of ecologically interested theologies, the natural world and its evolution remain distant from dominant theological interest. In the Christian churches, redemption and eschatology are still typically thought of in terms of a harvesting of human souls rather than the coming to fulfillment of an entire universe. Furthermore, the divorce of theology from the cosmos persists no less glaringly in what has come to be called "postmodern theology," most of which ironically seems unable to move beyond modernity's sense of the fundamental estrangement of both God and ourselves from the nonhuman natural world.

In view of the general failure of theology to respond adequately to evolution, we may ask here whether the impressive theological work of Paul

Tillich, on whose understanding of "depth" the previous chapters have so heavily relied, takes us deep enough to situate the new evolutionary picture of the universe that so energized Teilhard's own life and thought. Toward the end of his life, Tillich had become acquainted at least vaguely with some of Teilhard's ideas; and although he considered Teilhard's vision of the universe too "progressivistic" for his own tastes, he nevertheless felt "near" to the modest Jesuit in "so many respects."[9] Tillich did not say exactly what attracted him to Teilhard, so we can only guess. I suspect, though, that he found in Teilhard a deeply Christian thinker who mirrored many of Tillich's own religious and theological intuitions.

For example, Tillich and Teilhard both sought a reformulation of spirituality in a way that would permit believers to feel that they do not have to turn their backs on the universe or the Earth in order to approach the Kingdom of God. Additionally, they agreed that life in a finite universe is inevitably, and not just accidentally, riddled with ambiguity, and that the estrangement of the universe from its essential being somehow coincides with the very fact of its existence. They both wrestled in creative ways with how to balance the vertical (transcendent) and horizontal (immanent) dimensions of human aspiration. Together they looked for a way in which the human person could experience religious meaning without being subjected to a law alien to authentic being and freedom. That is, they longed for a kind of communion with God, with other humans, and with the universe that differentiates rather than obliterates human personality and freedom. They held in common an intuition that love is the key to all unity, but that *agape* (selfless love of others) should never be separated from natural desire, or *eros*. Not insignificantly they also shared an appreciation of the dimension of the inorganic which had been largely overlooked, and is still seldom noticed, by theology.[10] Similarly they both recognized that the materialist metaphysical foundation of modern science is, in Tillich's words, nothing less than an "ontology of death."[11] Yet they also sought to address this baleful modern perspective without reverting to vitalism. Above all, they each placed special emphasis on the need for religious thought to open itself to the category of the New.

Both Tillich and Teilhard were also extremely sensitive to the ways in which dualism and "supranaturalism" had sickened Christianity. Although Teilhard was not directly influenced as much by Friedrich Nietzsche as was Tillich, he was sensitive to Nietzsche's accusations that Christian piety often fosters a hatred of the Earth that saps human existence of a wholesome "zest for living."[12] He also agreed with modern secularistic complaints that Platonic influences in Christian thought had robbed the world's "becoming" of any real significance, of the capacity to bring about anything truly unprecedented.

In the end, however, Teilhard no less than Tillich found the Nietzschean and secularistic outlooks suffocating. Any vision of things that ultimately closes off the world to new being, however friendly to becoming it may initially seem to be, is no home for either the human spirit or the religious adventure. Both the Platonic metaphysics of eternity, in which everything important has already happened, and the modern materialist ideology that explains everything "new" as simply the outcome of a past sequence of deterministic causes, can have the effect of stifling hope and depleting human energy. Only a universe in which the truly new can occur will ever be a suitable setting for religious faith and hope in the future.

Another important point of comparison of Tillich with Teilhard is their respective interpretations of original sin. Aware that, after Darwin, the traditional explanation of a historical "Fall" of actual humans from an earthly paradise could no longer be taken literally as the explanation of our estrangement from "the essential," Tillich and Teilhard both sought new ways to account for the ambiguities of life and the presence of evil. They wrote at a time when biblical scholarship and a growing awareness of evolution had already exposed the questionable nature of a plain reading of Genesis; and they received harsh criticism as they sought deeper meanings in the story of the so-called Fall. In fact, they are still demonized by biblical or dogmatic literalists and anti-evolutionists.

On the question of original sin, what continues to require theological discussion is the role of human freedom and responsibility in accounting for evil. Both Tillich and Teilhard moved decisively in the direction of interpreting sin, evil, suffering and death as tragic, or as "somehow" inevitable. Their intention in doing so was in each case to magnify our sense of God by widening vastly the sweep of redemption along with creation. They shared the belief that a one-sidedly anthropocentric interpretation of evil always risks diminishing the cosmic compass of divine love. But by pointing to the tragic "inevitability" of evil they raised troubling questions about how much responsibility for evil can then be attributed to individual human persons.

In one of several early notes not intended for publication (reflections that may have led at least indirectly to his being virtually exiled to China by his religious superiors), Teilhard wrote that

> original sin, taken in its widest sense, is not a malady specific to the Earth, nor is it bound up with human generation. It simply symbolizes the inevitable chance of evil (*Necesse est ut eveniant scandala*) which accompanies the existence

of all participated being. Wherever being *in fieri* [in process of becoming] is produced, suffering and wrong immediately appear as its shadow: not only as a result of the tendency towards inaction and selfishness found in creatures, but also (which is more disturbing) as an inevitable consequence of their effort to progress. Original sin is the essential reaction of the finite to the creative act. Inevitably it insinuates itself into existence through the medium of all creation. It is the *reverse side* of all creation.[13]

For Teilhard the most noteworthy theological consequence of this universalizing of evil is that it considerably enlarges the scope and import of the redemption in Christ:

If we are to retain the Christian view of Christ-the-Redeemer it is evident that we must also retain an original sin as vast as the world: otherwise Christ would have saved only a part of the world and would not truly be the center of all. Further, scientific research has shown that, in space and duration, the world is vast beyond anything conceived by the apostles and the first generations of Christianity.[14]

It follows that by failing to expand our minds in a way that represents the temporal and spatial immensities portrayed by the new scientific epic of evolution, we shall also inevitably fail to do justice to the notions of Christ and divine redemption: "How, then, can we contrive still to make first original sin, and then the figure of Christ, cover the enormous and daily expanding panorama of the universe? How are we to maintain the possibility of *a fault as cosmic* as the Redemption?"[15] Teilhard's answer: "The only way in which we can do so is by spreading the Fall throughout the whole of universal history . . . "[16] And, he comments, "The spirit of the Bible and the Church is perfectly clear: the whole world has been corrupted by the Fall and the *whole* of everything has been redeemed. Christ's glory, beauty, and irresistible attraction radiate, in short, from his *universal* kingship. If his dominance is restricted to the sublunary regions, then he is eclipsed, he is abjectly extinguished by the universe."[17]

Tillich would surely sympathize with Teilhard's attempt to widen the scope of redemption. In fact, for Tillich, the redemption extends not only into the whole of the physical universe and its history, but into the very heart of being as such.[18] For Tillich, however, no less than for Teilhard, the question remains as to whether, by universalizing the primordial fault and, correspondingly, the compass of redemption, he has unduly lessened the role of human responsibility in accounting for evil. Many theologians have resisted a broad extension of the scheme of redemption precisely because such expansionism seems to dilute and even nullify the role of human freedom in accounting for the most horrendous evils in our world.[19]

Although Teilhard does not pretend to remove the mystery of evil, he rightly claims that the reality of evil has a cosmic dimension; and evil appears to be not quite the same thing when viewed in the context of evolution as when interpreted in terms of a static universe, although too few theologians have bothered to notice the difference. We may ask whether even as significant a theologian as Paul Tillich has taken evolution and the idea of an unfinished universe sufficiently into account in his own understanding of God and the theology of redemption.

Cosmic and biological evolution instruct us as never before that we live in a universe that is in great measure not yet created. The incompleteness of the cosmic project logically implies, therefore, that the universe and human existence have never, under any circumstances, been situated in a condition of ideal fullness and perfection. In an evolving cosmos, created being as such has *not yet* achieved the state of integrity. Moreover, this is nobody's fault, including the Creator's. The only kind of universe a loving and caring God could create, after all, is an unfinished one. For God's love of creation to be actualized, the beloved world must be truly "other" than God. And an instantaneously finished universe, one from which our present condition of historical becoming and existential ambiguity could be envisaged as a subsequent estrangement, would in principle have been only an emanation or appendage of deity and not something truly other than God. A world that is not clearly distinct from God could not be the recipient of divine love. And an instantaneously completed world could never have established an independent existence vis-à-vis its creator. The idea of a world perfectly constituted *ab initio* would, in other words, be logically incompatible with any idea of a divine creation emerging from the depths of selfless love.

Moreover, the pre-scientific sense of a non-evolving universe has tended too easily to sponsor scapegoating quests for the culprit or culprits that allegedly befouled the primordial purity of created being. If creation had been originally a fully accomplished affair, we would understandably want to identify whoever or whatever it was that messed things up so badly for us. The assumption of an original perfection of creation has in fact led religious speculation to imagine that the source of the enormous evil and suffering in the world must be either an original principle of evil—an idea unacceptable to biblical theism according to which the principle of all being is inherently good—or else some intraworldly being or event. That the latter supposition has led to the demonizing of various events, persons, animals, genders, aliens, etc., requires no new documentation here. It is enough for us simply to wonder what a salutary thing it would be if religious thought were now to take the reality of evolution with complete seriousness.

In 1933, Teilhard wrote, in words that apply to much Christian thought even today:

> In spite of the subtle distinctions of the theologians, it is a matter *of fact* that Christianity has developed under the over-riding impression that all the evil round us was born from an initial transgression. So far as dogma is concerned we are still living in the atmosphere of a universe in which what matters most is reparation and expiation. The vital problem, both for Christ and ourselves, is to get rid of a stain.[20]

As long as we had assumed that creation was instantaneous, and the cosmos fully formed in an initial creative act, the only way we could make sense of present evil and suffering was to posit a secondary distortion. But this assumption opened up the possibility of interpreting suffering essentially as punishment and fostered an ethic tolerant of retribution. Such a view, one that still informs both religious and social life, can only render expiation an interminable affair, thereby robbing suffering of the possibility of being interpreted as part of the process of ongoing creation itself. "A primary disorder," Teilhard goes on, "cannot be justified in a world which is created fully formed: a culprit has to be found. But in a world which emerges gradually from matter there is no longer any need to assume a primordial mishap in order to explain the appearance of the multiple and its inevitable satellite, evil."[21]

Evolution, to repeat our theme, means that the world is unfinished. But if it is unfinished, then we cannot justifiably expect it yet to be perfect. It *inevitably* has a dark side. Redemption, therefore, if it means anything at all, must mean—perhaps above everything else—the healing of the *tragedy* (and not just the consequences of human sin) that accompanies a universe *in via*. Especially in view of Darwin's portrait of the life-story, one through which we can now survey previously unknown epochs of life's tragic suffering and struggle preceding our own emergence, it would be callous indeed on the part of theologians to perpetuate the one-sidedly anthropocentric and retributive notions of pain and redemption that used to fit so comfortably into pre-evolutionary pictures of the world.

Imagine, once again, that the created universe *in illo tempore* had possessed the birthmarks of an original perfection. Then the evil that we experience here and now would have to be attributed to a contingent occurrence or perhaps a "culprit" that somehow spoiled the primordial creation, causing it to lose its original integrity. This, of course, is how evil and suffering have often been accounted for by religions, including Christianity. Accordingly, any "history of salvation" will consist *essentially* of a drama of "restoring" the original state of affairs. And although the *re*-storation may be garnished at its margins with epicycles of novelty, it will be essentially a *re*-establishment of the assumed fullness that once was and now has dissolved.

The central biblical intuition, of course, is that redemption means much more than the restoration of a primordial fullness of being. But the influence of Western philosophy on soteriology (the theology of redemption) has caused theologians to subordinate the expectation of novelty and surprise at the fulfillment of God's promises to that of the recovery of a primal perfection of being. This is why evolution is potentially such good news for theology. Paying close attention to evolution no longer allows us even to imagine that the universe was at one time—in a remote historical or mythic past—an integrally constituted state of being. As we look back into the universe's distant evolutionary past with Teilhard, we see only multiplicity fading into nothingness, accompanied at its birth by an almost imperceptible straining toward a future unity that still remains to be fully accomplished.

Thus, a scientifically informed understanding of redemption may no longer plausibly make themes of restoration or recovery dominant. The remote cosmic past, after all, consists of what Teilhard calls "the multiple," that is, the fragmentary monads not yet brought into relationship or unity. It would be absurd, therefore, to seek the restoration of a chonologically primordial state of material dispersal. The notion of an unfinished universe still coming into being, on the other hand, opens up the horizon of a new or unprecedented future. The prospect of truly new creation also foreshadows an end to the expiation that feeds upon a misleading sense of loss. After the emergence of evolutionary biology and cosmology, the whole notion of the future begs as never before to be brought more integrally into our ontologies as well as our cosmologies. Any notion of *esse* (timeless being) as the consummation of the vast cosmos must be qualified by the theme of being's essential futurity. Being must in some way mean the still-to-come. *Esse est advenire.* In its depths, nature is promise.

Is Tillich's Theology Adequate to Evolution?

How well then does Tillich's theology function as a context for understanding and appreciating the reality of evolution broadly speaking? We must ask here especially about Tillich's notion of redemption as New Being. Unfortunately, even Tillich, in spite of his awareness of the biblical theme of new creation, embeds his cosmic soteriology and eschatology in a conceptuality and terminology of "*re*-storation." This theme benumbs the power of his notion of New Being with suggestions of repetition. Certainly Tillich goes far beyond classical theology in taking us toward the metaphysics of the future that the logic of evolution requires. His interpretation of redemption as the coming of the New Being is philosophically rich, and it leads toward a theology that can at last take evolution seriously. But does it go far enough? Open to New Being though his system of theology is, has it fully absorbed the impact of Darwin and others who have introduced us to evolution?[22] Tillich, as I mentioned earlier, was suspicious of Teilhard's apparently progressivist optimism. But beneath this complaint lies a much deeper disagreement, one that places in question whether Tillich's thought can, after all, give us our "God for evolution," and whether his thought can move us forcefully beyond romantic nostalgia to the fullness of a hope proportionate to evolution.

Tillich distinguishes the actual state of estranged existence from what he refers to as "essential" being. Essential being is an idealized unity of all beings with God, the depth and "ground" of their being. But the Tillichian location of "the essential" in terms of a metaphysics of *esse* is in tension with Teilhard's sense of the inadequacy to evolution of any theological system that thinks of the divine in terms only of a philosophical notion of "being." Both Tillich and Teilhard interpret our ambiguous existence as an existential estrangement from the "essential." But where the comparison between them becomes most important—at least as far as the question of God and evolution is concerned—is in their respective ways of understanding just how and where "the essential" is to be located with respect to the actual or existential state of finite beings. It is on this point that I believe we can begin to notice a considerable divergence of one religious thinker from the other.

For Tillich, existence erupts as the *separation* from a primordial wholeness of being, from an undifferentiated "dreaming innocence."[23] Implied here are images of loss that can only be redressed by the idea of *re*-union with the primordial Ground of being. Tillich's ontological way of putting things is likely, in spite of his attempts to highlight the newness of being in redemption, to subordinate the novelty in creation and evolution to the motif of restoration. For even though his thought tries to introduce us to New Being, it is still in terms of the notion of "being" that he articulates the idea of newness. The New Being, after all, is defined as "essential being under the conditions of existence."[24] This way of putting things is unable to prevent us from thinking and imagining essential being in pre-evolutionary terms as an eternal sameness that resides somewhere other than in the dimension of the unprecedented,

still-not-yet future toward which a sense of evolution now turns our expectations. In Tillich's thought, as in the classical metaphysics of pre-evolutionary
theology, the futurity of being is still subordinated to the idea of an eternal
presence of being. For Teilhard, on the other hand, Tillich's somewhat Platonic view of things implies that nothing truly new can ever get accomplished in the world's own historical unfolding, since the fullness of being is
portrayed as already realized in an eternal present. Such a picture of things, as
Teilhard might put it, would only "clip the wings of hope."

For Teilhard, the fullness of being is what awaits at the end of a *cosmic* journey, not something that lurks either in an eternal present or in some misty
Urzeit (primordial time). In a sense, we can say that the universe is not yet, or
that it not yet *is*. Its being awaits it. The foundation of things is not so much a
"ground" of being sustaining from beneath—although this idea is partially illuminating—as it is a power of attraction toward what lies up ahead. "The
universe," Teilhard says, "is organically resting on . . . the future as its sole
support. . . ."25 This suggestive way of locating ultimate reality arouses a religious imagery quite different from Tillich's notion of God as the depth and
ground of being, or as the *Eternal Now*. The gravitational undertow of Tillich's
powerful metaphor of "ground"—together with his other earthy images of
"depth" and "abyss"—may have the disadvantage of pulling our theological
reflections toward a soteriology of return to what already is. Tillich's
metaphors of God as ground, depth and abyss do respond to Teilhard's concern that theology no longer locate the divine exclusively in the arena of the
"up above," but the same images may also fail sufficiently to open up for religious thought the horizon of the future as the appropriate domain of redemption and the fullness of being. In a sense, Teilhard is inviting us now to dig
deeper than "depth" in our endless search for metaphors of the divine.

Or, if we still wish to use Tillich's terminology, we must emphasize once
again that nature in its ultimate depths consists essentially of promise. Moreover, in a world not yet fully finished, it is important for theology still to acknowledge with Tillich that the actual condition of finite existing beings is
indeed that of estrangement from their true being. But the being from which
they are "estranged" must be, at least in the light of evolution, in some sense
not-yet-being, being that arrives from up ahead, *ab ante,* and not only a
depth and ground to which estranged beings eventually sink back. Perhaps
Tillich would agree with much of what Teilhard is haltingly attempting to
say about the future as the world's foundation, but his ontology places exces-
sively rigid constraints on what we can affirm and hope as far as the world's
future is concerned. There remains in Tillich's thought a spirit of tragic resignation that is hard to locate in terms either of evolution or biblical eschatol-

ogy. The New Being, an otherwise felicitous idea, is still portrayed as a futureless plenitude that enters only *vertically* into the context of our present estrangement. Consoling as such a conception may be, it still bears the weight of metaphysical traditions innocent of evolution and at least to some extent resistant to the biblical motif of promise.

Tillich's presentation of Christ as the New Being does indeed give an enormous breadth to redemption, and in this respect his theology goes a long way toward meeting the requirements of a theology of evolution. However, although Teilhard would be appreciative of Tillich's broadening of the scheme of redemption, he would still wonder whether the philosophical notion of "being," even when qualified by the adjective "new," is itself adequate to the reality of evolution. To Teilhard, it is less the concept of *esse* than those of *fieri* (becoming) and *uniri* (being brought into unity in the future) that a theology attuned to a post-Darwinian world requires.[26] Even his earliest reflections on God and evolution prefigured Teilhard's life-long disillusionment with the Thomistic metaphysics of being, beginning at a time when it was extremely audacious for a Catholic thinker to express such disenchantment. But the young Teilhard already realized that evolution requires nothing less than a revolution in metaphysics. It seems that evolution still awaits such a metaphysics, and it is doubtful that Tillich's theological system is revolutionary enough to accommodate this requirement.

For Teilhard, as I have noted, "the essential" from which the universe—including humans as part of it—is separated is the Future, the Up Ahead, the God-Omega who creates the world *ab ante* rather than *a retro*, the God who saves the world not so much by returning it to an Eternal Now, but by being the world's Future. The *essential*, therefore, is not for Teilhard an original fullness of being from which the universe has become estranged, but instead a yet unrealized ideal (God's vision or God's dream, perhaps) toward which the multiple is forever being summoned. In this eschatological setting, the universe can be thought of as essentially more of a promise than a sacrament. Correspondingly, nature may be seen as anticipative rather than simply revelatory of the ultimate Future on which it leans. If we still view the cosmos as participative being, then what it participates in is not a past or present plenitude, but a future pleroma (fullness). And its present ambiguity is of the sort that we might associate with a promise still unfulfilled, rather than the seductive traces of a primordial wholeness that has now vanished into the past. Evolutionary cosmology, in other words, invites us to complete the biblical vision of a life based on hope for surprise rather than allowing us to wax nostalgic for what we imagine once was.

In keeping with Teilhard's futurist location of the foundation of the world's being, our own existence and action can now also be thought of as possessing an intrinsic meaning and an effectuality that alternative metaphysical conceptions of the universe, including Tillich's, do not permit. Much more clearly than we ever realized before we learned that the cosmos is a genesis, we may now envisage human action as contributing to the creation of something that never was. Teilhard was especially concerned to develop a vision of the world in which young and old alike could feel genuinely that their lives and actions truly matter, that their existence is not just "killing time" but potentially contributing to the creation of a cosmos. Evolution provides the context for such a vision.

Evolutionary science, therefore, is both a disturbance and a stimulus to theology because it logically requires that we think of paradise (or "the essential") as something more than a condition to be restored or returned to after our having been exiled from it. Instead of nostalgia for a lost innocence, evolution allows a posture of genuine hope that justifies action in the world. Our existence here is more than just spinning our wheels as we await an alleged reunion with Being-Itself. The true "courage to be" is not therefore simply a Tillichian taking nonbeing into ourselves, but an orienting of our lives toward the Future Unity that is the world's true foundation. Concretely, this would mean "building the Earth" in a responsible manner as our small part in the ongoing creation of the cosmos. After Darwin, the power of being is the power of the future, and we affirm ourselves courageously by orienting ourselves toward this future in spite of the pull of the multiple that defines the past.

From the perspective of a theology of evolution, once the universe arrives at conscious self-awareness, it hopefully anticipates *arriving at* the being from which it is deprived, rather than merely longing for a reunion with it. In this setting, what Tillich refers to as our "existential anxiety" is not simply the awareness of our possible nonbeing, an awareness that turns us toward courageous participation in the "Power of Being."[27] Even more, it is the disequilibrium that inevitably accompanies our being part of a universe still-in-the-making, a universe whose inevitable ambiguity turns us toward what we might call the Power of the Future.[28] Pathological forms of anxiety (which Tillich distinguishes from "normal" or existential anxiety) could then be understood as unrealistically premature flights into nostalgic illusions of paradisal perfection cleansed of temporal process—far removed from the hopeful and enlivening disequilibrium of living in an unfinished universe.

Sin or moral evil, moreover, would be understood here as the consequence of our free submission to the pull of the multiple, to the fragmentary past of a universe whose perfected state of ultimate unity in God-Omega has yet to be realized. In an unfinished universe, we humans remain accomplices of evil, of course—even horrendous forms of evil. But our complicity in evil may now be interpreted less in terms of a hypothesized break from primordial innocence than as our systematic refusal to participate in the ongoing creation of the world. The creative process is one in which the multiple, the originally dispersed elements of an emerging cosmos, are now being drawn toward unity. Our own sin, then, is at least in some measure that of spurning the invitation to participate in the holy adventure of the universe's being drawn toward the future (the God-Omega) upon which it leans as its foundation. Here sin means our acquiescence in and fascination with the lure of the multiple. It is our resistance to the call of "being more," our deliberate turning away from participation in what is still coming into being.

Thus, there is ample room in this scheme for us to respect the traditional emphasis on our own personal responsibility for evil. But we can affirm our guilt in a way that no longer requires expiation or retribution so much as renewed hope to energize our ethical aspirations. Moreover, in an evolutionary context, we might wish to go beyond Teilhard and suggest that "original" sin is not simply the reverse side of an unfinished universe in process of being created. It is also the aggregation in human history and culture of all of the effects of our habitual refusal to take our appropriate place in the ongoing creation of the universe. It is this kind of corruption—and not the defilement of an allegedly original cosmic perfection—by which each of us is "stained." The lure of the "multiple" is inevitable in an unfinished universe, but there is also the cumulative history of our own species' "Fall" backward toward disunity. And yet, past evolutionary achievement also provides a reason for trusting that the forces of unity can emerge victorious in the future. Even if the universe eventually succumbs to entropy, as Teilhard predicted it would, there is something of great significance—he called it spirit—that is now coming to birth in evolution and that can escape absolute loss by being taken permanently into the life of God.

13

Darwin, God
and the Search for
Extraterrestrial Intelligence

To those convinced of Darwinism's extraordinary explanatory power, the temptation is nearly irresistible to apply its principles beyond our terrestrial sphere. If life exists elsewhere in the universe, would it not be subject to the canons of differential reproduction and natural selection that have driven the life-process here on Earth? And if life exists elsewhere, would it not increasingly complexify over time, perhaps to the point of becoming conscious? The underlying blend of contingency, law and deep time that grounds the narrative character of nature, and thus renders biological evolution possible on our planet, must surely permeate the entire Big Bang universe. And now that scientists are discovering other planetary systems in deep space, it seems quite natural that they would become increasingly optimistic that life, or something like what we call life, exists at least somewhere beyond the confines of Earth.

Of course, evolutionary materialists still view even life here on our own planet as having been an extremely improbable event. Life seems to have just popped up accidentally in an essentially lifeless and mindless universe. But many experts in the scientific community today are perceptibly shifting toward another view, namely, that the universe has a physical structure inclined almost inevitably to explode into life at some point(s) in its history. The cosmos, it turns out, is not essentially lifeless. And for all we know, the same universe that has generously let life loose here on Earth is extravagantly open to the evolution of life and intelligence in extraterrestrial domains as well. So far, we have no direct evidence of any such occurrence, and some skeptics insist that if there were intelligent beings elsewhere, we would have heard from them by now. But today, not least because of a growing confidence in the universal, creative and complexifying power of Darwinian processes, others argue that the prospect of our finding extraterrestrial life and intelligence seems more promising than ever before.

What, though, would be the religious and theological reactions to such a revelation, and particularly to the discovery of extraterrestrial intelligence (ETI)? Not necessarily absolute surprise. Religious thinkers have long entertained the idea of the existence of extraterrestrial intelligent "worlds," not only in "heaven" amidst the angelic hosts, but also in "the heavens" of the physical cosmos as well.[1] Nevertheless, the actual discovery of an extraterrestrial world of living and intelligent beings would, to say the least, be a most interesting new stimulus not only to evolutionary biology but also to a post-Darwinian theology. Obviously, given the distances that separate our planet from any other possible intelligent civilizations, it is doubtful that much of an encounter is going to take place for a long time. And if and when it does, communication along the electromagnetic spectrum will be maddeningly slow. Even in the neighborhood of our own galaxy, whole lifetimes would go by while initial greetings are being exchanged.

Still, even the mere entertainment of the prospect of eventual "contact"—whether this ever actually occurs or not—is a wholesomely expansive exercise for a theology interested in cosmic and biological evolution. It seems appropriate even now for religious thought to ponder some of the questions that an encounter with other worlds of living and intelligent beings would raise. What would happen to the notion of God? Would the sense of our own significance in the universe be diminished? What would be the implications for those earthly faith traditions that identify themselves as specially chosen, as people set apart (the question of religious particularity)? Would our own religions and theologies make any sense to intelligent beings from other planets? What implications would the discovery of other intelligent beings have for the large question of cosmic purpose? And can the world of religious thought even now perhaps provide us with conceptual frameworks that would not only be hospitable to, but also enthusiastic about, the prospect of ETI? I shall say only a few words in response to the first three of these questions, and then devote more attention to the others.

1. What Would Happen to the Idea of God?

At the very least, an encounter with alternative intelligent worlds would be one more in a series of occasions that modern cosmology has provided for theology to move beneath surface impressions and deepen its sense of nature and God. Contact with ETs would provide an exceptional opportunity for theology to widen and deepen its understanding of divine creativity. From a theological point of view, any intelligent provinces beyond Earth would be grounded in the same creative principle that our theistic creeds point to as the source of all things "visible and invisible." Radical monotheism believes that all beings, all forms of life, all peoples and all worlds have a common origin and destiny in a God who creates and encompasses everything. And monotheism, as H. Richard Niebuhr has carefully argued, is still the surest ground we have for embracing that which at first seems alien.[2] To learn to love what God loves is the vocation and the constant struggle to which our greatest religious prophets have already called us. Of course, tribalism and ethnic hatred, as well as disregard for nonhuman forms of life, still tragically persist here on Earth. But perhaps this is because radical monotheism, which emphasizes the ontological unity underlying all diversity, still has only a tenuous hold on human awareness, including that of avowed theists. Many people do not yet *really* believe in the ultimate unity of all beings even here in our own place, let alone elsewhere. And so, the discovery of other intelligent worlds would be a wholesome new challenge to radicalize our sense of the unifying principle that we associate with the ultimate ground and depth of nature.

Viewed theologically, all galaxies (and even all universes, if others exist) are rooted in an ultimate unity of being; so our travels could never bring us into an encounter with anything completely alien to us. *Nihil alienum.* Theology's relevance to the search for extraterrestrial intelligence (SETI) lies most fundamentally in its conviction that all possible worlds have a common origin and depth in the oneness of God. And by virtue of the omnipresence of the one God, we too would have an extended home in all the possible worlds to which we might eventually travel.[3]

Contact with extraterrestrial organisms and minds could also enlarge our appreciation of God's love of diversity. Divine creativity tends by its very nature to unfold in an unlimited plurality of ways, and in possibly a multitude of "worlds." In the *Summa Theologiae,* St. Thomas Aquinas poses the childlike question as to why God would create so many different kinds of beings. His answer: so that what is lacking in one thing, as far as expressing the infinity of God is concerned, can be supplied by something else, and what is lacking in that by something else, etc.[4] Diversity in creation and evolution, in other words, occurs precisely because of the nature of an infinitely re-sourceful creativity. A basic theistic belief is that the reality of God has al-ready become partially manifested in the extravagant multiplicity of non-living and living beings on our own planet. This belief should already have prepared the religious mind to anticipate a disclosure of rich diversity elsewhere—and in ways completely unfamiliar to us now. Perhaps, then, there is no better way for religious people to prepare themselves for "exo-theology" than by developing here and now an "eco-theology" deeply appre-ciative of the revelatory richness of the variety of life forms that have evolved here on Earth.[5]

2. The Question of Human Importance

Would knowledge of the existence of more intelligent, and perhaps more eth-ically developed, beings elsewhere perhaps undermine our self-esteem, thus making our religions seem woefully provincial and unduly anthropocentric in convincing their devotees that they are somehow special? What would be the theological implications of an extended "Copernican principle," one whereby the Earth's intelligent occupants would be shown to be just one more "aver-age" population in a universe of countless intelligent worlds?

In the first place, we should emphasize that, after Darwin, it is biologically inconceivable that there would be other *humans* anywhere else in the uni-verse; so our uniqueness as a species is virtually guaranteed in any case. The particularities of Earth history and the contours of life's adaptive landscapes here could not have been simulated exactly on other planets. "Of men else-where, and beyond, there will be none forever," wrote the naturalist Loren Eiseley. Natural selection has brought us about along roads that can "never be retraced" biologically.[6] Second, and more to the point, however, accord-ing to the great teachers in Islam, Hinduism, Judaism, Christianity, Bud-dhism and other religious traditions, we express our own unique human dignity and value not by looking for signs of our mental or ethical superior-ity over other forms of life but by following a path of service and even self-sacrifice with respect to the whole of life, wherever it may be present. Authentic existence, as Buddhism especially makes clear, consists of compas-sion for other kinds of life rather than competition with them. The meaning of our lives according to many religious traditions consists of the opportu-nity to surrender to something larger, more important and more enduring than ourselves. Thus, it is inconceivable that the eventual encounter even with beings that may in some ways be our superiors would ever render such instruction obsolete.

3. The Question of Religious Particularity

Perhaps, though, contact with ETI would be the occasion of heightened anguish to members of those faith communities that believe they have received special election or revelation from God. Wouldn't an encounter with other forms of personal, free and responsible beings put considerable strain on traditions that claim the status of being "a people set apart"?

The claim of special election might possibly undergo some stress after "contact." One response, of course, would be to treat ETs as potential subjects of conversion, in which case contact would simply provide new fields for missionary activity. Mary Russell conjures up such an approach—together with its potential hazards—in her imaginative science fiction novel *The Sparrow.*[7] However, at least in the context of contemporary Christian theology, the idea of special election is even now being divested of the connotations of rank and privilege that it may once have suggested. Election, the sense of being specially called or set apart by God, is increasingly understood as a vocation to serve the cause of life rather than extricating a people from its fundamental relatedness to the entire cosmic community of beings. It is worth recalling here also that, according to St. Paul, Jesus' own sense of being called by God did not prevent him from taking on the status of a "slave" (Philippians 2:5–11) and of being subjected to the most humiliating death available during his time, that of crucifixion. In the same spirit, solidarity with Christ today would still mean, at least if it follows St. Paul's instruction, belonging to one whose own life was itself a vulnerable openness to the estranged and alien, to what does not yet belong. After contact, "belonging to Christ" could then readily be thought of as requiring a more radical inclusiveness than ever before, one open to and supportive of the diversity of many intelligent worlds. Such an eventuality, once again, would not require an abandonment but instead a fuller appropriation of the central teaching and practice of Christian faith.

Most other religious traditions could also make similar adjustments. Among the teachings of the various religions there is the ideal of embracing rather than eliminating otherness and diversity. This is an ideal that beckons and challenges, no matter how much it has been ignored in practice. The history of religion is filled with failures to heed this calling, but in fact the encounter of various faiths with what they initially perceived to be alien cultures and practices has often led to the enrichment rather than the dissolution of their distinctive pathways. One may surmise that in the far distant future, if interstellar travel ever occurs, our terrestrial religions' contact with even more alien "cultures" will provide fertile opportunities for religious evolution.

4. Are Extraterrestrials Religious?

This brings us, however, to a fourth and perhaps more interesting question for religious thought as it hypothetically prepares for contact. Would the "Others"—I prefer this name rather than "aliens"—be able to make any sense at all of our own religious life and thought? And should we expect that other intelligent beings would practice anything like what we call religion, a trait that would render them deeply comparable to us? Let us put aside once again the sobering probability that, because of the enormous distances they would have to traverse, any messages flowing back and forth at the speed of light would not allow many exchanges in the course of a single human life-time, nor would they extend very far beyond our own cosmic neighborhood. Instead, let us suppose that we shall eventually be given the opportunity for prolonged conversation with other beings that impress us as being both alive and intelligent. What must their own kind of life and intelligence be like in order to allow us to share with them in a meaningful way our own deepest hopes, including ideas about "God" or "salvation"? What are some of the marks that other conceivable instances of intelligent life in this universe would have to possess in order for us to have an exchange with them about our own religious beliefs, and that might also open us up to an understanding of theirs, if they have any?

In contemplating such questions, we are reminded of just how extensively, in the way of both content and expression, our earthly religions borrow from the unique features of the terrestrial environment. We may assume therefore that religions in any other worlds would be idiosyncratically shaped by their own planetary surroundings. Our own most persistent religious metaphors are inseparable from the experience of *Earth's* own characteristics: rotation from day to night, and exposure to sun and moon; our planet's deserts, oceans, rivers and streams, clouds, rain, storms and whirlwinds, grass and trees, blood and breath, soil and sexuality, maternity, paternity, sisterhood and brotherhood. Think of how prominently our experience of trees, to give just one example, shapes religious imagery: the tree of life, the tree of "the knowledge of good and evil," the Bodhi tree, the tree of the cross, the cedars of Lebanon, etc. Likewise, we should note that the very earthy occurrence of fertility—for instance, when inert seeds miraculously sprout to life out of topsoil—has given us the highly significant religious metaphor of "resurrection." And the notion of "spirit," now ironically employed to refer to what is unearthly, comes from the Latin *spiritus* (in Hebrew *ruach,* and in Greek *pneuma*), a notion that originally meant the "breath of life" and that, as we now realize, requires the existence of Earth's enlivening atmosphere as its physical basis. Imagine what our religions would be like, Thomas Berry says, if we lived on something like a lunar landscape.[8]

Wouldn't extraterrestrial evolution and ecological systems breed other extraordinary blendings of land, life and religious longing? And is it not likely that we would have a very difficult time connecting with them? Difficult, perhaps, though not impossible. Yet in order to conceive of how we might be able to engage in anything like theological conversation with cosmic Others we need first to clarify our terms. What exactly do we mean by *life*, by *intelligence* and by *religion*?

First, *life*. What is it that allows us to identify living beings as "alive" at all, and thus to distinguish them from nonliving things or processes? Among many possible answers to this question, what stands out is that living beings share with us humans the trait of *striving* to achieve some goal, and therefore the possibility of failing or succeeding.[9] If an entity were not recognizable as a kind of striving, or of struggling against limits of some kind, and therefore as capable of succeeding or failing in the effort, we would not properly call it living. The great Jewish philosopher Hans Jonas remarks that even the most primitive instances of metabolism are in some rudimentary way constantly "striving" to overcome the threat of being dissolved into their inanimate surroundings.[10] We observe this striving less obviously in plants, fungi and insects than in reptiles, mammals and humans, but, as long as there is even the remotest possibility of success or failure, there is life.[11]

Scientist and philosopher Michael Polanyi argues that we humans recognize the distinctive features of life primarily through a *personal* knowledge, one shaped by what he calls "the logic of achievement."[12] Living beings, as we noted in Chapter 8, are capable of "achieving" in a way that does not apply to purely physical routines or chemical reactions. We spontaneously realize that all modes of life, ours included, can in many ways either "succeed" or "fail," in a way that nonliving processes logically cannot. I would suggest, then, that human persons are interested in the possibility of life elsewhere in the universe in great measure because deep down we want to know whether there are other striving, struggling beings around anywhere. And if we ever encountered any, we would feel a kind of connatural relatedness with them, a connection that we do not have with inanimate things. If nonterrestrial forms of life exist, perhaps they too are part of a larger history of life and a Darwinian struggle for existence.

So if we ever encountered life on other worlds, we would call it alive (regardless of its chemical make-up) only if we recognized—through what Polanyi calls a "personal" rather than objectifying knowledge—that it participates with us in a kind of striving that risks the possibility of failure. Of course, in our search for life elsewhere, we would also look for qualities like the transgenerational sharing of information we find in the genetic flow of life here on Earth. We would look for open, self-organizing systems that pump energy out of their environment and so maintain themselves at a high level of complexity far from thermodynamic equilibrium. But mostly we would be looking for instances of exquisite organismic fragility, beings that need to "exert" themselves in some degree even to maintain their biological identity against the constant threat of being dissolved into their inanimate surroundings. Life elsewhere as well as here, in other words, could be identified as such only if it conforms in some degree to the logic of achievement. How this logic of life bears on the question of ETI and religion will become clear shortly.

Next, though, what do we mean by *intelligent* life, that special set of traits for which SETI professes to be looking, and which we confidently think we could identify if we ever stumbled across it? First of all, if we find intelligent *life*, then it must be manifested in some sort of *striving*; and, second, if it is *intelligent* life, it must be the kind of striving that we associate in ourselves with *a desire to know*. If the desire to know is absent, then there may be life—sentient and even conscious life—but not intelligent life. Any being that is not somehow striving is not alive; and any being whose striving does not include the search for insight and knowledge is not intelligent, at least in the sense that we humans minimally understand the term. SETI already tacitly assumes such a notion of intelligent striving, of a desire to understand and know, when it scans the heavens for electromagnetic signals that only a technologically sophisticated and similarly insight-seeking and truth-desiring source is sending out.

Finally, what do we mean by *religion?* Building on arguments set forth in Chapters 10 and 11, let us once again understand by "religion" a specific kind of striving also. Before religion is anything else, it is a manifestation of *life*, and of a specific kind of intelligent life, striving toward a goal. Underneath all of its extravagant symbolic, ritualistic, doctrinal, ethical and institutional foliage, religion is an expression of life, of intelligent life, striving and exploring. Religion, I would go so far as to suggest, is intelligent life at perhaps its most intense level of striving. The whole terrestrial religious endeavor may be thought of as a kind of "route finding," a quest for pathways that promise to carry us through the most intractable limits on life.[13] Even from our perch here on Earth, therefore, can we not identify at least some of the most severe limits that *all* other forms of intelligent life would inevitably have to face along with us? And in identifying these limits, would we not be placing ourselves and the Others within a common (hermeneutical) circle, one that would allow meaningful conversation with them in spite of broad ecological and linguistic differences?

I think that, *if* they possess anything like what we call intelligent life, we can reasonably expect to discover that extraterrestrials would at least have the capacity for a religious mode of venturing. Since any possible Others we shall ever encounter will be inhabitants of the same Big Bang universe that we belong to, the general features of this cosmos as made known to us by our terrestrial science will presumably also apply to their own situation. We must expect to find, then, that any living, sentient and intelligent beings will be subject to the transience and perishability characteristic of all things positioned on the slopes of entropy. They would be subject to the physical forces that break orderly or complex arrangements down into disordered and simple ones. They too would be subject to selective evolutionary pressures. They, like us, would be subject to the threat of failure, and eventually nonbeing, that every living, finite being has to confront.

We may conclude, then, that since all living and intelligent beings would experience essentially the same physical limits on life that we do, a conversation about religious route finding through these limits could conceivably occur. Quite likely the Others, if they are truly striving centers, would also be in search of ways to transcend the limits on their own particular forms of life. If they are not striving, and therefore risking failure, then they would not qualify as being alive. And if they are truly intelligent, they would have an awareness of their possible nonbeing. They might even have, in other words, something like what Paul Tillich calls "existential anxiety." Existential anxiety, the awareness of finitude, is what drives intelligent life to find a courage that can conquer the threat of nonbeing.[14] In our human experience, it is the quest for courage in the face of possible nonbeing that leads many of us to seek the foundational support of religious faith. It is what leads in some cases to the idea of "God" as the depth and ground of our courage to continue life's striving in the face of fate, death, guilt and the threat of meaninglessness.[15] If any Others "out there" are truly alive and intelligent, it would not be surprising that they too need courage. If so, they would be no less potentially religious than we are.

5. Does SETI Have Implications for the
Question of Cosmic Purpose After Darwin?

Whether the universe has any "point" or "purpose" to it is a question that religions must always be concerned about, perhaps above all others. It is a question that for many religious people has become especially intense after Darwin. Religions can put up with all kinds of particular scientific ideas so long as these ideas do not contradict the sense that the whole scheme of things is meaningful. Religions can survive the news that Earth is not the center of the universe, that humans are descended from simian ancestors and that the universe is fifteen billion years old. What they cannot abide, however, is the conviction that the universe and life are pointless.[16]

It is worth asking, therefore, how SETI might bear upon the question of cosmic purpose and, by implication, on the meaning and mission of our own lives. Generally speaking, "purpose" means the realizing of a value. So, to say that the universe has a purpose would be to imply that it is oriented toward the implementation of something intrinsically good. Cosmic purpose does not have to imply a particular *finis* or end. Purpose is not identical with a predetermined plan or design, both of which, as Bergson points out, tend to close off the future in a suffocating way.[17] All we need in order to affirm cosmic purpose is an awareness that something of undeniable importance is going on in the universe, and that it is doing so in a way that is tied essentially, and not just accidentally, to the whole of the cosmos.

Of course, in an unfinished universe, as we have already admitted, there will by definition always be ambiguity. And so here and now we will look both intensely and tentatively for whatever indicators we can find to support our own suspicions, whether these be pessimistic or hopeful, about the ultimate character of the universe. Accordingly, it would seem relevant to our understanding of what this universe is all about that we try to find out whether intelligent life is abundantly distributed throughout the cosmos, or, for that matter, whether it exists only here on Earth. Certainly the existence of ETI would force us to reexamine the claim by evolutionary materialists that life and intelligence are the results of utterly improbable, purely random statistical aberrations in an overwhelmingly lifeless and mindless universe. A universe that features multiple instances of intelligent life would lead us to question the influential modern assumption that the physical universe is *essentially* mindless.

However, it is never good form, theologically speaking, to make the credibility of a religious sense of meaning or cosmic purpose contingent upon the vicissitudes of scientific exploration. And so the discovery of ETI could not be for theology a deciding factor on a question of such vital religious importance as that of cosmic purpose. Anyway, scientific thinkers already inclined to think of the universe as "pointless" or essentially mindless would persist in looking for ways to understand and explain even an abundant distribution of intelligent life in the cosmos as no less the consequence of blind chance and impersonal physical laws than life and intelligence on Earth now seem to them to be. For this reason, then, any theological reflections must be very cautious about SETI's prospects for helping us with the big question of cosmic purpose. It is theologically more prudent to deal more directly with the question of what our own intelligence, even if it turns out to be the sole instance of it in the cosmos, might imply as far as the character, and possible purposiveness, of the universe is concerned.

As I noted above, any process that moves incrementally toward the establishment or intensification of intrinsic value could be called purposeful. If so, then might we not plausibly claim that a universe that proceeds over the course of its history—however long and meandering the evolutionary journey through time may be—toward the establishment of intelligent life is a purposeful one? Even if intelligent life (as I have been understanding it in this chapter) manifests itself only in one of many universes on one of innumerable planets, it is still a property of the cosmos as a whole. The existence of our own intelligent life is, I believe, already sufficient of itself to render the universe meaningful, and the discovery of ETI would not add anything qualitatively new to this judgment.

With the help of physics and astrophysics we now understand how intricately the biological evolution of our own intelligence is connected to a fifteen-billion-year-old cosmic story, and to the physical features of this universe, features established from the very earliest microseconds of cosmic time. And even if ours is only one of many universes, there are still very subtle physical principles, and perhaps even historical connections, that tie them all together. Moreover, they all have *being*, and in having being there is a deep ontological unity that binds them one to the other. And so even one instance of intelligent life in such an array would be intertwined ontologically and historically with the totality.[18]

In light of the inseparability of our minds from the cosmos, to assert that the universe—or totality of universes—is inherently purposeless seems arbitrary at best. In view of the spontaneous (and undeniable) valuation you give to your own mind, on the one hand, and our new scientific understanding of the cosmic process constitutive of your intelligence, on the other, you cannot but wonder about the coherence of cavalier claims that the universe is inherently pointless. To argue in complete seriousness that the cosmos is ultimately unintelligible, or even to doubt the intelligibility of our patently mind-bearing universe, would seem to sabotage the very mind that is making such an assertion. The point to be made here with respect to SETI and cosmic purpose is that the undeniable existence of intelligent life on Earth, whether life exists elsewhere or not, may already tell us something about the *essential* nature of the whole universe. We do not need to have any other instances of intelligent life than our own in order to make a coherent argument that we inhabit an essentially mind-bearing universe.

However, even aside from the point I have just made, SETI may eventually have some implications for the question of cosmic purpose. Let us recall that the modern loss of a sense of cosmic purpose is ultimately rooted in the fictitious expulsion of mind from nature—by Cartesian dualism, classical mechanism and modern scientism. It is not from science itself, but from the assumed mindlessness of nature, that the historically recent and culturally provincial idea arose that the cosmos, in its depths, is just mindless stuff and that the appearance of our own intelligence, therefore, is purely accidental. An essentially mindless universe would seem to be a purposeless one, but a universe in which intelligent life is an essential rather than accidental property could hardly be called purposeless. Therefore, any future discovery that instances of intelligence occur abundantly in the universe could not help but place the burden of proof upon those who see no intrinsic connection between mind and the rest of nature.

6. Available Frameworks for a "Theology After Contact"

Theology is typically more responsive than predictive. Of course, a few prophetic voices can read the signs of the times and issue appropriate warnings about what is to come. But by and large religious thought, undertaken as it is by finite and shortsighted humans, seldom accurately anticipates, much less prepares us for, the crises that occur in connection with unprecedented events in human history or new discoveries in the realm of science. Indeed, most of the theological content of the dominant traditions comes from religion's reaction to crises rather than anticipation of them. So we cannot accurately predict here and now the actual shape theology would take if we ever do encounter ETI. Instead, we must await the event itself.

Still, I would suggest all too briefly here that the cosmic vision of Pierre Teilhard de Chardin as well as some ideas of the philosopher Alfred North Whitehead are already inherently open to being developed into a "theology after contact." Not the least of the reasons for their adaptability is that both religious thinkers have already enthusiastically embraced the evolutionary portrait of life as well as the notion that the entire universe is still in the process of being created. Although Teilhard reflected only occasionally on the possibility of ETI, keeping most of his speculation firmly anchored to our planet, the general thrust of his visionary writings is cosmic in scope. As such, the impetus toward increasing complexity and consciousness, so evident to Teilhard in his surveys of the history of life on Earth, could be a trend that is occurring throughout the cosmos. As we saw in the preceding chapter, according to this famous Jesuit evolutionist, the "point" or purpose of the universe has something to do with the emergence and intensification of "complexity-consciousness." As physical complexity increases in the universe, Teilhard claims, so does consciousness. But, he acknowledges, the cosmic evolution of consciousness is still far from being finished. Here on Earth the birth of a "noosphere," the complexification of consciousness now taking place on a planetary scale, is still in process. And, he admits, it is not inconceivable that parallel worlds of consciousness are evolving elsewhere.

Hence, it would not be very difficult for us to graft onto Teilhard's open-ended story of increasing complexity-consciousness other instances of intelligent life that we may eventually find, or that may find us. Religiously speaking, according to Teilhard, the whole universe is on an evolutionary journey into the mystery of God, while at the same time God humbly seeks to become increasingly incarnate in the universe. That this encounter would result in many planets that eventually burst forth into life, consciousness, freedom and finally even charity and worship, would not surprise any of those who find some plausibility in Teilhard's cosmic vision.[19]

Finally, Whitehead's vision of cosmic purpose is also expansive enough to accommodate the discovery of ETI. In Whitehead's mature thought, the purpose of the cosmos consists of its aim toward the intensification of beauty.[20] Since—at least for Whitehead—beauty is an intrinsic value, any process that leads toward its establishment could be called purposeful or "teleological," at least in a loose sense. "Beauty," in Whitehead's thought, means the "harmony of contrasts" or the "ordering of novelty," many diverse instances of which have appeared in the evolution of the cosmos and in the emergence of life, mind and culture in our terrestrial setting.

Intelligent life, however, is only one instance of cosmic beauty. We really have no idea of the many forms the cosmic aim toward bringing about beauty might assume within the totality of the universe. Perhaps, then, SETI has set its goals too narrowly for theology. What we call intelligent life might turn out to be too trivial a notion to capture what is already "out there," or the incalculable cosmic outcomes that may yet occur in the future of this unfinished universe. The notion of "beauty," however, is encompassing enough to anticipate a wide variety of cosmic evolutionary outcomes. As we explore the universe, we should ask not only about the meaning of intelligence, but also about what the existence of beauty implies as far as the essential character of the whole universe is concerned. It is clear that the universe has always been dissatisfied with the monotony of the status quo, and so it has produced innumerable instances of ordered novelty. Perhaps the aim toward beauty, then, is enough to endow the entire universe with purpose—and with a promise that provides a constant reason for hope.

Notes

Introduction

1. Alfred North Whitehead, *Science and the Modern World* (New York: The Free Press, 1967), 192.

2. Michael Ruse, *Can a Darwinian Be a Christian?* (Cambridge: Cambridge University Press, 2000), 77.

3. See, for example, Michael R. Rose, *Darwin's Spectre: Evolutionary Biology in the Modern World* (Princeton: Princeton University Press, 1998), 203–6.

4. Cited in Stillman Drake, *Discourses and Opinions of Galileo* (New York: Doubleday Anchor Books, 1957), 237–38.

5. See, for instance, my discussion of Frederick Crews in Chapter 9 below.

Chapter 1

1. Michael Ruse and Edward O. Wilson, "The Evolution of Ethics," in James Huchingson, ed., *Religion and the Natural Sciences* (New York: Harcourt Brace Jovanovich, 1993), 308–11.

2. Fuller development of this point and related bibliography are given in Chapter 8 below.

3. Not all Darwinian explanations of religion consider the gene to be the only or primary unit of selection. David Sloan Wilson in *Darwin's Cathedral: Evolution, Religion, and the Nature of Society* (Chicago: University of Chicago Press, 2002) has recently argued that religion, as a social organism, is adaptive at the group level as well as at the levels of the individual and the gene. Wilson's multi-level theory of selection, however, still leaves us with the question of whether he intends this expanded Darwinian understanding to be an ultimate and adequate explanation of religion.

4. See my discussion of Pascal Boyer in Chapter 8.

5. A good example of this view of art, poetry and religion as adaptive fiction is E. O. Wilson's book *Consilience: The Unity of Knowledge* (New York: Vintage Books, 1999).

6. See the attempt by evolutionist Michael R. Rose to explain religion in purely naturalist and Darwinian materialist terms: *Darwin's Spectre: Evolutionary Biology in the Modern World* (Princeton: Princeton University Press, 1998), 202–11.

7. The method known as "naturalizing" is exemplified throughout the important collection edited by Jerome H. Barkow, Leda Cosmides and John Tooby, *The Adapted Mind: Evolutionary Psychology and the Generation of Culture* (New York: Oxford University Press, 1992).

8. See Mircea Eliade, *Myth and Reality,* Willard R. Trask, trans. (New York: Harper Torchbooks, 1963).

9. See John Hick, *An Interpretation of Religion: Human Responses to the Transcendent* (New Haven: Yale University Press, 1989).

10. Sigmund Freud, *The Future of An Illusion*, W. D. Robson-Scott, trans. (New York: Doubleday Anchor Books, 1964), 83–92.

11. See Chapter 8 below for a more extended discussion and evaluation of this perspective.

12. "Dorothy, It's Really Oz," *Time*, Vol. 154 (August 23, 1999). See also Stephen Jay Gould, *Rocks of Ages: Science and Religion in the Fullness of Life* (New York: Ballantine, 1999).

13. Stephen Jay Gould, *Dinosaur in a Haystack* (New York: Harmony Books, 1995), p. 48.

14. Ibid.

15. Daniel C. Dennett, *Darwin's Dangerous Idea: Evolution and the Meaning of Life* (New York: Simon and Schuster, 1995); Richard Dawkins, *The Blind Watchmaker* (New York: W. W. Norton, 1986); *River Out of Eden* (New York: Basic Books, 1995); *Climbing Mount Improbable* (New York: W. W. Norton, 1996).

16. Stephen Jay Gould, *Ever Since Darwin* (New York: W. W. Norton, 1977), 12–13.

17. Ibid.

18. Gould, "Dorothy, It's Really Oz."

19. The works of E. O. Wilson, especially *Consilience*, also exemplify this seemingly benign, but in fact condescending and epistemologically self-contradictory, treatment of religion.

20. One of the outstanding examples of this approach is philosopher Loyal Rue's book *By the Grace of Guile: The Role of Deception in Natural History and Human Affairs* (New York: Oxford University Press, 1994). I will discuss Rue's work more extensively in Chapter 8.

21. Plato, *Phaedo*, in *The Last Days of Socrates: Euthyphro, The Apology, Crito, Phaedo,* Hugh Tredennick, trans. (New York: Penguin Books, 1969), 156–57.

Chapter 2

1. On the possibility of *reading* the universe, see Jacob Needleman, *A Sense of the Cosmos: The Encounter of Modern Science and Ancient Truth* (Garden City, N.Y.: Doubleday, 1975).

2. Here I am adapting an analogy set forth by E. F. Schumacher (following ideas of G. N. M. Tyrrell) in *A Guide for the Perplexed* (New York: Harper Colophon, 1978), 41–42.

3. Edward J. Larson and Larry Witham, "Scientists and Religion in America," *Scientific American*, Vol. 281 (September 1999), 90.

4. Gavin de Beer, for example, writes that "Darwin did two things: he showed that evolution was a fact contradicting scriptural legends of creation and that its cause, natural selection, was automatic *with no room for divine guidance or design*." *The New Encyclopaedia Britannica*, 15th ed. (London: Encyclopaedia Britannica, 1973–74); emphasis added. Geneticist Francisco J. Ayala similarly states that evolutionary science "excludes" the influence of God. He claims that after Darwin "natural selection *excluded* God as accounting for the obvious design of organisms." "Darwin's Revolution," in John H. Campbell and J. William Schopf, eds., *Creative Evolution?!* (Boston: Jones and Bartlett, 1994), 5; emphasis added. "Excluding" God is necessary methodologically for science, but the term is often used in a metaphysical sense also. Later I will show that science can be said to "exclude" theological explanation in a metaphysical sense only if one first assumes that only one "explanatory slot" or only one level of explanation is available to hu-

man inquiry. It is the essence of what I am calling "literalism" to flatten the work of understanding down to one explanatory level when in fact many levels or dimensions may be operative.

5. The academically neglected works of Ken Wilber are especially helpful in pointing out the need for *training* in order to have our consciousness opened wide enough to grasp the various dimensions of reality hidden from those who are untrained. See, for example, *The Marriage of Sense and Soul: Integrating Science and Religion* (New York: Random House, 1998).

6. Daniel Dennett, as interviewed in John Brockman, *The Third Culture* (New York: Touchstone Books, 1996), 187.

7. E. O. Wilson, *Consilience: The Unity of Knowledge* (New York: Knopf, 1998), 6.

8. Although physics is often thought of as more "fundamental" than other sciences, this adjective is very misleading, especially if "fundamental" is also taken to signify "deep," as it often is. In fact, physics itself is neither fundamental nor deep, but general and abstract. Perhaps it may also be called "elemental," but that is not the same as fundamental.

9. Steven Weinberg, *Dreams of a Final Theory* (New York: Pantheon, 1992), 241–61.

10. See especially Richard Dawkins, *River Out of Eden* (New York: Basic Books, 1995), 1–29.

11. Ullica Segerstråle, *Defenders of the Truth: The Battle for Science in the Sociology Debate and Beyond* (New York: Oxford University Press, 2000), 399–400.

12. Peter W. Atkins, *Creation Revisited* (New York: W. H. Freeman, 1992), 11–17.

13. Heinz Pagels, *Perfect Symmetry* (New York: Bantam Books, 1985), xv.

14. Francis Crick, *The Astonishing Hypothesis: The Scientific Search for the Soul* (New York: Charles Scribner's Sons, 1994), 3.

15. Joseph Wood Krutch, *The Modern Temper* (New York: Harcourt, Brace and Company, 1929), 6.

16. It is worth noting in passing that much so-called postmodern thought is now questioning just how "objective" even our scientific understanding can be, but most postmodern critics have so far themselves ironically remained thoroughly modern in their persistent negation of any inherent meaning to the cosmos.

17. Daniel Dennett interview in John Brockman, *The Third Culture* (New York: Touchstone, 1995), 187.

18. David Hull, "The God of the Galapagos," *Nature,* Vol. 352, 486.

Chapter 3

1. Paul Tillich, *The Shaking of the Foundations* (New York: Charles Scribner's Sons, 1948), 52–63.

2. Today, for example, this call from the depths is being felt by a number of thoughtful experts in the life sciences who, while not opposed to Darwinian or genes-eye readings of evolution, think there is room for yet deeper understandings of what is really going on in Earth's life-story. Those who oppose the reductionism of evolutionary materialism are likely to draw the accusation that they are reintroducing occult factors into biology. See David J. Depew and Bruce H. Weber, *Darwinism Evolving: Systems Dynamics and the Genealogy of Natural Selection* (Cambridge, Mass.: MIT Press, 1995); also Robert Wesson, *Beyond Natural Selection* (Cambridge, Mass.: MIT Press, 1991).

3. Tillich, 57.

4. See John Horgan, *The End of Science* (New York: Broadway Books, 1997).

5. Ursula Goodenough, *The Sacred Depths of Nature* (New York: Oxford University Press), 1998.

6. Ibid., 9–11.

7. See Connie Barlow, *Green Space, Green Time: The Way of Science* (New York: Copernicus, 1997).

8. See Steven Weinberg, *Dreams of a Final Theory* (New York: Pantheon, 1992), 244–45.

9. Albert Camus, *The Myth of Sisyphus and Other Essays,* Justin O'Brien, trans. (New York: Vintage Books, 1955); Bertrand Russell, *Religion and Science* (New York: Oxford University Press, 1961).

10. See Paul Tillich, *Theology of Culture*, Robert C. Kimball, ed. (New York: Oxford University Press, 1959), 127–32. In making this point Tillich was in the debt of the German Idealist philosopher Friedrich Schelling.

Chapter 4

1. Daniel C. Dennett, *Darwin's Dangerous Idea: Evolution and the Meaning of Life* (New York: Simon and Schuster, 1995), 48–60. As much as Dennett tries to soften his materialism by criticizing what he calls "greedy reductionism" (82–83), he remains a practitioner of what I shall later refer to as metaphysical impatience, the acquisitive habit of claiming to have reached the ultimate depth of nature while skipping the arduous *journey* into the depths. (See Chapter 7 below.)

2. Ernst Mayr claims that it was Darwin who first opened up to science the task of addressing "why" questions and not just "how" questions. This is because, unlike most other sciences, evolution requires narrative or historical kinds of explanation. *This Is Biology* (Cambridge, Mass.: Harvard University Press, 1997), 115–19.

3. Ibid. Here Mayr mentions neither Dennett nor Dawkins, but he is certainly aware of their ideas.

4. Biological accounts of life often distinguish between "proximate explanations," such as biochemical processes, and "ultimate" explanations, like Darwinian processes. The use of the term "ultimate" here does not *have* to carry metaphysical weight, but in the "hybrid readings" of many biologists Darwinian explanations often function as "ultimate" in a quasi-religious sense as well as scientific. This is perhaps less true in the case of Mayr than of some other Darwinians we shall encounter later on.

5. Holmes Rolston, III, *Science and Religion: A Critical Survey* (New York: Random House, 1987), 33–35.

6. This is a point that is often forgotten by theologians who wish to make religion scientifically palatable by forcing it into the mold of scientific discourse.

7. Alfred North Whitehead, *Process and Reality,* corrected edition, David Ray Griffin and Donald W. Sherburne, eds. (New York: The Free Press, 1978), 162. "It must be remembered that clearness in consciousness is no evidence for primitiveness in the genetic process: the opposite doctrine is more nearly true" (173). We should indeed seek clarity, of course, but then we should mistrust it, Whitehead says, for clarity comes about only as the result of our reading things abstractly. We should not mistake what are in fact abstractions for concrete reality. To do so is a logical fallacy, the "fallacy of misplaced concreteness." Whitehead thinks that much of modern thought is based on this fallacy. See Alfred North Whitehead, *Science and the Modern World* (New York: The Free Press, 1967), 54–55; 51–57; 58–59.

8. Paul Tillich, *Systematic Theology*, Vol. III (Chicago: University of Chicago Press, 1963), 130; and *Dynamics of Faith* (New York: Harper Torchbooks, 1957), 99.

9. Peter W. Atkins, *Creation Revisited* (New York: W. H. Freeman, 1992), 11–17.

10. Paul Tillich, *The Shaking of the Foundations* (New York: Charles Scribner's, 1948), 63.

11. Jacob Needleman, *A Sense of the Cosmos: The Encounter of Modern Science and Ancient Truth* (Garden City, N.Y.: Doubleday, 1975), 10–36.

12. See Stephen Jay Gould's remark in *Ever Since Darwin* (New York: W. W. Norton, 1977): "Yes, the world has been different ever since Darwin. But no less exciting, instructing, or uplifting; for if we cannot find purpose in nature, we will have to define it for ourselves" (13).

13. Louise Young, *The Unfinished Universe* (New York: Oxford University Press, 1986).

14. For vivid examples of this perspective, see Alan Lightman and Roberta Brawer, *Origins: The Lives and Worlds of Modern Cosmologists* (Cambridge, Mass.: Harvard University Press, 1990), 340ff.

15. Carl Friedrich von Weizsäcker, *The History of Nature* (Chicago: University of Chicago Press, 1949). See also Wolfhart Pannenberg, *Toward a Theology of Nature*, Ted Peters, ed. (Louisville: Westminster/John Knox Press, 1993), 86–98.

Chapter 5

1. Ernst Mayr, *This Is Biology* (Cambridge, Mass.: Harvard University Press, 1997), 115–19.

2. For a discussion of Darwinian explanations of religion, see Chapter 8 below.

3. St. Augustine, *The Literal Meaning of Genesis*, 2 vols., J. H. Taylor, trans. (New York: Newman Press, 1982), 252–54.

4. Deeper than these, of course, is the question why anything exists at all? To answer this question humans have almost universally devised creation myths, and it is in this category of narrative that the Darwinian story also finds its setting.

5. Martin Rees, *Just Six Numbers: The Deep Forces That Shape the Universe* (New York: Basic Books, 2000).

6. See, for example, John Gribbin's discussion of Lee Smolin's ideas in *In the Beginning* (New York: Little, Brown and Company, 1993), 252–55.

7. This is a cosmological extension of a suggestion that author and speaker Elie Wiesel has at times made with reference to the question of why God would have created humans, namely, because God loves stories.

8. This summary is suggested in many writings of Karl Rahner, S.J. See his book *Foundations of Christian Faith*, William V. Dych, trans. (New York: Crossroad, 1978).

9. The Gospel of Luke, 1:45.

10. I am speaking here of biological evolution prior to the emergence of humans and culture. With culture the grammar changes.

Chapter 6

1. Steven Weinberg, *Dreams of a Final Theory* (New York: Pantheon, 1992), 246.

2. Revised Standard Version.

3. For a more extended introduction to these three approaches, see my earlier discussion in *God After Darwin* (Boulder, Colo.: Westview Press, 2000), 23–44.

4. These are themes that run throughout most of Dawkins's books, especially *The Blind Watchmaker* (New York: W. W. Norton, 1986); *River Out of Eden* (New York: Basic Books, 1995); *Climbing Mount Improbable* (New York: W. W. Norton, 1996).

5. Dawkins, *River out of Eden,* 131–33.

6. Dawkins, *The Blind Watchmaker,* 6.

7. See especially *The Blind Watchmaker, River Out of Eden,* and *Climbing Mount Improbable.*

8. Stephen Jay Gould, *Ever Since Darwin* (New York: W. W. Norton, 1977), 12–13.

9. What follows is a précis of a theological position I have developed at more length in *God After Darwin.* However, here I shall be shaping the discussion more explicitly in terms of the question of Darwin and divine providence. Moreover, I am transposing the discussion into the context of the notion of "depth" that runs throughout the present book.

10. Some, though certainly not all, of the ideas presented here by the Engagement approach, are those of "process theology." The idea of a God "discontent with the status quo" and concerned with "adventure" is a deeply biblical one, but it has been given new life in the religious philosophy of Alfred North Whitehead. See John B. Cobb and David R. Griffin, *Process Theology: An Introductory Exposition* (Philadelphia: Westminster Press, 1976). Some of the terminology in the Engagement approach summarized here is that of Cobb and Griffin.

11. See Pierre Teilhard de Chardin, *Christianity and Evolution,* René Hague, trans. (New York: Harcourt Brace, 1969), 33, 82, 132, 149–50, 179, 218.

12. For further development of the Engagement approach see my book *God After Darwin.*

13. See Karl Rahner, *Foundations of Christian Faith*, William Dych, trans. (New York: Crossroad, 1984), 78–203.

Chapter 7

1. Michael Shermer, *How We Believe: The Search for God in an Age of Science* (New York: W. H. Freeman, 2000).

2. Michael J. Behe, *Darwin's Black Box: The Biochemical Challenge to Evolution* (New York: The Free Press, 1996); William Dembski, *Intelligent Design: The Bridge Between Science and Theology* (Downers Grove, Ill.: InterVarsity Press, 1999); Phillip E. Johnson, *Darwin on Trial* (Downers Grove, Ill.: InterVarsity Press, 1991); James Porter Moreland, ed., *The Creation Hypothesis: Scientific Evidence for an Intelligent Designer* (Downers Grove, Ill.: InterVarsity Press, 1994); Jonathan Wells, *Icons of Evolution: Science or Myth?* (Washington, D.C.: Regnery, 2000). For a critical discussion of Intelligent Design Theory, see Robert T. Pennock, *Tower of Babel: The Evidence Against the New Creationism* (Cambridge, Mass.: MIT Press, 1999).

3. Michael Behe, *Darwin's Black Box* (New York: The Free Press, 1996). The helpful notion of "brittle device" comes from Richard Dawkins: A device is brittle when it has to be "perfect and complete if it is to work at all." Dawkins's point is that there are no such devices in nature since evolution implies that design comes about only gradually. *River Out of Eden* (New York: Basic Books, 1995), 70.

4. For a fair and lucid critique of IDT, see Kenneth Miller, *Finding Darwin's God: A Scientist's Search for Common Ground Between God and Evolution* (New York: Cliff Street Books, 1999), 81–164.

5. William A. Dembski, *The Design Inference: Eliminating Chance Through Small Probabilities* (New York: Cambridge University Press, 1998).

6. Even when they allow vaguely for biological evolution, advocates of IDT reject "Darwinian" theory because they, along with some of the Darwinians I have discussed in previous chapters, do not distinguish clearly between the *science* of evolution and extraneous materialist ideology in which the scientific ideas are often packaged. This is especially obvious in the works of Phillip Johnson. See, for example, his book *The Wedge of Truth* (Downers Grove, Ill.: InterVarsity Press, 2000).

7. This criticism is implicit especially in the works of Phillip Johnson.

8. Evolutionary theism itself comes in many different versions. Some of my own attempts to contribute to it may be found in *God After Darwin* (Boulder, Colo.: Westview Press, 2000).

9. Perhaps in archeology or in the search for extraterrestrial intelligence, the notion of "intelligence" comes in as a legitimate category, but in biology, to introduce such an idea in place of, and at the same explanatory level as, the idea of natural selection seems logically strained.

10. Michael R. Rose, *Darwin's Spectre: Evolutionary Biology in the Modern World* (Princeton: Princeton University Press, 1998), 211.

11. Gary Cziko, *Without Miracles: Universal Selection Theory and the Second Darwinian Revolution* (Cambridge, Mass.: MIT Press, 1995).

12. In addition to Rose's book *Darwin's Specter,* see Michael Ruse, *Can a Darwinian be a Christian?* (Cambridge: Cambridge University Press, 2000), 77; E. O. Wilson, *Consilience: The Unity of Knowledge* (New York: Vintage Books, 1999); William Provine, "Evolution and the Foundation of Ethics," in Steven L. Goldman, ed., *Science, Technology and Social Progress* (Bethlehem, Pa.: Lehigh University Press, 1989), 261.

13. Such views are depicted by David J. Depew and Bruce H. Weber in *Darwinism Evolving: Systems Dynamics and the Genealogy of Natural Selection* (Cambridge, Mass.: MIT Press, 1995).

14. See, for example, Dembski's *Intelligent Design.*

15. Cziko, *Without Miracles,* 121.

16. Dembski, *Intelligent Design.*

17. See especially Richard Dawkins's *Climbing Mount Improbable* (New York: W. W. Norton, 1996).

18. Cziko, *Without Miracles,* 101–234.

19. Stephen Jay Gould, as I pointed out in Chapter 1, would claim that science and religion are not in competition, but in order to support this contention, he has to reduce religion to ethics or to an illusory source of meaning, denying in effect that it has any cognitional competency. See, for example, Stephen Jay Gould, *Rocks of Ages: Science and Religion in the Fullness of Life* (New York: Ballantine, 1999).

20. Cziko, *Without Miracles,* 121.

21. Incidentally, it will not help at this point to postulate that the search for truth is a purely cultural affair, liberated from the laws of evolution. After all, the creation of culture itself was also accomplished by the same minds that you tell me arose out of a purely mindless adaptive process.

22. See the following chapter for examples.

23. Notice that I am not saying that there is a contradiction between an *evolutionary* explanation and other ways of explaining mind. Evolutionary explanations can be quite illuminating in helping us understand the story of mind's emergence. But the claim that they are *exhaustively* explanatory subverts the credibility of that claim itself.

24. In my opinion the most thorough philosophical investigation of the pure, disinterested desire to know is that of Bernard Lonergan, *Insight: A Study of Human Understanding,* 3d ed. (New York: Philosophical Library, 1970). Lonergan shows in great detail how a close analysis of the *actual performance* of understanding and knowing always refutes any ideas, such as those of evolutionary materialists, that conceptually and formally place in question the capacity of the mind to arrive at *what is.*

25. Dennett comes close at one point in *Darwin's Dangerous Idea* to recognizing the self-contradiction of claiming *seriously* that Darwinism is a universal acid that cuts through everything, and would therefore have to subvert that claim itself. But he craftily sidesteps the contradiction in a distractingly illogical attempt to distinguish clearly between "good reductionism" and "greedy reductionism," Darwin's being an instance of the former. See *Darwin's Dangerous Idea* (New York: Simon and Schuster, 1995), 82.

26. Here again see Lonergan's *Insight.*

27. Alfred North Whitehead points out that the "sharp division between mentality and nature has no ground in our fundamental observation. We find ourselves living within nature. . . . We should conceive mental operations as among the factors which make up the constitution of nature." *Modes of Thought* (New York: The Free Press, 1968), 156.

28. See, for example, my discussion of Frederick Crews in Chapter 9, below.

29. Scientists must consciously acknowledge that the natural sciences, both individually and collectively, leave out a great deal that is part of the real world, not least the obvious fact of our subjective experience. As a rule, of course, evolutionary materialists forget that such a bracketing is only methodological, and so they end up with a view of the world from which ironically even the scientific thinker is absent. See B. Alan Wallace, *The Taboo of Subjectivity: Toward a New Science of Consciousness* (New York: Oxford University Press, 2000).

Chapter 8

1. For a discussion of evolution's implications for morality, see Robert Wright, *The Moral Animal: Evolutionary Psychology and Everyday Life* (New York: Pantheon, 1994); Matt Ridley, *The Origins of Virtue* (New York: Penguin, 1996); Michael Ruse and Edward O. Wilson, "The Evolution of Ethics," in James Huchingson, ed., *Religion and the Natural Sciences* (New York: Harcourt Brace Jovanovich, 1993), 308–11.

2. See Robert Hinde, *Why Gods Persist: A Scientific Approach to Religions* (New York: Routledge, 1999); Walter Burkert, *Creation of the Sacred: Tracks of Biology in Early Religions* (Cambridge, Mass.: Harvard University Press, 1996); Pascal Boyer, *Religion Explained: The Evolutionary Origins of Religious Thought* (New York: Basic Books, 2001).

3. There are, of course, a number of different Darwinian perspectives, but the present chapter will focus on the "genes-eye" approach of evolutionary psychology. A "group-selection" approach is taken by David Sloan Wilson in *Darwin's Cathedral: Evolution, Religion and the Nature of Society* (Chicago: University of Chicago Press, 2002).

4. George C. Williams, *Adaptation and Natural Selection: A Critique of Some Current Evolutionary Thought* (Princeton, N.J.: Princeton University Press, 1996); William D. Hamilton, "The Genetical Evolution of Social Behavior," *Journal of Theoretical Biology,* Vol. VII (1964), 1–52; John Maynard Smith, *The Evolution of Sex* (New York: Cambridge University Press, 1978).

5. Robert L. Trivers, *Social Evolution* (Menlo Park, Cal.: Benjamin Cummings, 1985); Richard D. Alexander, *Darwinism and Human Affairs* (Seattle: University of Washington Press, 1979).

6. Alexander, *Darwinism and Human Affairs*, 38. In this summary I am following in part an essay by Frank Miele, "The (Im)moral Animal: A Quick & Dirty Guide to Evolutionary Psychology & the Nature of Human Nature," *The Skeptic*, Vol. 4, No. 1 (1996), 42–49. The essay is on-line at: http://www.skeptic.com/04.1.miele-immoral.html.

7. See *The Adapted Mind: Evolutionary Psychology and the Generation of Culture*, Jerome H. Barkow, Leda Cosmides, John Tooby, eds. (New York: Oxford University Press, 1992).

8. Pascal Boyer, *Religion Explained: The Evolutionary Origins of Religious Thought* (New York: Basic Books, 2001).

9. Ibid., 145.

10. Ibid., 137–67.

11. As I noted earlier, David Sloan Wilson in *Darwin's Cathedral: Evolution, Religion, and the Nature of Society* proposes that religion, as a social organism, is adaptive at the group level as well as at the levels of the individual and the gene.

12. See Loyal Rue, *By the Grace of Guile: The Role of Deception in Natural History and Human Affairs* (New York: Oxford University Press, 1994). Rue, himself a professor of religious studies, is not reluctant to call religious illusions "lies."

13. The central argument of Michael Shermer's *How We Believe: The Search for God in an Age of Science* (New York: W. H. Freeman, 2000) is that religion is a consequence of the human longing for "pattern" and is therefore cognitionally suspect.

14. Even at the end of his previous book, *The Naturalness of Religious Ideas: A Cognitive Theory of Religion* (Berkeley: University of California Press, 1994), Boyer expressed a suspicion that evolutionary psychology will provide the ultimate explanation of religion.

15. For a discussion of the difference between evolutionary psychology and standard social science, see *The Adapted Mind*, Barkow, Cosmides, and Tooby, eds.

16. Walter Burkert, *Creation of the Sacred*. See also Robert Hinde, *Why Gods Persist*.

17. See Burkert, 2–8. Casting aside the contemporary rejoinder that "nature" itself might be a purely cultural construct, the new explanations of religion have now turned to biology in order to get to the bottom of it all.

18. Rue, *By the Grace of Guile*, 82–127.

19. Ibid., 125–26.

20. Ibid., 261–306. After insisting that only nihilism can be *true*, Rue arrives at the following breathtaking conclusion to his book: ". . . it is now for us to thank the nihilists and to send them on their way. We have a story to tell." And what is this (admittedly untrue) story that we need to tell if we are to survive? Rue answers: "Biocentrism is your story and mine. It is everybody's story. It presumes to tell us how things are and which things matter. It is, nevertheless, a lie. It is a lie because it is not nature's own story, not told by the earth, not the authorized version. It is merely a tale told by humans, full of contingency and distortion, signifying hope. But it is a noble lie, one that washes down with a minimum of deception and offers up a maximum of adaptive change. And if it is well and artfully told, it will reenchant the earth and save us from the truth." One can only ask whether Rue is asking us to accept as true what he has just told us.

21. See Ernest Becker, *The Denial of Death* (New York: The Free Press, 1973).

22. Whether deep Darwinism can also be the ultimate ground of the assumptions made by deep Darwinism itself is an interesting question. Can the evolutionary psychologist coherently naturalize human culture, which includes science, without sabotaging the authority of Darwinism itself?

23. Holmes Rolston, III, *Genes, Genesis and God: Values and Their Origins in Natural and Human History* (New York: Cambridge University Press, 1999), 347.

24. A very good example of this confidence is Michael Shermer's *How We Believe.*

25. For a discussion of such theories of religion, see Daniel Pals, *Seven Theories of Religion* (New York: Oxford University Press, 1996).

26. If at this point a few Deep Darwinians respond that they are not making claims that have anything to do with the truth of religion, and that they are only describing the necessary conditions for religious awareness, then they are no longer Deep Darwinians. Moreover, if the only thing evolutionary accounts can give us is an account of the necessary but not sufficient conditions for religious awareness, then they will have told us very little that we did not already know. As a matter of fact, however, the implicitly materialist assumptions that drive Deep Darwinism inevitably look for ultimate, adequate and final explanations, a quest that inevitably places it in a competitive rather than complementary relationship with theology.

27. See *The Future of an Illusion,* James Strachey, trans. (Garden City, N.Y.: Doubleday Anchor Books, 1964). In his later writings, Freud also linked *eros* to *thanatos,* the death instinct.

28. See Alan Wallace, *The Taboo of Subjectivity: Toward a New Science of Consciousness* (New York: Oxford University Press, 2000).

29. See Michael Polanyi, *Personal Knowledge* (New York: Harper Torchbooks, 1958), 327ff.

30. To strive means to be open to either success or failure. Nonliving entities, on the other hand, can neither succeed nor fail. A simple chemical reaction cannot meaningfully be said to strive—and therefore it can neither succeed nor fail. It does not fulfill a basic criterion of being alive. A scientist, however, may be striving to bring about a particular chemical effect for some particular purpose and, depending on the outcome, may either succeed or fail. The scientist, as a center of personal striving, is clearly alive, but the chemical reaction is not. The difference is defined by the logic of achievement.

31. Matt Ridley, *The Red Queen: Sex and the Evolution of Human Nature* (New York: Penguin Books, 1993), 92–93. [Emphasis added]

32. Ibid., 94. [Emphasis added]

33. Ibid., passim.

34. Richard Dawkins, *The Selfish Gene* (New York: Oxford University Press, 1989).

35. John Bowker, *Is Anybody Out There?* (Westminster, Md.: Christian Classics, 1988), 9–18, 112–43.

36. Ibid.

37. I cannot enter here into the whole discussion of whether by its own efforts our religious striving can be successful. In fact, religious striving by itself risks failure, and it is often in moments of failure that the religious personality allows itself to be grasped by "grace."

38. Richard Dawkins, *The Selfish Gene;* Susan Blackmore, *The Meme Machine* (New York: Oxford University Press, 1999).

Chapter 9

1. "Saving Us from Darwin," *New York Review of Books,* Part I, October 4, 2001; Part II, October 18, 2001.

2. "What interests me," Crews says, "is general rationality, of which science is a part. General rationality requires us to observe the world carefully, to consider alternative hypotheses to our own hypotheses, to gather evidence in a responsible way, to answer objections. These are habits of mind that science shares with good history, good sociology, good political science, good economics, what have you. And I summarize all this in what I call the "empirical attitude." "Criticism and the Empirical Attitude: Conversation with Frederick Crews" (Online interview at: http://globetrotter.berkeley.edu/people/Crews/crews-con0.html).

3. Phillip E. Johnson, *The Wedge of Truth: Splitting the Foundations of Naturalism* (Downers Grove, Ill.: InterVarsity Press, 1999); Jonathan Wells, *Icons of Evolution: Science or Myth? Why Much of What We Teach About Evolution Is Wrong* (Washington, D.C.: Regnery, 2000); Michael J. Behe, *Darwin's Black Box: The Biochemical Challenge to Evolution* (New York: The Free Press, 1996); William A. Dembski, ed., *Mere Creation: Science, Faith and Intelligent Design* (Downers Grove, Ill.: InterVarsity Press, 1998); William A. Dembski, *Intelligent Design: The Bridge Between Science and Theology* (Downers Grove, Ill.: InterVarsity Press, 1999); Robert T. Pennock, *Tower of Babel: The Evidence Against the New Creationism* (Cambridge, Mass.: MIT Press, 1999); Robert Pollack, *The Faith of Biology and the Biology of Faith: Order, Meaning, and Free Will in Modern Medical Science* (New York: Columbia University Press, 2000); John F. Haught, *God After Darwin: A Theology of Evolution* (Boulder, Colo.: Westview Press, 2000); Michael Ruse, *Can a Darwinian Be a Christian? The Relationship Between Science and Religion* (New York: Cambridge University Press, 2001); Kenneth R. Miller, *Finding Darwin's God: A Scientist's Search for Common Ground Between God and Evolution* (New York: Cliff Street Books, 1999); Stephen Jay Gould, *Rocks of Ages: Science and Religion in the Fullness of Life* (New York: Ballantine, 1999).

4. Crews, "Saving Us from Darwin," Part II, 51.

5. Ibid.

6. "So, too," Crews continues, "competitive pressures now form a more plausible framework than divine action" for understanding life, ethics and even religion. "Saving Us from Darwin," Part I, 24.

7. See my discussions of Boyer and Rue in the preceding chapter.

8. Crews, "Saving Us from Darwin," Part I, 24.

9. Crews views my own book *God After Darwin* as one such "evasion." "Saving Us from Darwin," Part II, 55.

10. See note 2 above.

11. Stephen Jay Gould's *Rocks of Ages* and Michael Ruse's *Can a Darwinian Be a Christian?* See note 3 above.

12. Crews, "Saving Us from Darwin," Part II, 55.

13. Ibid.

14. Pierre Teilhard de Chardin, *Activation of Energy*, René Hague, trans. (New York: Harcourt Brace Jovanovich, 1970), 239.

15. Paul Tillich, *Systematic Theology*, Vol. III (Chicago: University of Chicago Press), 19.

Chapter 10

1. The understanding of religion as a "route-finding" through the "limitations" on life is developed in the works of John Bowker: *The Sense of God: Sociological, Anthropological, and Psychological Approaches to the Origin of the Sense of God* (Oxford: Clarendon Press, 1973); *The Religious Imagination and the Sense of God* (New York: Oxford University Press, 1978); and *Is*

Anybody Out There? Religions and Belief in God in the Contemporary World (Westminster, Md.: Christian Classics, 1988). This chapter adapts some of Bowker's insightful interpretations of religion to the Darwinian context.

2. Paul Tillich, *The Courage to Be* (New Haven: Yale University Press, 1952).

3. The term "route-finding" is that of John Bowker in *The Sense of God*, 51, 60 and *passim*.

4. Sigmund Freud, *The Future of an Illusion*, W. D. Robson-Scott, trans. (New York: Doubleday Anchor Books, 1964), 41.

5. Cited in Bowker, *The Religious Imagination and the Sense of God*, 2.

6. Here, and in the following, I am adapting some of what Bowker says about Freud's projection theory to that of the Darwinian criticism of religion. *The Sense of God*, 116–34.

7. Strictly speaking, as Bowker comments, there is no sense (singular) of God, but only senses (plural) of God. However, with this qualification understood, I shall use the singular for the sake of simplicity, as Bowker's book title does also: *The Sense of God*, 44–45.

8. For a vivid example of such either-or literalism, see Gary Cziko, *Without Miracles* (Cambridge, Mass.: MIT Press, 1995).

9. The following interpretation of religion in terms of information systems is in part derived from, and in part an adaptation of, the fertile ideas of John Bowker developed in the three books cited in note 1, but especially in *Is Anybody Out There?*

10. John Bowker, *The Sense of God*, 131–33.

11. There is an imaginative and constructive aspect to science also, and, like religion, science too is responding to depth and truth, constantly called upon to revise its models of nature. At their best both science and religion are instances of critical realism. That is, they are oriented toward what is real, but they are willing to criticize their always inadequate understandings or images of what is real. The difference is that science works much closer to the surface of the universe, where sensory input is clearer and more distinct than the vaguer, but more momentous, signals from the depth that arouse religious life and symbolism.

12. It is especially in the writings of Teilhard de Chardin that the connection is made between the unfinished character of the cosmos and the inevitable present obscurity of our sense of God.

13. Jürgen Moltmann, "God's Kenosis in the Creation and Consummation of the World," John Polkinghorne, ed., *The Work of Love: Creation as Kenosis* (Grand Rapids, Mich.: Eerdman's Publishing Company, 2001), 149. Moltmann goes on to argue, along with Kierkegaard and Heidegger, that possibility is higher than actuality. "Possibility can become actuality, but actuality never again becomes possibility" (150). In the following two chapters I shall make a similar point as I attempt to locate evolution in terms of a non-materialist metaphysics.

14. Moltmann, 149.

15. See also Gerd Theissen, *Biblical Faith: An Evolutionary Approach*, John Bowden, trans. (Philadelphia: Fortress Press, 1985).

16. In my book *Science and Religion: From Conflict to Conversation* (Mahwah, N.J.: Paulist Press, 1995), I have discussed this function of religion under the category of "confirmation," by which I mean that religion supports or "confirms" the scientific trust in the world's intelligibility.

Chapter 11

1. See Paul Tillich, *The Courage to Be* (New Haven: Yale University Press, 1952), 78–85.

2. This is not to deny, of course, that geology, astrophysics and many other sciences have also contributed to the new awareness of nature as narrative.

3. For Whitehead's discussion of "perishing," see especially *Process and Reality,* Corrected Edition, David Ray Griffin and Donald W. Sherburne, eds. (New York: The Free Press, 1968), 34–51, 340–41. Much of the following is a summary and adaptation of reflections on perishing that first appeared in my book *The Cosmic Adventure* (New York: Paulist Press, 1984).

4. Alfred North Whitehead, *Science and the Modern World* (New York: The Free Press, 1967), 191–92; and Alfred North Whitehead, "Immortality," in Paul A. Schillp, ed., *The Philosophy of Alfred North Whitehead* (Evanston and Chicago: Northwestern University Press, 1941), 682–700.

5. Alfred Lord Tennyson, "In Memoriam" (from Stanzas 54 and 56).

6. "The Garden of Persephone."

7. "Dover Beach."

8. Whitehead, *Science and the Modern World,* 191–92.

9. From Arthur Hugh Clough's poem, "With Whom Is No Variableness, Neither Shadow of Turning."

10. Charles Hartshorne writes: "According to the view I adopt, there was once no such individual as myself, even as something that was 'going to exist.' But centuries after my death, there will have been that very individual which I am." *The Logic of Perfection* (Lasalle, Ill.: Open Court Publishing Co., 1962), 250.

11. Henri Bergson, *Creative Evolution,* Arthur Mitchell, trans. (London: Macmillan, 1911), 5.

12. Alfred North Whitehead, *Process and Reality,* 86–104.

13. Strictly speaking, after Einstein we must say that nature is spatio-temporal. The point is that "there is no nature at an instant." If time ceased to exist, the physical world would vanish along with it. Alfred North Whitehead, *Modes of Thought* (New York: The Free Press, 1968), 146.

14. Whitehead, *Process and Reality,* 29, 60, 81–82, 346–51.

15. Ibid., 340.

16. Ibid.

17. Ibid.

18. Paul Tillich, *The Eternal Now* (New York: Charles Scribner's Sons, 1963), 33–34.

19. Ibid.

20. Ibid.

21. William James, *Pragmatism* (Cleveland: Meridian Books, 1964), 76.

22. Tillich, *The Eternal Now,* 35.

23. Whitehead, *Process and Reality,* 345–51.

24. Ibid., 346.

25. Ibid.

26. See Alfred North Whitehead, *Adventures of Ideas* (New York: The Free Press, 1967), 62, 183–85, 265.

27. This is an insight that Teilhard de Chardin expresses in many of his works without developing it at length theologically.

28. Romans 8:24–25. *New American Bible.*

29. Paul Tillich, *The Shaking of the Foundations* (New York: Charles Scribner's Sons, 1948), 151.

Chapter 12

1. Carl Friedrich von Weizsäcker, *The History of Nature* (Chicago: University of Chicago Press, 1949); see also Stephen Toulmin and June Goodfield, *The Discovery of Time* (London:

Hutchinson, 1965); Wolfhart Pannenberg, *Toward a Theology of Nature,* Ted Peters, ed. (Louisville: Westminster/John Knox Press, 1993), 86–98.

2. Pierre Teilhard de Chardin, *The Human Phenomenon,* Sarah Appleton-Weber, trans. (Portland, Ore.: Sussex Academic Press, 1999).

3. Pierre Teilhard de Chardin, *Christianity and Evolution,* trans. René Hague (New York: Harcourt Brace and Co., 1969), 240.

4. Teilhard de Chardin, *The Human Phenomenon,* 191–94.

5. Pierre Teilhard de Chardin, *The Future of Man,* Norman Denny, trans. (New York: Harper Colophon Books, 1964), 83.

6. Ibid., 272–81.

7. Pierre Teilhard de Chardin, *Toward the Future,* René Hague, trans. (New York: Harcourt Brace Jovanovich, 1975), 92–100; 203–8.

8. Teilhard de Chardin, *Christianity and Evolution,* 240.

9. Paul Tillich, *The Future of Religions,* Jerald C. Brauer, ed. (New York: Harper and Row, 1966), 90–91.

10. See Michael Drummy, *Being and Earth: Paul Tillich's Theology of Nature* (Lanham, Md.: University Press of America, 2000).

11. Paul Tillich, *Systematic Theology,* three volumes (Chicago: University of Chicago Press, 1963), Vol. III, 19.

12. Pierre Teilhard de Chardin, *Activation of Energy,* René Hague, trans. (New York: Harcourt Brace Jovanovich, 1970), 231–43.

13. Teilhard de Chardin, *Christianity and Evolution,* 40.

14. Ibid., 54

15. Ibid. Emphasis in original.

16. Ibid.

17. Ibid, 39. Emphasis in original.

18. See Part II of Tillich's five-part *Systematic Theology,* Vol. I, 163–210.

19. See, for example, Reinhold Niebuhr, "Biblical Thought and Ontological Speculation in Tillich's Theology," in Charles W. Kegley and Robert W. Bretall, eds., *The Theology of Paul Tillich* (New York: Macmillan, 1952), 219.

20. Teilhard de Chardin, *Christianity and Evolution,* 81.

21. Ibid., 83–84.

22. In some of Tillich's sermons, the sense of the future seems more alive than in the *Systematic Theology.* Tillich talks about being religiously grasped by the "coming order": "The coming order is always coming, shaking this order, fighting with it, conquering it and conquered by it. The coming order is always at hand. But one can never say: 'It is here! It is there!' One can never grasp it. But one can be grasped by it." *Shaking of the Foundations* (New York: Charles Scribner's Sons, 1948), 27.

23. Tillich, *Systematic Theology,* Vol. II, 33–36.

24. Ibid., 118.

25. Teilhard de Chardin, *Activation of Energy,* 239.

26. Teilhard de Chardin, *Christianity and Evolution,* 51.

27. Paul Tillich, *The Courage to Be* (New Haven: Yale University Press, 1952), 32–57.

28. See Ted Peters, *God—The World's Future: Systematic Theology for a Postmodern Era* (Minneapolis: Fortress Press, 1992).

Chapter 13

1. See Michael J. Crowe, *The Extraterrestrial Life Debate 1750–1900* (Cambridge: Cambridge University Press, 1986); Stephen J. Dick, *Plurality of Worlds: The Origins of the Extraterrestrial Life Debate from Democritus to Kant* (Cambridge: Cambridge University Press, 1982); Ted Peters, "Exo-Theology: Speculations on Extraterrestrial Life," in James R. Lewis, ed., *The Gods Have Landed: New Religions from Other Worlds* (Albany: State University of New York Press, 1995),187–206.

2. See H. Richard Niebuhr, *Radical Monotheism and Western Culture* (London: Faber and Faber, 1943).

3. Roch Kereszty, as quoted by Thomas F. O'Meara, "Extraterrestrial Intelligent Life," *Theological Studies,* Vol. 60, 29.

4. *Summa Theologiae* I, 48, *ad* 2.

5. The term "exo-theology" (a take-off on "exo-biology," which studies the prospects of life outside of our planet) is used by Peters, 188.

6. Quoted by Stephen J. Dick, *Life on Other Worlds: The 20th-Century Extraterrestrial Life Debate* (Cambridge: Cambridge University Press, 1998), 194.

7. Mary Russell, *The Sparrow* (New York: Fawcett Columbine, 1996).

8. This question has often been raised by Thomas Berry. See his book *The Dream of the Earth* (San Francisco: Sierra Club Books, 1988), 11.

9. See Michael Polanyi, *Personal Knowledge: Towards a Post-Critical Philosophy* (New York and Evanston: Harper and Row, 1958), 327, 344.

10. Hans Jonas, *Mortality and Morality* (Evanston, Ill.: Northwestern University Press), 60.

11. This perspective is not identical with vitalism, a philosophy that attributes striving primarily to a life-force that transcends matter and the universe. If some readers remain skeptical about placing plants or fungi within the logic of achievement, it is sufficient for our purposes here simply to acknowledge the fact of "centered striving" as a characteristic of animals and humans.

12. Michael Polanyi, *Personal Knowledge,* 327.

13. John Bowker, *Is Anybody Out There?* (Westminster, Md.: Christian Classics, Inc., 1988), 9–18; 112–43. See the other references to Bowker's work in Chapter 10.

14. Paul Tillich, *The Courage to Be* (New Haven: Yale University Press, 1952), 40–45.

15. Ibid.

16. See W. T. Stace, "Man Against Darkness," *The Atlantic Monthly,* Vol. CLXXXII (September 1948), 54.

17. Henri Bergson, *Creative Evolution,* Arthur Mitchell, trans. (New York: Henry Holt and Company, 1913), 103–5.

18. The very fact that human intelligence could tell a story about the genesis and demise of many worlds—however tenuously related they may be physically—gives a historical unity to the totality. Moreover, metaphysically speaking, there can really be only one universe, even though this overarching unity might comprise the many possible *facets* that physicists misleadingly refer to as separate universes.

19. See Pierre Teilhard de Chardin, *Activation of Energy,* René Hague, trans. (New York: Harcourt Brace Jovanovich, 1970), 99–127. In 1944 Teilhard wrote that the hypothesis of other planets inhabited by intelligent beings has a "positive likelihood," in which case "the phenomenon of life and more particularly the phenomenon of man lose something of their disturbing loneliness" (127). There may be many "noospheres" or "thinking planets." "It is

almost more than our minds can dare to face," he continues, but the evolutionary tendency toward complexification and centration might well have a "cosmic" scope. Yet "there can still be only a single Omega," that is, a single transcendent Reality whose being enfolds the entire universe (127).

20. See Alfred North Whitehead, *Adventures of Ideas* (New York: The Free Press, 1967), 265.

Index